Student
MENTAL HEALTH
& WELLBEING
IN HIGHER EDUCATION

Sara Miller McCune founded SAGE Publishing in 1965 to support the dissemination of usable knowledge and educate a global community. SAGE publishes more than 1000 journals and over 800 new books each year, spanning a wide range of subject areas. Our growing selection of library products includes archives, data, case studies and video. SAGE remains majority owned by our founder and after her lifetime will become owned by a charitable trust that secures the company's continued independence.

Los Angeles | London | New Delhi | Singapore | Washington DC | Melbourne

Student
MENTAL HEALTH
& WELLBEING
IN HIGHER EDUCATION

A practical guide

Edited by
NICOLA BARDEN & RUTH CALEB

Los Angeles | London | New Delhi
Singapore | Washington DC | Melbourne

Los Angeles | London | New Delhi
Singapore | Washington DC | Melbourne

SAGE Publications Ltd
1 Oliver's Yard
55 City Road
London EC1Y 1SP

SAGE Publications Inc.
2455 Teller Road
Thousand Oaks, California 91320

SAGE Publications India Pvt Ltd
B 1/I 1 Mohan Cooperative Industrial Area
Mathura Road

New Delhi 110 044
SAGE Publications Asia-Pacific Pte Ltd
3 Church Street
#10-04 Samsung Hub
Singapore 049483

Editor: James Clark
Assistant editor: Diana Alves
Production editor: Katherine Haw
Copyeditor: Jane Fricker
Proofreader: Brian McDowell
Marketing manager: Dilhara Attygalle
Cover design: Naomi Robinson
Typeset by: C&M Digitals (P) Ltd, Chennai, India
Printed in the UK

Library of Congress Control Number: 2019933233

British Library Cataloguing in Publication data

A catalogue record for this book is available from
the British Library

ISBN 978-1-5264-2121-0
ISBN 978-1-5264-2122-7 (pbk)

At SAGE we take sustainability seriously. Most of our products are printed in the UK using responsibly sourced
papers and boards. When we print overseas we ensure sustainable papers are used as measured by the PREPS
grading system. We undertake an annual audit to monitor our sustainability.

Contents

Acknowledgments

All books are shared productions. For this book, the editors would like to give particular acknowledgement and thanks to:

- The chapter authors, for their valuable contributions and their ongoing enthusiasm for and commitment to the book
- The Mental Wellbeing in Higher Education Working Group (MWBHE)
- Professor Julia Buckingham CBE
- Professor Elizabeth Stuart
- Sally Olohan MBE
- The Counselling Team, Brunel University London
- The Student Services Team, University of Winchester

About the Editors

Dr Nicola Barden is a Professional Services Fellow at the University of Winchester, where from 2013 to 2018 she was the Director of Student Services. Prior to this she led counselling and mental health teams at the Universities of Portsmouth and Aston. She has over 30 years' experience as a counsellor and psychotherapist, spending some time in the voluntary sector working with young people and those with alcohol problems. She has chaired the Heads of University Counselling Services group, and contributed significantly to the work of the British Association for Counselling and Psychotherapy (BACP) as Chair of their Accreditation and then Professional Standards Committee before becoming Chair of the Association from 2005 to 2008. She remains a Fellow of BACP, was a Fellow of the Higher Education Academy, and was also registered with the United Kingdom Council for Psychotherapy (UKCP). She has edited the BACP journal *Therapy Today*, been a lecturer and external examiner on several counselling programmes, and has published in the field of gender, sexuality and therapy. From 2012 to 2018 she was the Secretary of the Mental Wellbeing in Higher Education Working Group, and from 2016 to 2018 was on the Executive Committee of AMOSSHE, the Student Services organisation.

Dr Ruth Caleb MBE is a wellbeing consultant, trainer and psychotherapist, BACP member and registered with UKCP, who specialises in the mental health and wellbeing of students and staff in higher education. She is also a supervisor and tutor on the Metanoia Institute / Middlesex University Doctorates in Psychotherapy and Counselling Psychology programmes. She has over 30 years' experience as a counsellor and psychotherapist in a wide variety of settings, including the National Aids Helpline, ChildLine, fertility counselling and private practice. Over the last 25 years she has specialised in mental health and wellbeing support for university students and staff. She was Head of Counselling at Brunel University London from 1999 to 2017. Ruth was Chair of the Mental Wellbeing in Higher Education (MWBHE) Working Group from 2012 to 2018 and was a member of Universities UK's Mental Health in HE programme working group. She has worked strategically at a national level, including addressing and contributing to All-Party Parliamentary Group meetings on student health and informing Members of Parliament speaking in parliamentary debates involving student wellbeing. Previously Ruth was Chair of the British Association for Counselling and Psychotherapy's Universities and Colleges Executive Committee (2008–10) and a member of the BACP International Research Committee (2003–6). She has published articles and book chapters on student mental health and wellbeing, ethical practice, organisational support and the role of a counselling service.

About the Contributors

Professor Dinesh Bhugra CBE is Emeritus Professor of Mental Health and Cultural Diversity at King's College, London. He was Dean (Lead Educational Officer) of the Royal College of Psychiatrists (2003–8) and then President of the Royal College (2008–11). He was Vice-Chair of the Academy of Medical Royal Colleges responsible for education. During this period he led on the Royal College of Psychiatrist's campaign for a Fair Deal for people with mental illness. He established a strategy for public mental health and was part of the group developing policy for mental health. As President of the World Psychiatric Association he led on the development of 20 Position Statements and various other initiatives including a Bill of Rights for people with mental illness and a campaign to back this. As President of the British Medical Association (2018–19) he has led on a large survey on the mental health and wellbeing of medical students globally. He chaired the Board of Trustees of the Mental Health Foundation (2011–14) and is on the Boards of the Psychiatry Research Trust and Sane charities. Since 2014 he has been a Non-Executive Director of the Tavistock and Portman NHS Foundation Trust.

Dr Ann-Marie Houghton is Director of REAP: Researching Equity, Access and Participation, a group based in Lancaster University's Department of Educational Research. REAP's work contributes to the work of the department's Centres for Social Justice and Wellbeing and Higher Education, Research and Evaluation. Working in Educational Research since 1996, she currently teaches on the Doctoral Programme in Educational Research and supervises PhD students, and is an Educational Developer based in Lancaster's Organisational Educational Development unit where she works with disciplinary colleagues based at Lancaster and at Lancaster's International Teaching Partnerships in Malaysia, Ghana and China. She is a Senior Fellow of the Higher Education Academy, and has engaged in HEA projects relating to inclusive curriculum design and embedding wellbeing in the curriculum. She led the Lancaster team on two national projects for the Higher Education Funding Council for England (HEFCE) including a review of support for students with mental health difficulties and models of disability. Within the institution she is a member of the University's Equality, Diversity and Inclusion Committee and several networks which bring her into regular contact with academic and professional service colleagues; she has recently taken on facilitation of a university Inclusive Learning Network. She is Chair of Governors of the Loyne Specialist Special School, Lancaster.

Siân Jones-Davies is an education law expert and a solicitor with Eversheds Sutherland (International) LLP. She has significant experience of providing legal and strategic advice to higher education institutions and further education colleges on student-related issues, including in the area of student mental health. She advises across the wide range of student-related issues which arise for institutions, including in connection with admissions, the student contract and consumer law, student complaints (including to the Office of the Independent Adjudicator for Higher Education), court claims (including for discrimination and judicial review), student conduct and discipline, fitness to practise, fitness to study, duty of care, sexual misconduct, data protection and freedom of speech. Siân also drafts and reviews student regulations, policies and procedures and advises institutions on their lawful implementation. She regularly delivers public training courses in addition to in-house training events to institutions and speaks at national sector conferences on a variety of student-related topics. Siân contributed to the Universities UK and MWBHE *Student Mental Wellbeing in Higher Education: Good Practice Guide* (2015).

Dr Gurvinder Kalra is a psychiatrist at the Monash Gender Clinic in Victoria, Australia; he also works in an in-patient unit in a regional setting. He completed his psychiatric training in India before moving to Australia, where he gained his Fellowship with the Royal Australian and New Zealand College of Psychiatrists. He has over 80 publications, including peer reviewed scientific papers and book chapters. His areas of interest include culture, migration and sexuality within the context of psychiatry. He has also focused on psychiatric training, with some of his key work being the use of commercial films through psychiatry movie clubs to teach sensitive issues related to psychiatry and sexuality. These days his work is focused on gender minorities seeking gender affirmative treatments, and he is in the process of setting up a private practice.

Dr Denise Meyer is a BACP Senior Accredited Counsellor and Chartered Counselling Psychologist. She has worked in university support services since 1995, at four very different institutions, and is currently Head of Wellbeing at the University of Portsmouth. She has advisory positions with national mental health charities Student Minds and the Charlie Waller Memorial Trust (CWMT), and has published and spoken at numerous sector conferences on a range of student mental health topics. Denise has a longstanding interest in innovation in student support, especially through integration with learning, and in the development of empowering discourses related to psychological health. Her doctoral research, which included collaborative action research with students, investigated practical applications of empowering discourses around depression and resulted in CWMT's award-winning Students Against Depression website, which has supported millions of users nationally and internationally. Other previous projects with national impact include the widely-used Mood Boost course and Student Minds' Positive Minds peer support course. Denise's innovative student Welcome Ambassadors project has recently been promoted by the Universities Minister and Department for Education as an example of good practice in supporting student transitions. Her current interest is the integration of compassion-focused psychoeducation into the curriculum.

Dr Andrew Reeves is a BACP Senior Accredited Counsellor/Psychotherapist and a Registered Social Worker. He is also an Associate Professor in the Counselling Professions and Mental Health at the University of Chester. He works as the Director of Colleges and Universities for the Charlie Waller Memorial Trust, regularly working with colleges and universities across the UK in developing mental health training strategies with institution-wide impact. He has written extensively around his research area of working with suicide risk and self-injury. He is the author of seven books and numerous articles and book chapters. He is on the Steering Committee for the International Pluralistic Conference and holds external examiner roles at both UK and international institutions. He is previous Editor-in-Chief of the *Counselling and Psychotherapy Research* journal and is current Chair of the British Association for Counselling and Psychotherapy.

Nic Streatfield is Head of Student Services at York St John University, managing a wide range of student support teams. He is Vice Chair (Professional Development) of AMOSSHE, the Student Services organisation, and was a trustee at Mental Wealth UK, helping to merge that student-led charity into what is now Student Minds. Nic has an MA in Counselling, is a BACP Accredited Counsellor/Psychotherapist and since 2003 has worked in university counselling and wellbeing services at the Universities of Manchester, Sheffield, York, Leeds and at Royal Holloway, University of London. Nic has completed the Leadership Foundation's 'Future Professional Directors' course and is also a Yorkshire Accord coach. Nic has co-written the Advance HE 'Governors' Guide to Safeguarding' and has spoken at national conferences on a range of student wellbeing and mental health subjects. Nic previously worked in Family Services while living in Australia and worked in the private sector as Operations Director for a company providing psychological outcome measure software to NHS, Universities and Third Sector services. Outside of work Nic is an FA-qualified football coach who manages his daughter's football team, and has run three marathons.

Dr Dominique Thompson is a GP, young people's mental health expert, TEDx speaker, author and educator, with over 20 years of clinical experience caring for students, most recently as Director of Service at the University of Bristol Students' Health Service. It was for this work that she was named Bristol Healthcare Professional of the Year 2017. She is a Clinical Advisor for the Royal College of GPs, and for Student Minds, the UK's student mental health charity. She was the GP member of the NICE Eating Disorders guideline development group, and the Universities UK StepChange and Minding Our Future committees. Dominique is also a member of the Mental Wellbeing in Higher Education Working Group (MWBHE), and was on the Board of an NHS Mental Health Foundation trust. Dominique has helped design apps and websites to support student mental health, writes books on the topic and is author of a series of short practical guides on student wellbeing at university, including topics such as anxiety, depression, staying well (surviving the first year) and resilience (what to do if things go wrong). She has been interviewed widely, including by *The Guardian* and Radio 4's *Today* programme. Dominique has now launched her own student health and wellbeing consultancy, Buzz Consulting, to assist organisations in improving their student support offer.

Dr Antonio Ventriglio is a psychiatrist and psychotherapist at the Department of Mental Health in Foggia, Italy. He is an honorary researcher at University of Foggia and has completed two PhD programmes there. He also has a Research Fellowship at Harvard University (Schizophrenia and Bipolar Disorder Program). He has been a member of the Ethics and Review committee of the World Psychiatric Association (WPA, triennium 2014–17). He is currently an Honorary Member of the WPA, a member of the Italian Society of Psychiatry and the Italian Society of Social Psychiatry. He is Editor for Letters of the *International Journal of Social Psychiatry* and has authored more than 100 peer reviewed articles and chapters for several international books.

Definition of Terms

Mental health, mental wellbeing, mental health difficulties and mental illness are terms that are in common use, but often without clear or shared definitions or understandings. This is to a degree a reflection of the changing narrative around mental health that is current in society. For the purposes of this book, as editors we propose that the following definitions/usages are adhered to. They are congruent with the definitions to be found in the Higher Education Policy Institute (HEPI) report on student mental health (Brown, P. [2016] *The Invisible Problem? Improving Students' Mental Health*), the Royal College of Psychiatrists' report (2011) *Mental Health of Students in Higher Education* (report CR166) and the Mental Wellbeing in Higher Education Good Practice Guide (MWBHE/UUK [2015] *Student Mental Wellbeing in Higher Education*).

Mental health

Good mental health encompasses the emotional resilience that enables us to enjoy life and to survive pain, disappointment and sadness, and an underlying belief in our own and others' dignity and worth. It also allows us to engage productively in and contribute to society and our community. Mental health can be described as spanning a spectrum, dependent on each individual's feelings, experiences and life events, and there is no absolute divide between mental health, mental health difficulties and mental illness.

Mental wellbeing

This is allied to mental health, but is often used as a broader concept, taking in a range of aspects that together constitute 'wellbeing'. A positive sense of mental wellbeing is for all of us to consider all of the time, as we might consider our physical, social and spiritual wellbeing. It is quite possible to have a good sense of mental wellbeing and yet be living with a diagnosed mental illness.

Mental health difficulties/Mental health problems

There is also a spectrum of what can be considered mental health difficulties, from mild to severe. What might be considered 'mild' can still have a significant effect on a student's ability to be a student; and an individual with 'severe' difficulties can, with appropriate support, find themselves with a good sense of mental wellbeing. Symptoms of mental health difficulties such as depression and/or anxiety may beset anyone at any time, giving rise to ongoing conditions that could interfere with the student's university experience and have implications for academic study. Such symptoms may follow major life events such as the end of a relationship, bereavement or leaving home, and can impact significantly on how students feel about themselves and how they engage with the transitions and challenges of university life.

Mental illness/ill health

Mental illnesses are conditions that are beyond what would be seen as the anticipated experience of the ups and downs of life and usual development. They may arise from organic, genetic, psychological or behavioural factors (or combinations of these) that occur in an individual, or an individual in relation to their environment. Mental illness can be acute (for example, a sudden or one-off episode) or chronic, and may fall within the definition of a 'disability' as defined in the Equality Act 2010. A diagnosis of mental illness is formally made by suitably qualified medical practitioners, and this is usually necessary for entry into secondary or tertiary care within the NHS.

Disability

Some mental health difficulties will constitute a disability under the Equality Act 2010, and disabled students are entitled to reasonable adjustments in respect of their particular support needs. The Act defines a disability as a physical or mental impairment which has a substantial and long-term adverse effect on someone's ability to carry out normal day-to-day activities. It should be noted that some mental health difficulties will not be defined under the Equality Act as a disability qualifying for protection or adjustments, and others will not require a formal diagnosis to qualify.

Foreword

'Universities have always acknowledged that the emotional and psychological wellbeing of their students is part of their remit'. So begins the editors' introduction to this timely volume. I am not entirely sure about 'always', but it is indisputable that there has never been a time when matters of health and wellbeing have had such prominence both within and without our universities or schools, or, indeed, received such funding, a reasonable quantitative measure of concern. Similar rises are also seen in metrics such as the number of students seeking help, declaring to the university that they have mental health problems, or answering affirmatively to similar questions in surveys.

It is a moot point if students actually have higher rates of mental disorders than appropriate comparison groups, but it probably matters little. Although the enormous expansion in student numbers since 'my day' (rather a long time ago I am afraid) means it is certain that proportionately more young people with known mental health disorders are now able to go to university (a good thing), it is still the case that going to university is not random, and that those at higher risk of poor mental health are less likely to be in full-time education. It is for that reason that it was not unexpected that the first national data on student suicide showed a lower, not higher, rate than the corresponding population. And whilst population rates of mental disorders have remained remarkably stable for decades, the only exception to this is in young women between 16 and 24, so whether or not students are at higher or lower risk, the absolute numbers of those at university with mental health disorders are likely to be increasing.

What is indisputable is that more and more students recognise themselves to have mental health problems, and are prepared to come forward and ask for help. And, as this volume shows, it is also indisputable that this has created something of a crisis in universities, with no consensus on what lies behind these changes, and hence, and not surprisingly, no consensus on what should be the appropriate response. It is for that reason that this volume is so timely.

Going to university is a time of transition, and like all times of transition it is accompanied by challenges, strains, upset, turmoil and occasionally mental disorder. When I was elected President of the Royal College of Psychiatrists in 2014 I made a promise to visit every university with a medical school to talk about mental health and ill health. I had not kept up with the expansion of medical schools, or perhaps I would not have made that commitment, but in any event I fulfilled it. Usually the venues were packed, and on occasion we needed an overflow room. Most of the student unions I visited had conducted some form of mental health survey, which often reported high rates of mental health problems, usually in the 70 to 80% range, well above what more formal studies using standardised interviews found. The stories were varied, but many told of loneliness, anomie, homesickness, difficulties establishing relationships, relentless academic pressure, financial worries, especially around debt, and so on. These are not normally constructed as 'mental disorders' which probably explains some of the difference in prevalences between epidemiological rigorous studies and others organised more locally. Others talked about the struggle to get help with what professionals such as myself would definitely consider mental disorders, such as eating disorders, obsessive compulsive disorder, or development disorders such as autism. Waiting lists for support were sometimes long, especially if help was needed from secondary mental health services within the NHS.

I was left in no doubt that if any progress was to be made, it was going to have to come from within the universities, including from those who are not mental health professionals, namely the staff and students themselves. Expecting the NHS to come to the rescue for anything other than the most serious of disorders was simply never going to happen. I would go further and say not only won't it happen, it probably shouldn't either for the majority of the stories that I heard. The dangers of over-professionalising and medicalising problems was apparent to me, and to much of the audience as well.

At the end of these talks I would share my own experience. I had moved from a Northern state school to an Oxbridge college, encountering for the first time in my life public school boys (and it was boys, as we are talking about the era when only two colleges were not single sex). My first term was not happy. I felt excluded, gauche and lonely. Half way through I had returned home, miserable and wondering if I should carry on. After a week my parents gently persuaded me to return. Things picked up – not least when early exam results showed I was the intellectual equal of my more sophisticated fellow students. I wasn't sporty – I did coxing but largely as an anthropological project rather than out of any sporting desire. However, music and a minor talent at comedy writing created social networks, some of which still survive. So after a stuttering start I had settled down, and started to enjoy myself.

And the point is what? Not to bemoan the lack of informal support from my peers on arrival, although that was true and would have made a difference. Nor the fact that my college barely registered what was going on – also true, but I am still unsure if that would have helped much. My unhappiness was definitely related to my lack of an early peer group. But I used my own experience to tell my modern audiences that university is a time that changes nearly all fortunate enough to experience it. The experience is complex, but in the end we know that the benefits usually outweigh the problems. Perhaps the worst thing we can do is create the impression that a university is a 'toxic environment' for health and wellbeing, which runs the danger of becoming self-fulfilling. And the second worst thing is to pretend the opposite, that it will be a nirvana in which everyone will smile and thrive all of the time. Because you won't.

Now unlike my Round Britain Tour, this book is not aimed specifically at students. Its audience is those who have to decide on how they will address the real and present problems that universities and their students now face. And there will inevitably be disagreements – there is nothing wrong in that, indeed I would be more concerned if everyone was in agreement, because the state of the evidence, especially around interventions, does not at the moment support such certainties.

But where there is no dispute or argument is that the inevitable result of the awareness that has already been raised, let alone any yet to come, is an increasing pressure on universities to devote more resources to addressing mental health needs. And that is most easily and speedily done by increasing resources for, and access to professional mental health interventions, especially where the waiting lists are long, and tested triage and risk management procedures have not yet been adopted. Ensuring then that such interventions are directed towards those in most need is an essential part of any response.

But, as this book shows, that is very much not the end. First, everyone must remember the known risks of over-reaction and over-professionalisation. This is particularly likely if we fail to match up skills and need. Using people like me to treat normal emotional reactions to life experience is not just a waste of money, it can do more harm than good. Second, if used alone then this is an approach that is directed at individuals, and not the whole university approach that this book describes and endorses.

This approach I would summarise as putting mental health and wellbeing at the heart of what a university does – but without needing to make that explicit. Creating an atmosphere in which social networks flourish will counter loneliness and isolation, as will encouraging cultural diversity. Teaching good learning and examination techniques and skills will reduce anxiety, Adjustments to the built environment, accommodation and so on can have an immediate impact on wellbeing.

It is the whole university workforce who really deliver not just the teaching, but the culture and ethos of the university. Most of those in the Armed Forces never meet a general or admiral, just like in any office few people meet the chief executive or the board of directors. It is just the same in a university. Few students know or even need to know the name of their vice chancellor or head of school. What matters are the lecturers, tutors and so on. As has been shown in the armed forces, and in 'blue light' organisations, a little bit of mental health training goes a long way when given to the right people, the ones in daily contact with those in need.

And even more important than training is the wellbeing and morale of those in those 'frontline' jobs. This is one topic on which we can for once say that no further research is needed. In health services around the world, a work force that is well supported and has good job satisfaction delivers better clinical care and makes fewer mistakes than one that isn't. In the NHS we are constantly told to 'put the patient at the heart of everything that we do' – true enough, but the easiest way to do that is to pay more attention to the morale of the workforce. Sort that out, and the rest follows. I doubt that universities are different.

So read and enjoy this book. It contains all the research evidence that you need, including much that I didn't know existed. But it is also full of good advice and practical support. A lifetime in academia has persuaded me that a good case study is more compelling than a Lancet paper, and this volume is also full of them.

But overall what I commend to you is the importance of taking a whole university approach to the issue of mental health, and that must be owned at all times by the university itself. It cannot be farmed out to external organisations, no matter how glossy their brochures. Let's not pretend that even if you follow everything outlined in this book there will be no problems, no disasters, no unhappiness – there will be, but implementing some of the strategies in this book is a good start. And finally, you are probably reading this book because you believe that going to university remains a life-enriching experience. And you are right. It is.

Professor Sir Simon Wessely

Director, King's Centre for Military Health Research

Regius Professor of Psychiatry, Institute of Psychiatry, Psychology and Neuroscience, King's College London

President, Royal Society of Medicine

Past President, Royal College of Psychiatrists

Introduction

Ruth Caleb and Nicola Barden

Universities have always acknowledged that the emotional and psychological wellbeing of their students is part of their remit. While the student population is a mix of full-time and part-time, undergraduate and postgraduate, young adults and mature, the majority are still school leavers, coming away from home for the first time to live and work somewhere new. For this reason tutors, counsellors and advisers have long been an integral part of student support. Students are in a time of transition, living in an unfamiliar environment, frequently separated from their established family and social networks and any existing professional support. Good mental health is vital in order for them to manage the challenges that university life presents, to progress through their studies and to achieve their full potential.

The *Student Mental Wellbeing in Higher Education: Good Practice Guide* states that good mental health not only gives students the enthusiasm to flourish in their degree and personal life but also 'encompasses the emotional resilience to enable us to enjoy life and survive pain, disappointment and sadness, and an underlying belief in our own and others' dignity and worth. It also allows us to engage productively in and contribute to society or our community' (MWBHE/ UUK, 2015: 8).

The purpose of this book is to support all university staff, whatever their role, to offer the best care for the mental health and wellbeing of their students. All staff have a part to play in this. The book may also be of interest to students themselves, their friends and families, prospective students and student unions, who wish to know more about the student experience and how universities can support them, so that their experience of university life can be positive. As well as giving the background that will help readers to understand mental health in the context of HE, the book will also address the concerns of academics and professional services in terms of how to respond to wellbeing needs.

The book offers a collection of chapters written by contributors who are specialists in their field and who share their expertise and lived experience with readers. While offering a professional perspective, they have written for a broad audience with varying levels of knowledge and experience of engaging with mental health issues. They have written their chapters with the aim of sharing practical suggestions and solutions to challenging issues.

Please note that the case scenarios used by the authors to illustrate particular elements of their chapters are fictitious or composite and none relate to individual cases, though the situations and challenges they describe are true to the experiences of the authors. If they seem familiar that is because, sadly, similar struggles with mental health are repeated over and again in different university contexts. It is intended that they feel recognisable so that they can be related to; but at no point do they tell any individual's story.

There are three main sections which combine together the major elements that need to be understood in order to ensure that good practice takes place in supporting the mental wellbeing of students in higher education.

Part I – The Context

This outlines the political and economic context of Higher Education (HE) in the UK today, and examines the legal considerations that need to be thought about by universities.

- Chapter 1, *Higher Education in the Twenty-first Century: Changes and Challenges for Mental Wellbeing*, examines the context of HE in UK universities, outlining the many changes that have occurred since the last century. It also outlines the impact of these changes on the student profile and explores the current undergraduate and postgraduate body.
- Chapter 2, *The Legal Position: Obligations and Limits*, explores the key legal obligations which higer education institutions owe to their students in the context of mental health and wellbeing and the implications for the role of university staff at all levels, from policy writing to individual student care, taking into consideration what students can reasonably expect in terms of mental health care and pastoral support during their student journey. It emphasises how staff need to be aware of their responsibilities and limitations within the boundary of their roles, in order to best support students and at the same time protect the institution and themselves from complaints and legal challenge.

Part II – Mental Health

This section demonstrates what needs to be understood by staff in terms of the development of the mind, the influence of transition on student wellbeing and the impact of moving to and living in a new culture.

- Chapter 3, *Student Mental Health and the Developing Mind*, examines the development of the mind and how this may affect mental health. The contribution of neuroscience as well as biological, psychological and social aspects of mental health are explored, along with their implications for how an understanding and response to student wellbeing is shaped.
- Chapter 4, *The Student Lifecycle: Pressure Points and Transitions*, explores the student experience and how it may impact mental health and wellbeing at different stages of a student's university career, including transition from home to university and, finally, into employment.
- Chapter 5, *Cultural Approaches to Mental Health Among Migrating Students*, addresses student mental health in relation to different cultural approaches which may affect both on how a student communicates any mental health difficulty and how their communication is understood and perceived.

Part III - Policy and Practice

This section concentrates on policy and procedure, exploring a whole-university approach that offers strategic best practice, academic and departmental support, and professional support, both internal and external to the institution. It also explores the challenges of how universities manage mental health risk and crisis, the role of university staff members and staff mental wellbeing.

- Chapter 6, *From Strategy to Policy and Procedure: Making Mental Health Policies Work*, considers a whole-university approach to raise staff and student awareness about student mental health issues. It clarifies the range of concerns that mental health policies and procedures should address.
- Chapter 7, *Academic and Departmental Support*, addresses the crucial role of departmental and academic staff in relation to student mental health and wellbeing, in both their pastoral and their teaching responsibilities.
- Chapter 8, *Professional Support in Higher Education*, explores how professional support for mental health problems may be offered both within the university and externally from partners in the community.
- Chapter 9, *Risk and Crisis: Managing the Challenges*, explores the need to prevent crises, where possible, and to anticipate and manage crises that will inevitably occur, by having measures in place and clear procedures which are understood by all staff.
- Chapter 10, *Supporting Staff: Creating the Conditions for Confident Support*, emphasises the need for university staff to support the mental wellbeing of students and the consequent importance of all staff being supported to do this through training and access to effective consultation.

Finally, the Conclusion brings together the roles played by staff of all levels, and also looks at the wider role that government and society can play, to ensure that good mental health for students and staff is constantly on a university's agenda.

Student mental wellbeing is the responsibility of all university staff, and examples of collaboration and good practice will be offered. The overall aim of the book is to support the whole university community to study and work in an atmosphere of confidence that mental wellbeing is understood and promoted, and mental ill health is addressed and supported in an active and positive way. The book will provide readers with a supportive tool to help them to consider how best to support the mental health and wellbeing of their students and staff in their higher education institutions.

References

MWBHE/UUK (Mental Wellbeing in Higher Education and Universities UK) (2015) *Student Mental Health and Wellbeing: Good Practice Guide.* www.universitiesuk.ac.uk/policy-and-analysis/reports/Documents/2015/student-mental-wellbeing-in-he.pdf (accessed 29 January 2019).

PART I
THE CONTEXT

1

Higher Education in the Twenty-first Century: Changes and Challenges for Mental Wellbeing

Ruth Caleb and
Nicola Barden

Objectives

This chapter aims both to provide a snapshot of the many changes that have occurred in relation to higher education mental health in the United Kingdom, and to set the scene for the chapters that follow, many of which will pursue this theme from their own perspectives.
   It will examine:

- The political and social changes that have impacted the HE sector
- Changes in mental health in the wider population
- Changes in the student cohort
- Changes in student mental health

The political and social changes that have impacted the HE sector

The UK university sector has grown significantly in size since the last century and has changed beyond recognition. In 1910–11 there were 639,000 students who attended grant-aided establishments of further and higher education (FE and HE) in England and Wales. In 2016–17, there were 2.32 million students studying at UK higher education institutions alone. In 1950, only 17,337 students were awarded first degrees and 2400 were awarded higher degrees at UK universities. By 2010/11 this number had risen to 331,000 and 182,600 respectively. By 2016/17, the number of undergraduate degrees had yet again risen to 491,170 and postgraduate degrees to 266,125 (HESA, 2018a).

There was an increase in undergraduate degree attainment in the late 1940s due to government schemes to support those who had served in the armed forces. In the early 1990s the extension of university status offered to polytechnics caused the number of university degrees awarded to more than double. There were only 22 universities in 1918 when the Committee of Vice-Chancellors and Principals (CVCP), now Universities UK (UUK), came into existence. In 2016–17, there were 162 higher education institutions in the UK in receipt of public funding (UUK, 2018).

A significant growth in undergraduates came from the increase in attendance from traditionally under-represented groups. A clear direction was set for this widening of participation, as it came to be known, when the then Prime Minister Tony Blair before the 2001 general election committed to a target for 50% participation in higher education by school leavers. The Higher Education Initial Participation Rate (HEIPR), an estimate of the likelihood of a young person participating in higher education by age 30, gives the latest provisional initial participation rates for higher education as having risen from 42% in 2011 to 49% by September 2017, almost meeting this objective (Department for Education, 2018).

The intention was that this would provide young people with better opportunities to gain more skilled and highly paid employment, improving social mobility and at the same time addressing the skills shortage in the national economy. However, in 2004, while 79% of the children of professional parents moved from school to further and higher education, only 15% of children of unskilled parents did so, leaving questions around how much of the increase in numbers was actually reflected in wider participation.

The link made between education and employment prospects contributed towards justifying a change in the funding systems for students. With higher graduate earnings being marketed as one of the reasons for entering university, it became arguable that students should contribute to their own education; it no longer seemed reasonable for the taxpayer to fund an experience that would itself improve someone's future wealth. The Dearing Report of 1997 examined different options to fund the expansion of higher education and concluded that graduates in employment should be asked to contribute to the cost of the education that had improved their financial prospects. The Teaching and Higher Education Act 1998 introduced tuition fees into all four countries. Students could take out government-backed loans to cover these fees, paying them back from earnings at a later date and over a long period of time. The first tuition fee was set at £1000 per year in 1998; at the time of writing it stands at £9250 per year in England. A similar system followed for living costs shortly thereafter, gradually replacing maintenance grants with maintenance loans. The Scottish system developed differently, with no tuition fees being required from the majority of Scottish undergraduate students and lower fees being in place for those who did have to pay, and means-tested grants as well as loans being available for maintenance. Welsh students can apply to the Welsh government for a combined grant and loan to cover fees and maintenance, and while Northern Ireland does operate a loan system, the fee level is significantly lower than in England and there is again access to a means-tested grant as well as a loan for maintenance. So while students do contribute to the funding of their higher education throughout the UK, there are national variations in degree. While the financial investment was expected to deter poorer students from applying, it has not in fact done so, but it is likely to make affordability one factor impacting on student choice.

An unanticipated but notable additional impact of tuition fees has been the increased involvement of parents and those with parental responsibilities in everything from the choice of university to the management of university life. Now that education is experienced in effect as an expensive financial investment, parents want to make sure that it is a wise investment with the potential for a good return. It is parents who accompany prospective students to open days, who want to understand how the loans and repayments work, and who ask questions about additional bursaries or awards that each university provides. For mature students the financial questions are equally important as they are taking on a significant additional debt, but they will at least have more knowledge of managing finances and have something on which to build their decision making. Now that loans for postgraduate study have also become available the financial pressure has increased along with the opportunity, and undergraduates must consider whether they feel the need to undertake a Master's degree qualification to be distinct from the increasing undergraduate crowd.

Fees were initially set up with the possibility of differential charging between universities, with the purpose of raising standards by encouraging competition. This largely failed, with lower fees running the risk of being seen as an indication of a less prestigious institution, and most universities quickly raised their fees to the maximum allowed. Competition as a mechanism for improvement has continued to be a government strategy, visible in a proliferation of league tables. The Office for Students' National Student Survey (NSS) in particular has a high profile in reporting on teaching, learning, engagement and support through student feedback, gathered annually from final year undergraduates. The government has also established excellence frameworks for teaching, research and knowledge exchange that enable students, and their parents, to compare results between universities before making their choice, with the Teaching Excellence Framework awarding gold, silver and bronze ratings to institutions based on students' satisfaction (including NSS ratings), employment outcomes and retention rates. These awards have been controversial in terms of their assessment mechanisms and there is little evidence as yet that they have had significant influence over student choice, although that may change with time.

The sector is in continual change and subject to political insecurity. Different political parties may change the fee regime yet again; the UK's changing relationship with the European Union may change not only education but also employment patterns and prospects that will themselves impact on the place of British higher education in the future. It is feared that there could be particular challenges if the UK leaves the EU. At the time of writing, there is no cap set on the numbers of international students able to come to the UK to study at university and overall there has been a 30% growth in the number of international students in higher education over the past nine years (Migration Advisory Committee, 2018). International and European students may start to see the UK as a less friendly and welcoming place and seek other overseas study opportunities. More restrictive immigration laws, particularly on the ability to stay and work post-degree, have already had a negative impact on some international markets such as India, which has reduced its UK student numbers by more than half since 2010/11 (UUK, 2017).

Changes in mental health in UK society

There has been a significant increase in the recognition of mental illness in the UK, accompanied by an increase in the recognition of student mental health problems within universities. This is immensely positive and is due in no small part to the efforts of campaigners and educators to get mental health talked about and mental health difficulties normalised. The social movement Time to Change's 'Time to Talk' campaign with its celebrity support, and the impact of Princes William and Harry and their 'Heads Together' initiative have contributed in no small way towards this.

At the same time, the Mental Health Foundation survey (MHF, 2017) suggested that mental health is actually deteriorating in the UK population. It stated that 'while there may be an element which reflects a greater ease at acknowledging a mental health problem, nevertheless these statistics suggest a real and emerging problem. It is possible that it is linked to greater insecurities in life expectations for work, relationships and homes' (MHF, 2017: 1). There is also a gender element to this: according to McManus et al. (2016) there is a substantial and growing gap in mental health between men and women. In England, among all age groups, women are more likely than men to experience common mental health conditions, but it is in the 16–24 age group that there is the widest difference between the sexes, with young women almost three times more likely to experience a mental health condition than young men (28% compared to 10%). Mental ill health is likely to have more impact on young people, those on low income or benefits, or people living alone (McManus et al., 2016). A further survey in 2018 indicated that three in four adults in the UK have felt so stressed at some point in their life that they have felt overwhelmed or unable to cope, and around a third had experienced suicidal feelings. Again, the group most vulnerable to stress were young adults aged 18–24 years, the age of much of the UK undergraduate population, of whom 83% had experienced stress to the level where they had found themselves unable to cope (MHF, 2018). Perhaps this worsening of wellbeing is noticeable in part because society is more prepared to listen and to talk about thoughts and feelings; if this is the case it is all to the good, but makes it no less real.

Over the last few years there has been growing concern about this increase in mental ill health in the UK, matched with pledges of action to address it. The Royal College of Psychiatrists' (RCPsych) report 'Whole-person care: From rhetoric to reality (Achieving parity between mental and physical health)' (Bailey et al., 2013) outlined the strong relationship between mental health and physical health. It stated: 'This report should be seen as the first stage of an ongoing process over the next five to ten years that will deliver parity for mental health and make whole-person care a reality' (Bailey et al., 2013: 9). The NHS blueprint for the future, the *Five Year Forward View for Mental Health*, written by the Mental Health Taskforce (see Mental Health Taskforce, 2016), acknowledged that mental health must be a priority for health care. The report aimed to achieve equality between mental and physical health for children, young people, adults and older people. The Prime Minister Theresa May assured parliament in her speech to introduce the 2017 Conservative Party Manifesto that what she termed 'the burning injustice of mental illness' (May, 2017) would be challenged, and made clear that 'we will introduce the first new Mental Health Bill for thirty years to put parity of esteem at the heart of treatment and end the stigma of mental illness once and for all' (Conservative Manifesto, 2017).

However, the pledges seem some way from becoming reality. The *State of Care in Mental Health Services* Care Quality Commission report (2017) described mental health services as 'at another crossroads in its journey of transformation' (2017: 12). The report explored services for children and young people and for 'working age adults' but made no mention of students in further or higher education. Nor were student problems discussed in the Parliamentary and Health Service Ombudsman's 2018 report *Maintaining Momentum: Driving Improvements in Mental Health Care*, outlining serious failures and injustices within the NHS mental health services (Parliamentary and Health Service Ombudsman, 2018). The government's Green Paper on children and young people's mental health provision, though purporting to go up to the age of 25, made no mention about the specific challenges and needs of students, other than to state the intention to support the launch of a new University Mental Health Charter which aims to escalate the promotion of student and staff mental health and wellbeing, leading to an award recognising the meeting of improved standards (House of Commons, 2018a: 35). This absence of higher education students from government reports is curious, given the numbers that are now involved. The reality is that all of these age groups are poorly served in terms of mental health support while simultaneously being high risk. While there are generally more support services available to students at university, these are necessarily focused on supporting them in their education and do not replace statutory services, which are often poorly designed to meet the needs of a student population. This apparent wealth of HE resources is in danger of having the effect of reducing statutory resources for the student population as their needs are believed to be addressed by the institution.

Changes in the NHS mental health provision

Though funding for the Department of Health increases year on year, according to the King's Fund (2018) the rate of growth has reduced in recent years and the Department of Health budget is set to grow by only 1.2% in real terms between 2009/10 and 2020/21. This is far below the long-term average increases in health spending of approximately 4% a year (above inflation) since the NHS was established and below the rate of increase needed based on projections by the Office of Budget Responsibility (4.3% a year). In terms of mental health spending, the King's Fund briefing (2015) evidenced how the funding for adult mental health had fallen in 2011/12 and in addition showed that around 40% of mental health trusts continued to experience year-on-year cuts to their budgets. The number of NHS beds available for patients with acute mental health conditions has fallen by 72% between 1987/8 and 2016/17 (King's Fund, 2017). The NHS itself acknowledges that 'historically, treatment options for mental health compare unfavourably with those for physical conditions, particularly for children and young people'. Formed in March 2015, the independent Mental Health Taskforce brought together health and care leaders, people who use services and experts in the field to create a *Five Year Forward View for Mental Health for the NHS in England*.

As well as facing major challenges in their own academic funding, universities face the decrease of mental health funding in the NHS, which has led to reduced specialist mental health services such as eating disorder clinics and psychological therapies, and the lengthening of waiting lists for psychiatric care and psychological therapy. Figures obtained through a Freedom of Information request showed the budgets for mental health trusts fell by 2% from 2013/14 to 2014/15. In England, 29 of 53 trusts had reported a drop in income and there was a 1.4% fall in the number of nurses working in psychiatric sectors between 2010/11 and 2014/15 (Bloch, 2016).

The House of Commons briefing *Mental Health Statistics for England: Prevalence, Services and Funding* (2018b) showed that waiting times for first therapy treatment for those who had completed therapy in 2016/17 varied enormously within the UK, from an average of five days in Stoke-on-Trent to 135 days in Leicester. Waiting times for first and second treatment combined varied from 16 days in Waltham Forest to 167 days in Leicester. Those who did not complete therapy or who failed to attend their second or subsequent sessions may have been impacted by an even longer waiting time before their treatment was due to begin.

Like many statutory services, the NHS is designed around the idea of permanent residence while students will generally be living in two residences, at their original home and at university. This means a lost connection with mental health services when they move home if their GP is at university, or vice versa. It is also designed around funding streams, leading to divisions between child and adult services and between social and health care, as well as between regions. This makes it difficult for students who are moving from child to adult services; are likely to need to transfer their GP to a new area; and those who, while being on a waiting list for treatment, may be invited for an appointment during the vacation period when they are unable to engage and, as a result of non-attendance, have to go back to the beginning of the waiting list, or even start afresh.

Changes in the student cohort

The impact of the widening participation agenda and the removal of the numbers cap on higher education has been profound. While the increase in overall numbers entering universities does not yet reflect the wider society, there has been movement in the right direction. In the academic year 2002/3, there was only 10.5% participation in HE for 18-year-olds from the lower four socio-economic groups, whereas participation for those who were eligible for free school meals was up to 40% in 2012/13. In 2017, English pupils receiving free school meals were 83% more likely to go to university than they were in 2006 (UUK, 2018).

In terms of ethnicity, the news is more mixed. The number of full-time under-graduates from black and minority ethnic groups rose by 38% between 2007/8 and 2015/16 (HESA, 2018c), and, at the point of writing, students from minority ethnic groups are now overall slightly more likely to become undergraduates than their white peers, although this is unevenly distributed between the groups. However, numbers and proportions alone should not reassure the sector that they have succeeded in addressing the problems experienced by BAME (Black, Asian and Minority Ethnic) students, who remain less likely to go to the more traditional highly competitive universities and more likely to stay at home with their families and commute to local institutions. This can be a positive decision in terms of remaining connected to family support and having a strong base from which to deal with racism or bias, whether unconscious or otherwise, in the institution; it can also potentially be limiting in terms of choosing the type of university and the specific course that would be a first preference. In terms of progression, 78% of white students graduating in 2017 gained a first or a 2:1 degree classification, whereas only 66% of Asian students and 53% of black students achieved the same (HESA, 2018a). This does not relate to previous attainment or experience and Guiffrida et al. (2018) suggest it may be something to do with the university experience itself rather an earlier deficit.

The attainment gap is a priority focus for the Office for Students (2019) in their Access and Participation plans for universities, and Universities UK (UUK) and the National Union of Students (NUS) are working together in a project to sup-port and inform the sector's efforts to tackle the BAME attainment gap (Amos, 2018). The retention of BAME students is worse than that of their white peers and their overall student experience and the occurrence of hidden or overt racism may have an impact on their academic achievement and personal life. So while the increase in BAME students coming to university is to be welcomed, there are considerable challenges faced by them in staying and succeeding once here, and this is a challenge for the sector as a whole to deal with.

A clear change has also occurred in the male–female proportion of students in higher education. In 1950, just 3.4% of young people went to university, with only 23% being female (House of Commons Educational Briefings, 2012). By 2016/17, 1,314,035 students were female, 57% of the total cohort (HESA, 2018b). Men tra-ditionally find it more difficult to ask for help and this is borne out in the records on usage of counselling services. It is important to celebrate the achievements of women and girls after years of being denied equal access to education, while also noting that for male students being in a minority and losing a previously dominant position in terms of both access and progression, whether sought or not, will have a psychological impact.

Over the past 10 years, the number of first year students who disclose a men-tal health condition has increased enormously, from 3145 in 2006/7 to 15,395 in 2015/16 (HESA, 2018b). Given that many students prefer not to disclose a mental health condition, or may not have a diagnosis or thought of their strug-gles in terms of a mental health condition, or indeed not develop mental health problems until their second or third year at university, this is likely to be a considerable underestimate of the number of students at university who have diagnosable mental health difficulties, including those that count as a disability. Those who do make a declaration on their application form may also be underestimated: multiple disabilities may be logged only once, whereas mental health will often sit alongside other conditions.

Universities are working hard to encourage prospective students with mental health disabilities to disclose their condition before entry. When they do, it enables their Disability Services to meet with the students early in their course or even pre-arrival to establish their learning needs for when they start. This will facilitate academic departments to offer appropriate academic help and to have made reasonable course adjustments prior to the start of the programme, minimising the impact of the disability on the student's progression. Disability Services may also help home students to apply for the Disabled Students' Allowance (DSA), and as this takes time to arrange an early disclosure is again useful. Universities will also support students who are not entitled to DSA funding, for example due to their international student status, or the mental health difficulty not falling within a recognised diagnosis. The changes in funding to the DSA look set to continue, with impact on government-funded support for some students with mental health difficulties. However, it is clear that whether or not the support is funded, the responsibility of universities under the 2010 Equality Act will not diminish.

The student body is more diverse than previous generations: more students come as young parents, asylum seekers, young carers or having been in care, or the first in their family to come to university. There are different forms of study, such as work-based learning, degree apprenticeships, two year degrees, distance learning, and different university types, including both small and private institutions. With all these changes, most UK university students are still young adults: in 2018 two-thirds of all university students were aged under 25, including 89% of the full-time undergraduate cohort (Thorley, 2017). This should not limit thinking about the perspectives of older students, but does mean that additional thought must be given to the needs and difficulties of this dominant age group. They are more vulnerable in terms of developing mental health difficulties, and young adults have a higher risk than the rest of the population of developing major ongoing mental illnesses such as psychotic and bipolar disorders (RCPsych, 2011). It has long been understood that young adulthood is a challenging time, as new experiences such as living away from home and having to find a new sense of belonging may lead to distress and dislocation as well as a sense of pride and achievement. Many untested practical and social as well as academic skills are required in the movement towards independent life. Living together is not a new part of university life but living in such huge halls of residence is, with many now provided by the private sector and not in-house. With the arrival of the private sector there is even more variety in levels of support provided in accommodation, with the added complication of finding ways for these to articulate with the university services.

It was in part this awareness of the additional transitional challenges that students faced that led to counsellors being introduced into universities in the UK and USA in the mid-1940s. Counselling and mental health services can now be found in almost all universities, and the demand on them continually increases. The IPPR *Not by Degrees* report (Thorley, 2017) noted that almost two-thirds (61%) of HE institutions saw an increase in the use of their counselling services by more than 25% over the past five years, and overall there has been a 94% increase in demand for counselling services and an 86% increase in attendance at disability services in the last five years. While this may in part demonstrate the higher level of stress that students are now under, on the positive side it may also indicate a normalisation of support and hopefully a reduction of the stigma that seeing a counsellor and seeking help has previously generated.

Changes in student mental health

Universities and other higher education institutes (HEIs) have entered a marketplace that was not even conceived of 50 years ago. From being a privilege for the few, higher education is now within reach of the many, with the 2001 target of 50% close to being a reality. This has very welcome implications for equality of opportunity, but has also brought pressures of a wholly different kind to students embarking on a degree, as well as to the institutions and staff teaching them. There is an altogether new customer narrative in education, casting it as a transaction rather than a journey, with an outcome increasingly defined in terms of financial success. With many more graduates in the job market the need to stand out has never been greater. So-called 'good' first and upper second class degrees are seen as essential by many employers and students alike; extra-curricular activities are assessed less for pleasure or personal development and more for their relevance to future employment; time is a carefully measured resource and often includes students finding paid work to supplement insufficient incomes. Even the maximum maintenance loan or grant is unlikely to meet the most frugal costs of living. This is not the picture of a 'snowflake' generation that is often drawn, but of a stressed and anxious cohort for whom the demands of the degree are being juggled with the need to earn money and invest in themselves as a marketable product.

The impact of the changes to the financing of higher education outlined above has made most students very aware that they will carry a large debt. The Institute for Fiscal Studies report (IFS, 2017) stated that students in England will graduate with average debts of £50,800, including increases in interest rates. Ironically, students from the most economically impoverished backgrounds will graduate with even greater debts of over £57,000 on average, following the scrapping of university maintenance grants and their conversion into loans since the academic year of 2016/17 (Sutton Trust 2019).

Year on year the Higher Education Policy Institute (HEPI) Student Academic Experience Survey has found that the wellbeing of students is lower than the wellbeing of the general population, and indeed continues to fall in spite of the fact that satisfaction in their courses in terms of their perceived value for money has risen. The survey found that only 17% of undergraduates felt happy most of the time compared with 32% of all 20- to 24-year-olds, and only 18% of undergraduates reported the lowest level of anxiety compared with 36% of all 20- to 24-year-olds (HEPI and Advance HE, 2018).

The number of suicides in UK higher education has risen from 77 in 2006/7 to 95 in 2016/17, which is in proportion to the rise in student numbers in that decade. Most of the students who took their own life were undergraduates, with 66% being male. However, the rate of student suicide overall is significantly lower than in the general population (ONS, 2018); as the Royal College of Psychiatrists (RC Psych 2011) points out, university can be considered to some extent as having a protective factor.

Some groups will come with pre-existing vulnerabilities to poor mental health, often related to oppression, dislocation and less sense of belonging in the HE environment. Two examples are given below, and there are many others: care leavers with no family to fall back on who may arrive with few if any close ties; estranged students in similar positions; young carers with additional responsibilities at home; asylum seekers with uncertain futures and traumatic pasts – while there will be resilient and positive individuals in these groups, sometimes better equipped precisely because of the challenges they have already overcome, it is also easy to see how past experience may make the transition to and ongoing engagement with university and academic life more difficult.

LGBTQ+ students

Changes in perceptions of sexuality and gender have been profound in society over the last 40 years. Students are more able to openly identify as lesbian, gay, bisexual, trans, or queer (LGBTQ+). But this is not yet as easy as it sounds, even in the comparatively open environment of a university, and there are likely to have been stresses in managing identity and coming out at home, at school and in home communities prior to arrival. LGBTQ+ groups are more likely to suffer from poor wellbeing, with only one in 10 reporting low levels of anxiety, compared to 18% of all students (HEPI and Advance HE, 2018). The Stonewall/YouGov 2013 survey on homophobic hate crime (Guasp et al., 2013) noted that one in six lesbian, gay or bisexual people experienced a homophobic hate crime or incident over the previous three years. As an interviewee in the report said, 'it messes with your confidence and affects your work and health' (2013: 30). It takes time for the experience of equality to catch up with the legislation, so while LGBTQ+ students are theoretically in an equal position to their heterosexual, cisgender counterparts the actual experience is seldom like this, even though it is vastly improved from the days of criminalisation.

International students

International students may also encounter difficulties in embedding into UK student life and the educational system. The additional transitional demands of leaving home and familiarity hundreds or thousands of miles away may be added to by enormous financial pressures and family hopes of success, with no backstop should things go wrong. Initial high expectations can be met with culture shock, and sometimes racial discrimination (Newsome and Cooper, 2016). Feeling welcomed particularly with some of the rhetoric that has accompanied discussions about leaving the EU can be challenging, even when prepared for. Different ways of thinking about wellness and origin-specific views of mental health can impact on help-seeking behaviour, and if the help when approached is not culturally sensitive it is easy to quietly go away.

Identities and pressures are, of course, intersecting. An international student away from home, where the home country is less liberal in its views on sexuality, may explore or affirm a gay or lesbian identity for the first time, with the complex stresses and liberations that might bring. The personal, social and political worlds all contribute to mental health.

Conclusion

This chapter has set the scene for the pages that follow by giving a sense of the changes that have occurred in higher education within the UK in terms of student numbers, the profile of university cohorts and the pressures that students are now under in the current highly competitive climate. It has also noted some of the moves that there have been in society's attitudes to and understanding of mental health. Pollard et al. (2015) attributed the increased demand for mental health support in universities to four factors: greater acceptance of talking about mental health in society generally; better and earlier diagnosis and treatment; universities becoming known for their ability to provide support; and increasing academic and financial pressures on students during their degrees. As other chapters in this book will demonstrate, most universities have taken on the challenge to adapt their services, programmes and student experience opportunities to the evolving student profile, including the changes in expectation and responsibility in relation to mental health support. However, constant societal and political shifts and the concomitant insecurity that this engenders make clear the continual need to build flexibility into support structures, which will – like their universities – be responding to persistent and often unpredictable change for the foreseeable future.

This contextual kaleidoscope impacts on the experience of being a student. Considering the developments within higher education in terms of the impact on students enables universities to better plan for and respond to students' needs and expectations, in order to effectively teach and support them.

References

Amos, V. (2018) Tackling ethnicity attainment gaps – we want to hear from you. www.universitiesuk.ac.uk/blog/Pages/Tackling-ethnicity-attainment-gaps-we-want-to-hear-from-you.aspx (accessed 3 March 2019).

Bailey, S., Thorpe, L. and Smith, G. (2013) Whole-person care: From rhetoric to reality. Achieving parity between mental and physical health. http://publiche althwell.ie/node/436048 (accessed 30 January 2019).

Bloch, S. (2016) NHS mental health funding falls in England. 14 February. *BBC Online.* www.bbc.co.uk/news/health-35559629 (accessed 30 January 2019).

Care Quality Commission (2017) *The State of Care in Mental Health Services 2014 to 2017.* www.cqc.org.uk/sites/default/files/20170720_stateofmh_report.pdf (accessed 30 January 2019).

Conservative Manifesto (2017) Mental HEALTH. https://fullfact.org/health/conservative-manifesto-2017-mental-health/ (accessed 30 January 2019).

Department for Education (2018) *Participation Rates in Higher Education.* https://assets.publishing.service.gov.uk/government/uploads/system/uploads/attachment_data/file/744087/Main_text_participation_rates_in_higher_educa tion_2006_to_2017_.pdf (accessed 30 January 2019).

Guasp, A., Gammon, A. and Ellison, G. (2013) *Homophobic Hate Crime: The Gay British Crime Survey 2013.* London: Stonewall and YouGov. www.stonewall. org.uk/sites/default/files/Homophobic_Hate_Crime__2013_.pdf (accessed 27 January 2013).

Guiffrida, D., Boxell, O., Ponicsan, I., Hamell, S. and Akinsete, R. (2018) Supporting black British university students, part one: Understanding students' experiences with peers and academic staff. *University and College Counselling Journal,* 6 (3): 4–11.

HEPI (Higher Education Policy Institute) and Advance HE (2018) *Student Academic Experience Survey.* https://www.heacademy.ac.uk/knowledge-hub/student-academic-experience-survey-report-2018 (accessed 10 April 2019).

HESA (Higher Education Statistics Agency) (2018a) Student outcomes dataset. www.hesa.ac.uk/data-and-analysis/students/outcomes (accessed 30 January 2019).

HESA (Higher Education Statistics Agency) (2018b) Who's studying in HE dataset. www.hesa.ac.uk/data-and-analysis/students/whos-in-he (accessed 30 January 2019).

HESA (Higher Education Statistics Agency) (2018c) Students in higher education dataset. https://www.hesa.ac.uk/data-and-analysis/students/whos-in-he/charac teristics (accessed 15 March 2019).

House of Commons Educational Briefings (2012) https://researchbriefings.files. parliament.uk/documents/SN04252/SN04252.pdf (accessed 10 June 2019).

House of Commons (2018a) Transforming children and young people's mental health provision: A Green Paper and next steps. www.gov.uk/government/consultations/transforming-children-and-young-peoples-mental-health-provi sion-a-green-paper (accessed 10 June 2019).

House of Commons (2018b) *Mental Health Statistics for England: Prevalence, Services and Funding*. http://researchbriefings.parliament.uk/ResearchBriefing/Summary/SN06988 (accessed 30 January 2019).

IFS (Institute for Fiscal Studies) (2017) Living standards, poverty and inequality in the UK. July. www.ifs.org.uk/publications/9539 (accessed 31 January 2019).

King's Fund (2015) Mental health under pressure. www.kingsfund.org.uk/publications/mental-health-under-pressure (accessed 30 January 2019).

King's Fund (2017) NHS hospital bed numbers: Past, present, future. www.kingsfund.org.uk/publications/nhs-hospital-bed-numbers (accessed 30 January 2019).

King's Fund (2018) The NHS budget and how it has changed. www.kingsfund.org.uk/projects/nhs-in-a-nutshell/nhs-budget (accessed 30 January 2019).

May, T. (2017) The shared society: Prime Minister's speech at the Charity Commission annual meeting. www.gov.uk/government/speeches/the-shared-society-prime-ministers-speech-at-the-charity-commission-annual-meeting (accessed 30 January 2019).

McManus, S., Bebbington, P., Jenkins, R. and Brugha, T. (eds) (2016) *Mental Health and Wellbeing in England: Adult Psychiatric Morbidity Survey 2014*. NHS Digital. http://content.digital.nhs.uk/catalogue/PUB21748/apms-2014-full-rpt.pdf (accessed 30 January 2019).

Mental Health Taskforce (2016) *The Five Year Forward View for Mental Health*. www.england.nhs.uk/wp-content/uploads/2016/02/Mental-Health-Taskforce-FYFV-final.pdf (accessed 30 January 2019).

MHF (Mental Health Foundation) (2017) Surviving or thriving? The state of the UK's mental health. www.mentalhealth.org.uk/publications/surviving-or-thriving-state-uks-mental-health (accessed 30 January 2019).

MHF (Mental Health Foundation) (2018) Stress: Are we coping? www.mentalhealth.org.uk/file/3432/download?token=709ABkP8 (accessed 30 January 2019).

Migration Advisory Committee (2018) *Impact of International Students in the UK*. https://assets.publishing.service.gov.uk/government/uploads/system/uploads/attachment_data/file/739089/Impact_intl_students_report_published_v1.1.pdf (accessed 30 January 2019).

Newsome, L.K. and Cooper, P. (2016) International students' cultural and social experiences in a British university: 'Such a hard life [it] is here'. *Journal of International Students*, 6 (1): 195–215 .

Office for Students (2019) Our new approach to access and participation. www.officeforstudents.org.uk/advice-and-guidance/promoting-equal-opportunities/our-new-approach-to-access-and-participation/next-steps/ (accessed 27 January 2019).

ONS (Office for National Statistics) (2015) More children using social media report mental ill-health symptoms. www.ons.gov.uk/peoplepopulationandcommunity/wellbeing/articles/morechildrenusingsocialmediareportmentalillhealthsymptoms/2015-10-20 (accessed 30 January 2019).

ONS (Office for National Statistics) (2018) Student suicide statistics. www.ons.gov.uk/peoplepopulationandcommunity/birthsdeathsandmarriages/deaths/

articles/estimatingsuicideamonghighereducationstudentsenglandandwalesex-
perimentalstatistics/2018-06-25 (accessed 30 January 2019).

Parliamentary and Health Service Ombudsman (2018) *Maintaining Momentum:
Driving Improvements in Mental Health Care*. https://assets.publishing.service.
gov.uk/government/uploads/system/uploads/attachment_data/file/693175/
Maintaining_momentum-driving_improvements_in_mental_health_care-_
Report-Final-Web-Accessible.pdf (accessed 30 January 2019).

Pollard, E., Williams, M., Coare, P., Marvell, R., Houghton, A. and Anderson, J.
(2015) *Understanding Provision for Students with Mental Health Problems and
Intensive Support Needs*. Brighton: Institute for Employment Studies and
Lancaster University, Researching Equity, Access and Partnership.

RCPsych (Royal College of Psychiatrists) (2011) *Mental Health of Students in
Higher Education*. www.rcpsych.ac.uk/publications/collegereports/cr/cr166.
aspx (accessed 30 January 2019).

Sutton Trust (2019) English students face highest graduate debts, exceeding Ivy
League average. www.suttontrust.com/newsarchive/english-students-face-
highest-graduate-debts-exceeding-ivy-league-average/ (accessed 30 January
2019).

Thorley, C. (2017) *Not by Degrees: Improving Student Mental Health in the UK's
Universities*. London: Institute for Public Policy Research (IPPR). www.ippr.
org/files/2017-09/1504645674_not-by-degrees-170905.pdf (accessed 26 January
2019).

UUK (Universities UK) (2017) *International Facts and Figures: Higher Education
May 2017*. www.universitiesuk.ac.uk/policy-and-analysis/reports/Documents/
International/International_Facts_and_Figures_2017.pdf (accessed 26 January
2019).

UUK (Universities UK) (2018) Higher education in numbers. www.universi
tiesuk.ac.uk/facts-and-stats/Pages/higher-education-data.aspx (accessed 30
January 2019).

2

The Legal Position: Obligations and Limits

Siân Jones-Davies

Objectives

This chapter will:

- Discuss the key legal obligations which higher education institutions owe to their students under English law in the context of mental health and wellbeing
- Address the part that staff play in assisting to discharge those legal obligations and manage the expectations of students (and, increasingly, parents) in respect of the provision of pastoral support
- Highlight the importance of institutions delivering the pastoral support they promise whilst making clear the limitations on that support
- Consider the importance of staff awareness of the boundaries of their roles in supporting students, drawing a distinction between legal obligations and perceived moral duties
- Emphasise the importance of institutions providing support to staff who are supporting students with mental health difficulties

---

Whilst outside the scope of this chapter, support for student mental health and wellbeing should be considered in the context of the wider student-related legal and regulatory frameworks in which institutions operate.

This chapter discusses key legal obligations owed under English law. Obligations may differ for Scottish and Irish institutions, and some differences also exist for Welsh institutions, in respect of which specific legal advice should be taken. The basic legal principles addressed in this chapter will be of general application, however, as will the factual scenarios which may arise in practice.

Compliance versus challenge

Student mental health is a multifaceted area of law which draws on various distinct legal topics including, but by no means only, an institution's duty of care. It is also an area influenced by governmental, sector and societal agenda and policy, and largely untested in the Courts.

Institutions which stray outside the legal framework discussed below and breach their legal obligations may expose themselves to challenge. Challenge may come in the form of complaint or appeal under internal institutional processes or complaint to external bodies such as the Office of the Independent Adjudicator (OIA) or (in respect of alleged privacy breaches) the Information Commissioner's Office (ICO) (the UK regulator). Breach may also give rise to court claims.

Dealing with challenges can result in expenditure by institutions of valuable management time and legal costs, exposure to reputational damage and failure to support students effectively. On the other hand, compliance with legal obligations and management of students' expectations of the support which the institution provides can have very positive implications, including increased recruitment of students from under-represented groups, improved student retention, success and satisfaction, and a better student experience as a whole.

As such, senior leadership teams with ultimate responsibility for exercise of the institution's duties, functions and powers should ensure (with appropriate involvement of the governing body, academic board and relevant committees) that robust arrangements, policies and procedures are in place and regularly reviewed to assist the institution to comply with its legal obligations and provide appropriate pastoral support. Governors, too, should have a clear overview of the institution's legal obligations in order to exercise appropriate oversight and scrutiny.

The discussion which follows is designed to assist staff to understand better their institution's legal obligations and their role in assisting their institution to comply with those obligations.

The role of staff

Whilst this chapter addresses legal obligations owed by institutions, those obligations will be largely discharged in practice by staff and so it is crucial that staff understand the role they play in this regard and the limits on what is expected of them.

In this regard, it is important to keep in mind the nature and function of the institution – as a scholarly (primarily adult) community engaged in tertiary education teaching, learning and research. The pastoral services it provides should be tailored to supporting students in this context and staff should remember this when carrying out their roles so as best to support students with their scholarly pursuits and protect the institution (and themselves) by not going further in providing support than is appropriate in the circumstances.

Quite what an individual staff member may be expected to do in any given situation will depend on their role and the facts and circumstances of the situation, but senior leadership teams should look to ensure that all staff (whatever their roles) are aware of the implications of the institution's legal obligations on their day-to-day employment duties. This might include, for example, staff awareness-raising activities and training and the provision of 'what to do if' guides and posters.

For example, cleaners, refectory, security and library staff may, in the course of their normal duties, identify student behaviours which indicate wellbeing concerns such as to put the institution on notice of mental health problems. Whilst such staff may not be expected to address concerns directly themselves, ensuring that they are aware of 'what to look out for' and 'what to do' in such instances will assist the institution to deal with concerns appropriately and provide timely support to students. All staff should know from where to seek guidance and to whom to refer concerns (for example, student wellbeing teams or heads of student services) and where to signpost students for support, particularly out-of-hours or in crisis situations.

Some staff (such as university counsellors or nurses) may owe their own professional obligations to students in light of the professional roles in which they are employed.

Supporting staff who support students

Supporting students who are experiencing mental health difficulties can be difficult and stressful for staff, particularly where staff are receiving frequent out-of-hours communications from students seeking support or in situations involving serious self-harm or attempted suicide. Senior leadership teams should ensure that support is provided to staff who are supporting students experiencing mental health problems not only to assist staff to support students (see Chapter 10) but also to assist the institution to act reasonably to protect the health, safety and welfare of its staff and discharge its duty of care to them.

CASE STUDY 2.1

A university's business school has seen a dramatic rise in the number of students experiencing significant mental health difficulties, especially amongst international students. A junior lecturer complains he is being overwhelmed by students demanding support and contacting him at all hours of the day and night (including at weekends) and who often disclose serious concerns. He says he recently received an email from a student late on a Saturday night expressing suicidal thoughts and did not know how to respond. He says he is finding it very stressful dealing with these communications in addition to his teaching duties and is very worried that a student may suffer harm as a result of his not responding appropriately or quickly enough.

The university should provide all academic and administrative faculty staff with mental health awareness training and ensure they are informed about where they can seek guidance and to whom they can refer concerns within the university and where they may signpost students for support, particularly out-of-hours or in crisis situations. It should also consider the nature and parameters of the junior lecturer's employment and whether he has been stepping outside those (for example, in how he has been dealing with out-of-hours communications from students). In addition, the university should consider what support the junior lecturer may need in light of the concerns he has raised in order to assist discharging its duty of care to him.

Provision of a challenging student experience

Whilst not a definitive legal guide to student mental health and wellbeing, this chapter addresses institutions' key legal obligations. Given the specific higher education context in which these obligations arise, tensions may occur in practice between an institution providing a suitably challenging and demanding tertiary education experience and one that is not overly stressful. Whilst some degree of tension may be inevitable, institutions should look to ensure that demands placed on students are reasonably appropriate for the programme of study or research in question. For example, it may be anticipated that the academic and related demands of a PhD programme will be greater than those for an undergraduate programme of study. In addition, the more general demands of student life should be clearly described to prospective students so that they may make informed decisions about whether to apply to the institution or accept an offer of a place there.

Student-facing literature should make clear that prospective students will be joining an environment in which they will be intellectually challenged and expected to be critical thinkers, self-disciplined and self-reliant. It should explain that they will be members of a community in which views and beliefs are routinely tested and freedom of speech and expression within the law protected. It should describe the manner in which programmes are delivered, contact hours and anticipated workloads, requirements for self-study, the demands of particular components such as work placements or overseas study, and site locations so that students can understand travel demands. In addition to pastoral support, information should be provided about more general learning support designed to assist students to undertake and progress with their studies. This may include guidance on the format and referencing-style of essay writing and warnings about academic malpractice, including plagiarism.

In this way, institutions will be assisted to provide a more positive student experience, tailored to the academic nature of that experience, and reduce what students may (rightly or wrongly) perceive to be unnecessary or unacceptable pressure.

Pastoral support and the student contract

The nature and extent of the pastoral support which an institution offers may be instrumental in an individual's decision whether to apply to the institution or accept an offer of a place there, and accurate descriptions should be given of its support services together with any limitations on those. As the relationship between an institution and its students is, as a matter of law, a contractual one, an institution may be susceptible to challenge for breach of contract if it fails to deliver educational and pastoral services in the manner it has promised. A student who successfully sues an institution in the Courts for breach of contract could be entitled to damages to compensate them financially for loss arising from the breach.

It is also important to keep in mind that students commonly contract as consumers with the result that consumer law applies to the contract. As such, its terms should be fair, and surprising or onerous provisions (such as powers to terminate registration, including under fitness to study procedures) brought expressly to students' attention before the contract is entered into. In addition, statements about educational and pastoral services made by or on behalf of institutions upon which students rely in entering into contracts (or making decisions connected with the contract during the course of the contract) may be regarded as contractual terms, and institutions may be in breach of contract if they do not provide the services in the way stated.

To limit exposure to challenge, senior leadership teams should ensure processes are in place to identify and avoid or close any gaps between what pastoral support the institution has promised and what it delivers in practice. Staff involved in student-facing roles (including marketing, recruitment, admissions and student services, as well as academics) should have a clear understanding of what services their institution has promised so as not to overstate them, and staff (and student ambassadors and overseas agents) involved in events such as open days, outreach activities and overseas recruitment should ensure services are described accurately to prospective students (and to their parents).

Similarly, staff involved in the preparation of student-facing literature such as prospectuses should be careful to paint realistic impressions of what student life will be like at the institution, on a particular course, undertaking a particular placement or other opportunity, living in particular halls of residence, and so forth, so that prospective students can make informed decisions as to what, where, when and how to study.

CASE STUDY 2.2

A university has received a complaint from a student about the brochure it distributes to prospective students on undergraduate open days. She complains its glossy photos of smiling young students playing rugby and lacrosse, attending black-tie events and cooking with friends in high-specification shared kitchens in the university's new, award-winning halls

(Continued)

(Continued)

of residence are elitist and bear little resemblance to her own student experience at the university. She says her personal financial situation meant she had to opt for a shared student bedroom in one of the university's older catered halls some distance from campus which means a daily, lengthy and unpleasant commute, especially when she has to work late in the library, and has made it difficult to socialise and form friendships. She says she has found it difficult to manage her eating disorder as her hall has a restricted menu of catered meals served at limited hours and inadequate general kitchen facilities. She says she feels very isolated and unhappy and, had she known what this year was going to be like, she would not have applied to the university – and would recommend to anyone looking to apply to think twice.

In determining whether there is merit in the complaint and seeking to resolve it, the university should consider whether it has failed to provide a service or experience in the way promised, or misled the student about a service or experience, and whether the negative aspects complained about could have been avoided or mitigated. More generally, it should look to ensure the environment in which prospective students will find themselves is clearly and accurately described.

Where institutions require contractual powers to manage student behaviour and risks arising from mental health concerns (including powers of suspension or termination of registration), they should ensure that policies and procedures under which they would deal with such matters (for example, disciplinary, professional suitability or fitness to study processes) are drafted fairly and lawfully and incorporated into the student contract by being brought to students' attention before the contract is made. Leaving it until registration or induction to bring such information to students' attention may be too late to enable institutions to rely on those provisions – something which staff responsible for making offers of programme places to prospective students should bear in mind.

Limitations on pastoral support

Student-facing information (such as student terms and conditions, prospectuses and webpages) should make clear any limitations on the pastoral support an institution offers, not only to assist in defining the boundaries of the institution's legal obligations but also to manage the expectations of students (and parents) and reduce the risk of challenge for failure to provide support. Limitations on pastoral services might include access to counselling services being subject to opening/appointment times, student demand or a limit on the number of sessions available.

Institutions should equally make clear those services which they do not provide (such as 24/7 counselling services or out-of-hours support), or may not at certain times be able to provide (for example because of over-demand or staff shortages), and ensure that students are clearly signposted from the outset of the relationship to where they can seek and access statutory and other third party services (such as NHS provision and nightlines), particularly in emergencies.

Institutions should also make explicit any limitations on access to pastoral services for particular cohorts such as students on placement or studying overseas, enrolled with partner institutions or on distance-learning courses, or those whose studies have been interrupted. They should make clear what entitlements (if any) alumni have to access pastoral services (for example, if they re-enrol on short courses).

Senior leadership teams should ensure (for example, through training) that staff (including academic staff) are aware of these limitations and are able to signpost students appropriately.

Duty of care

The term 'duty of care' is frequently used when discussing student mental health. Although staff may have a general understanding of the duty of care owed to students, they may be less aware of the nature and extent of the duty, and where it starts and ends.

In broad terms, institutions owe a general legal duty of care to students to deliver their services (such as teaching and pastoral support) to the standard of the reasonably competent higher education institution and to act reasonably to protect the health, safety and welfare of their students.

Questions of potential breach of duty of care are not restricted to crisis situations (such as where a student has self-harmed or attempted suicide) but may arise also in less extreme cases (such as where a student has achieved low academic results or received a poor student experience due to lack of support). Save in exceptional cases where an institution employs specialist medical staff such as a consultant psychiatrist, the duty of care will not include diagnosing mental health conditions.

For an institution to be found liable in the civil courts for negligence for breach of a duty of care, a student will need to prove (on the balance of probabilities) not only the existence of a duty of care in the particular circumstances but also its breach by the institution, and that the breach caused the student loss which was reasonably foreseeable and not too remote. Loss may include psychiatric injury and distress.

Students in higher education will be joining and participating in an essentially adult environment and institutions will not generally be 'in loco parentis' to their students (that is, acting in the place of a parent). Institutions should avoid unintentionally assuming such a role.

Standard of care

The law expresses the standard of care which institutions must meet to discharge a duty of care as that of the ordinary skilled man exercising and professing to have that special skill (*Bolam* v. *Friern* 1957); that is, in practice, the standard of the reasonably competent higher education institution acting through a reasonably competent member of staff exercising the particular skill in question. In the case of an institution's wellbeing services where specific elements are delivered by qualified health or therapeutic professionals (such as counsellors or mental health advisers), or academic staff with specific pastoral roles (such as personal tutors) – that is, by individuals exercising particular skills – the standard of care to be met by those individuals will almost certainly be higher than that required of other staff not exercising such special skills (for example, academics, cleaners or library staff).

In practice, institutions will need to break down into their constituent parts the pastoral services they deliver (for example, hall warden services, personal tutor support, financial support advice, disability support and counselling) and deliver each part to the standard of the reasonably competent institutional staff member exercising that special skill.

How much pastoral support should institutions provide?

An institution's duty of care to its students will inevitably include the provision of some form of pastoral support but the nature and extent of the support is largely down to an institution's choosing. It should be anticipated that the more extensive the pastoral services provided (for example, a counselling service, psychiatric consultations or residential nursing unit), the greater may be the risk of breaching the duty of care. It is therefore vital that institutions deliver their services competently.

Although generally untested in the Courts, it may reasonably be anticipated that (as a matter of law) institutions should at the very least be offering a basic student welfare service providing confidential advice and guidance on matters of health and disability as they affect students' academic studies and progression. That basic service should, crucially, include some form of effective triage system and enable institutions to identify those cases in which they are able to provide appropriate assistance and those in which they need to direct or refer a student to external specialist and/or emergency support services. Many, if not most, institutions go well beyond this minimum to support the students and to seek to gain advantage in a competitive sector marketplace. Where wellbeing services are extensive, and students actively encouraged to access them, even where problems are not serious, institutions will need to meet the demand which may consequently be generated. Senior leadership teams should ensure that all staff (in particular those with student-facing roles such as marketing, recruitment, admissions, registry, faculty, learning support and residences) are aware (for example through training) of the extent and limitations on the support provided and the internal and external contacts to which students may be signposted and from which staff themselves may seek guidance.

Signposting and referral of students (generally and in specific matters), and following up where appropriate to do so, is crucial to discharging the duty of care, as is working in partnership across internal functions and with external parties such as the NHS, voluntary organisations and placement providers. Arrangements with external partners should be robust and documented, including in respect of data sharing and referrals, and make clear which partner is responsible for what and when. Institutions should also work in partnership with their students' unions in the provision of support services and the promotion of student wellbeing generally.

In determining the level of service to be provided, institutions may have regard to factors such as:

- Their mission and ethos, including their focus on attracting and retaining students from under-represented groups
- The nature of the academic and research programmes they offer
- Their student demographic and any particular cohorts which may require a greater degree of support such as widening participation or international students or those under the age of 18
- Their resources and the extent and accessibility of external provision, including lengths of NHS waiting lists and alignment of external support with academic terms/vacation periods
- The type of support students expect to be in place
- Previous trends or incidents.

Institutions should inform prospective students, and remind current students, of the steps they should take to safeguard their own welfare (such as registering with a local GP and noting numbers to call in the case of emergency).

Moral versus legal duty

Whilst staff should be careful not to act beyond their roles and what is legally required of their institution, in order to avoid assuming additional legal obligations unintentionally and failing to support students appropriately, staff may in some instances consider they have a moral (if not legal) duty to act.

Issues may arise, for example, in respect of students whose registration is terminated under internal processes (such as fitness to study) where staff feel a moral obligation to assist students financially or otherwise with transition arrangements. It is important in such cases that institutions discharge their legal obligations (for example, depending on the circumstances, taking reasonable steps to signpost or refer students, in good time and before termination of registration takes effect, to external mental health, welfare, immigration or other support) as part of the internal process. Staff should not, however, go further than is legally required (for example, providing students after termination of registration with accommodation or financial support) without a considered decision having been taken by suitably senior managers that this is an appropriate course of action in the circumstances, in the interests of both the institution and the student.

On notice of risk

To discharge a duty of care, an institution will need to take reasonable steps to remove or reduce risks to students' health, safety and welfare of which the institution is (or ought reasonably to be) aware. What may constitute reasonable steps for an institution to take will depend on the specific risks it has identified (or ought reasonably to have identified) and the facts and circumstances of the matter. If an institution is subsequently scrutinised, it is likely to face questions of 'what did it know' and 'what did it do' at the relevant time. There is also the question of when an institution is on notice of risk.

Where institutions know that students are experiencing mental health difficulties (for example because students have disclosed them or it is reasonably clear from their behaviour), assessment of support needs and any risks (for example to self or others) should be more straightforward. Senior leadership teams should ensure that the institution has in place robust and effective processes for identifying, assessing and managing risks, that staff and students are aware of those processes and they are implemented properly in practice, and that contemporaneous written records are made of risk assessments carried out and the conclusions they reach. In the event of challenge, the Courts will require evidence of the institution's policies and processes and whether or not they were followed.

Particular difficulties can arise where institutions only suspect (or should reasonably suspect) that students are experiencing mental health difficulties, for example in respect of students with undisclosed mental health problems whose behaviour is noted not by support staff such as wellbeing advisers, wardens or personal tutors but by other staff such as lecturers or cleaners. Such instances will turn on their own facts but can be addressed in part by senior leadership teams raising awareness of student mental health across the institution to assist staff to feel confident in recognising when students may be experiencing difficulties and signposting staff to where they may refer concerns and seek guidance. This should be in addition to fostering an environment in which students are encouraged to disclose support needs and seek support at an early stage (including pre-application/admission).

Issues may also arise where different functions of the institution are concerned about a student, for example where a student is known to its wellbeing services and, distinctly, their academic department is concerned about their attendance or academic progression, and/or accommodation staff have been alerted to changes in their behaviour. Institutions should take a coordinated and integrated approach to dealing with matters and have arrangements in place for the fair and lawful sharing of students' personal information so that wellbeing concerns can be addressed whilst respecting students' privacy rights.

Student suicide

In the event of a violent or unnatural death (including suspected suicide), the local coroner is obliged to investigate. Police often act as coroner's officers and collect evidence to help the coroner determine the answer to four questions: who the deceased was; when they died; where they died; and how they died (including whether by suicide). The coroner will normally hold an inquest following a student death to answer those questions in a public forum, to which the family of the deceased and the institution will normally be invited to listen to the evidence and potentially ask questions of any witnesses. The coroner is under a duty to make reports to a person or organisation where the coroner believes action should be taken to prevent future deaths. The standard of proof for determining death by suicide has recently been reduced by the Courts from the criminal standard of beyond reasonable doubt to the civil standard of balance of probabilities (although, at the time of writing, permission to appeal the decision to the Supreme Court has been granted).

Inquests into suspected student suicides will be held in open court and are ordinarily freely reportable. It follows that such inquests may present institutions with potential reputational risks and this aspect should be both anticipated and managed by the institution.

Dealing with the aftermath of a student death can be particularly distressing and stressful for staff, and senior managers should consider what support staff may need to assist them to deal with such matters, in addition to support which might be offered to students and staff generally affected by the incident. It would be probable that staff and/or senior managers would be called by the coroner to give evidence at any inquest.

Criminal liability under the Health and Safety at Work Act 1974 (HSWA), or civil liability in negligence, on the part of an institution following a student suicide will, in part and crucially, depend on whether the institution had, or should reasonably have had, knowledge of a problem and failed to take reasonable steps to avoid or reduce the harm. The standard of proving criminal wrongdoing on the part of an institution will be beyond reasonable doubt, and for civil wrongdoing the balance of probabilities.

What will constitute reasonable steps for an institution to have taken will depend on the facts but, in essence, what will have been called for is a risk assessment by the institution, preferably carried out in accordance with published process or protocol, which identified the nature of the suicide risk posed by the student and the steps which the institution could reasonably take to eliminate or reduce the risk. It will be important not only that institutions carry out robust risk assessments but also that they have in place written, contemporaneous records of the assessments undertaken and conclusions reached, and the steps taken in response to those conclusions and any assessment reviews. Depending on the perceived level of risk, reasonable steps may call for institutions to refer students to internal and/or external professional mental health/emergency services.

CASE STUDY 2.3

Baz was a second year student who disclosed depression and obsessive-compulsive disorder (OCD) on admission. He progressed well academically but struggled to manage his mental health problems. He saw a university counsellor regularly but last term talked increasingly of having suicidal thoughts. He missed his last two counselling appointments. This morning, Baz was found dead in his room having taken a suspected overdose.

The university is on notice of Baz's mental health problems as he disclosed them at the outset, was known to its counselling service and disclosed suicidal ideation. The university should carry out a prompt and proportionate investigation into the matter, reviewing what it knew and when, and what it did to support Baz, including whether it followed up his missed counselling appointments. It should review its actions against what the reasonably competent institution would have done in the circumstances. This will assist the university to respond to any complaint or claim made by Baz's family and identify whether changes should be made to existing processes to avoid/reduce the risk of recurrence. The university should notify its insurers of the death and its intention to carry out the investigation and review. Where appropriate the university should seek to attract legal professional privilege for the documents it creates as part of its investigation and review in order to protect them from disclosure (for example to Baz's family or the Courts in the event of a legal claim, or to the press) and assist to manage and control information generally. As such privilege only applies to confidential communications between the university and its legal advisers for the purposes of getting or giving legal advice or in connection with litigation, the university should work with its legal advisers from the outset to attract and protect the privilege.

HSWA offences are investigated and prosecuted by the Health and Safety Executive (HSE) and the primary penalty upon conviction following criminal prosecution is an unlimited fine. Whilst the HSE does not regard mental health in universities as an enforcement priority, it will be interested when investigating matters following incidents such as a student death on campus to identify what arrangements, policies and procedures the institution had in place to support student welfare.

While suicidal and self-harming behaviours can be observed and preventive measures taken (see Chapter 9), suicide itself is often unpredictable and difficult to prevent if an individual is determined. Provided institutions properly manage those risks of which they have notice, and take the obvious precautions, they are unlikely to be held criminally liable.

Distinct from any criminal prosecution, a civil claim may be brought by family or dependants following a student death, for which the lower civil standard of proof (balance of probabilities) would apply. Whilst such a claim, if successful, may have limited financial value, it could have wider implications for an institution such as adverse publicity and reputational damage. Where a civil claim is threatened, it is important for institutions to engage insurers and legal advisers early to assist to manage the litigation and reputational risks which may arise.

Disability and reasonable adjustments

Under the Equality Act 2010 institutions must not discriminate, harass or victimise applicants or students in respect of the protected characteristics defined in the Act, and must make reasonable adjustments for applicants and students with disabilities. The protected characteristic of disability is of relevance in the context of student mental health. The duty to make reasonable adjustments arises where a disabled applicant or student is put at a substantial disadvantage in comparison with non-disabled individuals. Disabled applicants and students are entitled to specific reasonable adjustments in respect of their particular support needs. In addition, institutions have an anticipatory duty to provide reasonable adjustments in respect of their student body at large.

The Act contains a specific definition of disability: 'a person has a disability if they have a physical or mental impairment which has a substantial and long-term adverse effect on their ability to carry out normal day-to-day activities'. Not every mental health problem will be a disability qualifying for protection under the Act; where it is not, an institution may still owe a duty of care to the student.

Relevant reasonable adjustments in the context of student mental health might include (depending on the circumstances): making changes to the manner in which part of a student's course is delivered or assessed, or in respect of the process by which their conduct is managed; affording rights to be accompanied or represented at a meeting or hearing; permitting additional time to comply with procedural steps such as time limits for submitting mitigating circumstances; or providing for an interruption from studies. (These may also be appropriate forms of support, in respect of discharging a duty of care or in the interests of fairness generally, where a student's mental health problems do not constitute a disability.) What makes an adjustment reasonable will depend on the circumstances but may include the effectiveness of making the adjustment, resources available and the cost of the adjustment.

The Act also applies the public sector equality duty to non-private institutions, covering all the protected characteristics (not just disability) under which institutions must, in the exercise of their functions, have due regard to the need to eliminate discrimination, harassment and victimisation and advance equality of opportunity and foster good relations in relation to persons sharing a relevant protected characteristic and persons not sharing it.

Forward planning and a strategic approach is required to address barriers that may impede disabled applicants and students, including in the context of student mental health. Institutions should have arrangements in place for encouraging early voluntary disclosure of mental health problems by students and prospective students and for assessing their support needs and putting in place reasonable adjustments where mental health difficulties are considered to fall within the statutory definition of disability. There should also be arrangements for encouraging early disclosure and providing support where mental health difficulties do not meet the statutory definition of disability, as discussed elsewhere in this chapter. Staff, including those involved in making admissions decisions and allocating accommodation, should ensure they are familiar with these arrangements and the institution's legal obligations.

There should also be mechanisms for assessing and monitoring the impact of disability and mental health on recruitment, retention, achievement, the student experience and employability, and on programme design, delivery and assessment and student regulations generally.

The Prevent duty

Under section 26 Counter-Terrorism and Security Act 2015 institutions must, in the exercise of their functions, have due regard to the need to prevent people (including, but not limited to, students) from being drawn into terrorism. In discharging the Prevent duty, institutions should have regard to the general and sector specific statutory guidance issued by HM Government.

There are important safeguarding aspects to the Prevent duty both in terms of the vulnerability of individuals who may be susceptible to being drawn into terrorism (although not all such individuals will have, or be vulnerable to having, mental health difficulties) and of others who may be harmed or at risk of harm by their actions. Institutions should consider student welfare when putting in place and implementing specific Prevent-related arrangements, policies and procedures. Conversely, the implications of the Prevent duty should be considered in the context of institutions' pastoral support generally.

Human rights

The Human Rights Act 1998 (HRA) gives effect to rights and freedoms guaranteed under the European Convention on Human Rights, in particular the rights: to life (Article 2 of the Convention); not to be subjected to inhuman or degrading treatment (Article 3); to respect for private and family life (Article 8, where case law has established that mental health is regarded as a crucial part of private life); and to the prohibition of discrimination (Article 14). These provisions are generally considered not to apply to private higher education providers.

A student may argue, for example, that their institution has caused them acute anxiety by implementing an internal process against them in a disproportionate and unduly intrusive manner, or exacerbated a mental health problem by failing to deal promptly with allegations of sexual harassment made by them against a member of staff or other student, thereby breaching their right to respect for private and family life. To reduce the risk of such challenge, staff dealing with student matters should ensure that they are dealt with promptly, proportionately and without unnecessary delay, and that a dialogue is maintained with the student (including keeping them informed of the progress of matters).

Data protection and confidentiality

Information about students' mental health will inevitably be sensitive in nature and require appropriate handling by institutions. Such information is also more likely to be disclosed by students in circumstances such as to attract a duty of common law confidentiality (for example, to a university counsellor during a counselling session). Under data protection legislation, information about mental health or disability is regarded as sensitive (referred to now, following the introduction of the General Data Protection Regulation (GDPR) on 25 May 2018, as 'special category data', as well as 'sensitive personal data' as was the case previously). The legislation places obligations on institutions in relation to the processing of sensitive personal information as outlined below.

The GDPR and Data Protection Act 2018 (DPA) requires institutions to process applicants' and students' general personal data and sensitive personal data transparently, fairly and lawfully. Processing means any action taken with personal data until the point of its destruction, including each instance of disclosure and data sharing.

To be transparent and fair, institutions should be open with individuals about how they will process their data, particularly in scenarios where the processing (and/or with whom data will be shared) is unusual or might not be anticipated by the individual. Often this is achieved via a fair processing, or privacy, notice. Data protection legislation prescribes substantial minimum information which such notices must contain. All data processing (internally and externally) should be within the reasonable expectation of the individual, and, in all the circumstances, should be fair and not detrimental to the individual.

To be lawful, processing should not breach any other legal obligations, such as a duty of confidentiality. It should also be justified by one or more of the lawful bases for processing prescribed in the legislation. Where sensitive personal data is concerned, a further lawful basis is required, which may, additionally, also require compliance with an extra condition for processing set out in the DPA. These additional lawful bases and conditions are narrower and restricted. One possible lawful basis is the provision by an individual of their freely given, prior, specific, informed and unambiguous consent. Depending on the circumstances, consent can be difficult for institutions to obtain, partly because of the actual or perceived imbalance of power between the institution and the student which can jeopardise the consent being freely given. In addition, where institutions are looking to rely on consent as a lawful basis for processing, they should bear in mind that consent provided by an individual may later be withdrawn. If this happens, institutions cannot simply 'swap in' a new justification – if institutions are going to process personal data regardless of the consent being in force, then an alternative lawful basis should be selected from the beginning.

Another possible lawful basis is the use of sensitive personal data where it is necessary to protect an individual's 'vital interests', which in practice will be a high hurdle to meet and require significant risk of harm to an individual (for example serious self-harm or suicide) in circumstances in which the individual is unable to provide their consent to the use of their sensitive personal data.

Staff should ensure that they have identified the relevant lawful basis for processing information in advance of the processing (including sharing) of that information, and should not look to retro-fit justifications to processing after the event. As part of the transparency obligation, mentioned above, institutions are required to specify in advance what their lawful basis for processing is.

In addition to ensuring that they have identified a relevant lawful basis for processing, staff should also ensure that they:

- Only use personal data for the purpose for which they have said it would be used
- Do not collect or accumulate more personal data than they actually need
- Hold personal data which is accurate and kept up to date
- Do not retain personal data for longer than is necessary, and securely and permanently delete it once it is no longer needed
- Keep personal data secure.

Staff should be particularly mindful of the above legal obligations when undertaking and recording risk assessments and reaching decisions, which will inevitably involve processing students' personal data. Institutions should also remember that the personal data they hold and process on individuals are subject to the right of access (and other individual rights) under data protection legislation and, should an individual request this information, the institution will (subject to any applicable exemptions) have to provide it to them. Staff should ensure when creating records (including in the course of dealing with individual matters) that the content of those records is such that they would be happy to disclose copies to individuals who make valid data subject access requests.

Students who are dissatisfied about the way in which institutions have dealt with their personal data may complain to the ICO, which may impose regulatory sanctions (including monetary penalties, but also enforcement notices) and institutions may be liable to compensate students financially (by way of a civil claim brought by the individual) where a breach of data protection obligations has caused the student loss or distress. Institutions are accountable for the personal data they process and will, if challenged, have to demonstrate compliance with data protection laws.

Information sharing

All staff involved in sharing sensitive student personal data should be familiar with the instances in which a lawful basis for processing (as explained above) other than consent may arise, and whether a student should be informed of any information sharing and the reasons for it in the absence of their consent, in addition to the wider requirements of data protection legislation and any related duty of confidentiality generally. Whilst dependent on the individual facts and circumstances of a matter, institutions should generally inform students of a decision to share their personal data without their consent as part of their transparency obligations outlined above, and the reasons for that decision. The lawfulness of sharing personal data may depend on with whom the information is being shared. Disclosure to a health professional, who are themselves subject to obligations of confidentiality, may be permissible, for example, for the purposes of preventive medicine or the provision of health care or treatment.

Institutions should ensure that the expectations of students (and parents) are managed as to the extent of privacy they can expect and to which they are entitled. Institutions need to strike a balance between not deterring students from disclosing mental health difficulties and seeking support, and not guaranteeing absolute confidentiality. Students should be provided (including as part of fair processing notices) with clear, unambiguous explanations of the type of circumstances in which personal data (including sensitive personal data) may be lawfully disclosed in the absence of their consent, what kind of information may be disclosed in these circumstances, and to whom.

Practical and legal difficulties may arise in particular in relation to situations in which information may be disclosed to third parties such as parents, external health practitioners or placement providers. It is not the role of data protection legislation to prevent an institution from taking action in emergency situations which could have beneficial consequences and avoid harm to a student or to others, notwithstanding that the institution has promised to keep that information confidential. Institutions will need, however, to balance the various interests involved and be mindful that disclosure may cause harm in some circumstances. Staff involved in dealing with such situations should ensure that they are familiar with the requirements of data protection legislation and can identify a lawful basis for disclosing the information in question.

Whilst institutions may be keen to secure an up-front general consent (obtained, say, at registration) from students to share their sensitive personal data with named individuals (such as parents) in the future, there may be legal and other risks associated with doing so. Contacting a person who was named by a student at the start of the student–university relationship, when the student's circumstances may have been very different, may not be appropriate where a situation involving the student occurs down the line. A student may also not understand or contemplate the situations where such disclosures may be made – and may even have forgotten about the consent by the time a disclosure is imminent. An institution would need to consider the legal basis for contacting a particular third party and sharing sensitive personal data about a student in light of the circumstances arising at the relevant time, and should not look to rely on a previously obtained, up-front, general consent for sharing such information.

Where future concerns did arise about a student's welfare (whether or not the student had previously named a person to contact in the event of such concerns arising), an institution would need to address, on the facts and circumstances at the relevant time, what steps it might take to mitigate a risk of harm to the student (or to others) and whether it was necessary to share specific information with a specific third party (who may or may not be a person previously named by the student) to that end. The starting point might well be for the institution to have a conversation with the student to get their response to any proposal that the institution contact a particular third party and to seek the student's explicit consent for such contact to be made and their sensitive personal data so shared. There might be very good reason, however, why a student might object to an institution contacting a particular third party, and contacting a third party might exacerbate a situation, depending on the circumstances. Where the student did not provide their explicit consent (or was unable to provide consent), the institution would need to identify another lawful basis for sharing personal data with the third party – and consider whether a student's refusal to give consent meant that disclosure in contravention of that refusal remained 'fair'.

To assist in managing these aspects (and matters generally), and reducing the risk of challenge, information sharing (internally and externally) by staff should be necessary, proportionate and lawful and on a need-to-know basis to appropriate contacts only, and subject to published policies and protocols which reflect the requirements of data protection legislation. Depending on the lawful basis relied upon, as discussed above, having in place a relevant policy to govern the processing of sensitive personal data may indeed be mandatory under the DPA.

The issues discussed in this section can be tricky ones for institutions to deal with and require a judgement to be made which balances the risks of sharing particular information with a particular third party with the risks of not sharing that information with that third party. Each instance will call for careful consideration in light of the circumstances arising in the particular matter and for a reasoned decision to be made, and blanket-decisions should be avoided. Institutions should ensure that all staff are aware of to whom within the institution such issues should be referred for determination and that staff responsible for making such determinations have the expertise, confidence and support to do so.

Policies and procedures

The existence and fair implementation of transparent, published, accessible and lawful policies and procedures for promoting student wellbeing and dealing with individual student matters (including assessing and managing risks) will assist institutions to discharge their legal obligations not only to students experiencing mental health difficulties but also to other students or staff who may be at risk from their conduct. Relevant policies and procedures include those relating to admissions, fitness to study, equality and diversity, professional suitability, mitigating circumstances, discipline and interruption of studies. The appropriateness and effectiveness of implementing a particular internal process should be considered and processes should not be invoked to take inappropriate or arbitrary action against students with mental health problems. Depending on the facts, expulsion of students or other disciplinary action may not only be ineffective in dealing with concerns and supporting students but also, where a student's mental health difficulties constitute a disability under the Equality Act, discriminatory and unlawful.

Staff responsible for the drafting and implementation of policies and procedures (for example, registry and academic staff, investigating and presenting officers and panel members) should be aware of the implications for those processes of the legal obligations discussed in this chapter.

Staff should avoid making decisions under internal processes which should only properly be taken by medical professionals (for example in relation to the diagnosis of mental health conditions) whilst ensuring that they do not avoid decision making which properly falls within their remit for the management and regulation of students (for example deciding whether or not students are fit to study or to return to study). Where staff are considering removal of students from university accommodation, careful thought should be given to the ability to do so lawfully under the terms of the student accommodation contract and protection from eviction legislation.

Conclusion

In order to widen participation, support students effectively, promote wellbeing agendas and comply with the law, institutions need to have a clear understanding of their legal obligations and what they mean in practice for programme design, delivery and assessment, marketing and recruitment, and provision of a positive student experience in an increasingly competitive and consumer-focused sector. Whilst not a definitive guide, this chapter has aimed to provide some assistance to institutions in this regard.

In terms of key themes, it is crucial that institutions:

- Create realistic impressions of what life is like at the institution and what support is available so prospective students can make informed decisions about whether to apply or accept offers of places
- Eliminate gaps between what support is promised and what is actually provided, and make clear any limitations on the support available
- Take reasonable steps to protect student health, safety and welfare
- Support staff who support students with mental health difficulties.

This chapter contains a general legal overview only. It does not constitute legal advice, and is not a substitute for taking independent legal advice.

Further reading

Advance HE (for all four UK nations). www.advance-he.ac.uk/
For information, advice and guidance about equality and diversity for students and staff in higher education institutions for all four UK nations and in colleges in Scotland.

Equality and Human Rights Commission, Commission in Wales and Commission in Scotland. https://equalityhumanrights.com/en
For information, advice and guidance on equality and human rights across England, Wales and Scotland.

Equality Commission for Northern Ireland. www.equalityni.org/
For information, advice and guidance on equality in Northern Ireland.

Irish Human Rights and Equality Commission. www.ihrec.ie/
For information, advice and guidance on human rights and equality in Ireland.

Competition & Markets Authority 'UK higher education providers – advice on consumer protection law. Helping you comply with your obligations' (12 March 2015).
For information about the consumer law obligations of higher education providers to undergraduate students and how consumer protection law applies to the higher education sector.
www.gov.uk/government/publications/higher-education-consumer-law-advice-for-providers (accessed 22 February 2019).

Reference

Bolam v. Friern Hospital Management Committee [1957] 2 All ER 118 at 121.

PART II
MENTAL HEALTH

3

Student Mental Health and the Developing Mind

Dominique Thompson

Objectives

This chapter will consider:

- What constitutes good mental health and how this differs from mental health difficulties
- Introduction to common mental health problems in the student population
- Understanding the development of mental health issues in the young brain
- How to notice if students are suffering from mental health difficulties
- Suicidal thoughts and risk assessment (referral)

Introduction

One of the most striking facts about the human brain is its ability to adapt to new experiences. Students arriving at university have to similarly adapt, arriving, as they do, from very wide and varied backgrounds. Differing schools, countries, cultures, family expectations and past life experience will have an impact on how they adjust to their new environment. All of this and more will have shaped how their brains, emotions, character, personality and spirit will respond in the higher education setting. This chapter will lay out some of the context of mental health, difficulties and illness, whilst reviewing the evidence to date on how everyone's brains, environment and experience affect their mental wellbeing. This approach will follow the author's own view of mental health, whereby a combination of factors, including genetic, environmental and emotional, affect psychological wellbeing. This holistic approach, putting the student at the centre, considers the interplay between innate biological and genetic tendencies, the impact of the environment each person is immersed in and inhabits, along with their experiences throughout life. This leads to every individual having a unique experience of mental wellbeing or difficulties. All of these factors should ideally be taken into account when trying to understand mental health issues, and when trying to manage them or support others in doing so.

What constitutes good mental health and how does that differ from mental difficulties?

People exist along a fluctuating spectrum of mental health. When it is good they enjoy life, engage in it, feel resilient and positive. Like physical health, mental health can be adversely affected by clinical conditions, such as depression. Such disorders are considered mental illnesses, and more than the emotional consequences of life's 'ups and downs'. Mental illnesses must meet certain criteria to be considered as such, even if not yet formally diagnosed by a clinician. These criteria are defined by the World Health Organization in the *International Statistical Classification of Diseases and Related Health Problems*, or ICD for short. It references diseases and injuries and lists the key features which must be present for a diagnosis to be made. From it, other manuals have been derived, such as the American Psychiatric Association *Diagnostic and Statistical Manual of Psychiatric and Mental Disorders* (DSM).

Wellbeing is considered to be a broader concept than mental health, whereby an individual is feeling and functioning well in their life. It is possible for a person to have a mental illness but also have good mental wellbeing, or for a person to have no mental illness but have poor wellbeing. Physical health, social support and spiritual disposition can all interplay with mental health to create good or poor wellbeing.

It is more challenging to define the variety of mental health difficulties that can befall anyone at any time in life, be they mild, moderate or severe, and which are variously referred to in everyday, non-clinical conversations as stress, worry, pressure, distress and trauma. Such symptoms are real and difficult to manage but do not meet clinical thresholds for diagnosis, whilst still having a genuine and adverse effect on daily activities such as academic study, relationships, family life and jobs. These mental health difficulties should be managed sensitively and with care, to support the students through challenging times and try to ensure that they do not spiral down into more clinically significant disorders. A student might for example suffer the bereavement of a close relative, and naturally feel tearful, flat, listless and unmotivated for a while. This normal reaction could resolve with support, empathy and space to grieve, or could deteriorate into a prolonged depressive episode if additional stressors are placed on the student, such as exams or relationship breakdown. The key feature suggesting a clinical diagnosis of depression would be the prolonged and all-pervasive nature of the low mood, preventing the student from being able to enjoy their usual activities even after several weeks had passed. The grieving reaction is a normal mental health difficulty, whereas the depressive episode is a mental health illness.

It is worth noting that different cultural backgrounds will affect beliefs and behaviours around mental health or illness, and may change help-seeking behaviour, or recognition and interpretation of changed behaviour and emotions. Cultural differences may come from religious, ethnic and country-specific influences (addressed particularly in Chapter 5), as well as in language use around mental health or difficulties. Stigma may be much more significant for certain demographic groups, preventing them from seeking help or leading to denial of issues. There are alternative views on topics such as therapy, evidence-based medicine, diagnoses and medication. Holding such diversity of experience and opinion in mind may allow for better support for students, viewing their issues through a different mental health and wellbeing lens than the dominant one.

Introduction to common mental health problems in the student population

The first presentation of mental health problems typically occurs in childhood or adolescence, with phobias appearing at the lowest ages and anxiety and mood disorders following later. Schizophrenia typically occurs in late teens to early twenties (Kessler et al., 2007). Roughly half of all lifetime mental health disorders start by around 14 years of age and three-quarters start by 24 years of age (Kessler et al., 2005).

It is estimated that around a third of all GP appointments in the UK have a mental health component (Mind, 2016) and from audits at the author's previous university GP practice around half of all GP appointments were for a mental health problem. In the UK nine out of 10 people receiving care for a mental health problem are doing so only in primary care, not in specialist NHS services (Gask et al., 2009). Primary care general practice is therefore likely to be the most common setting within the NHS for students with mental health difficulties to be seen in and cared for.

A recent survey of 12 UK university GP practices published in *Not by Degrees: Improving Student Mental Health in the UK's Universities* (IPPR, 2017) outlined the most common mental health diagnoses recorded and managed by the GPs, of which the most prevalent was depression, followed by anxiety. This reflects the results of the Global Burden of Disease study (Whiteford et al., 2013), which similarly shows that depression is also the leading worldwide mental health problem, followed by anxiety. Students, who are often dismissed as being fit, healthy, and having the 'best years of their lives', do in fact reflect national and global mental health prevalence. This is further supported by Macaskill's study of undergraduate university students screened using a population mental illness screening tool (GHQ-28) on entry and mid-way through their first, second and third years, which showed them to have similar rates of illness overall to the UK general population (17%), apart from half-way through the second year when significantly more (one in four) were found to be symptomatic (Macaskill, 2013).

Comparing students with their non-student peers in the UK is also interesting, as it indicates that students are considerably less happy, more anxious, have lower levels of life satisfaction and are less likely to feel that life is worthwhile (Neves and Hillman, 2017). In other words, UK students have demonstrably lower levels of wellbeing (defined by the four categories mentioned) than their non-student peers. This means that being at university is not, as some might expect from potential educational, career or earning benefits conferred, protective against mental health issues, but instead seems to add pressure which lowers overall wellbeing.

Some specific groups

Specific groups of students face further barriers to wellbeing. Research into Chinese and Malaysian student mental health in the UK has found that they face challenges in seeking support, including a lack of understanding about the NHS and the Western medical model, language and cultural barriers (University of Nottingham, 2011). Additionally, the HEPI Student Academic Experience Survey of 13,500 students concluded that LGBTQ+ students scored significantly lower for all four areas of wellbeing (life satisfaction, life worthwhile, happiness and low anxiety) compared to non LGBTQ+ students (Neves and Hillman, 2017).

A briefing by the National Union of Students, *Black Students and Mental Health* (NUS, 2014), identified specific barriers to accessing help for black students, namely stigma, lack of a cultural context in which to view mental health (which was described by some as 'taboo'), fear of stereotypes around black people and mental health being applied to them, and experience of a perceived lack of training on the part of medical staff when approached about mental health issues. Having black role models in the Student Union was seen as a very positive way to break down some of these barriers. Lack of awareness of support services was apparent in both this research, and in a HEA 2016 survey that found that Black, Asian and Minority Ethnic students had the lowest awareness of campus support available, of all student groups.

At a population level the most recent national Adult Psychiatric Morbidity Survey 2014 (digital.nhs.uk, 2017), carried out every seven years since 1993, showed a surprising and significant increase in the rates of mental health conditions in young women aged 16–24 in the UK. They are three times more likely than their male peers to have a mental health condition, with one in four suffering from a common mental health problem (defined by the survey as depression, anxiety, phobia, obsessive-compulsive disorder and panic disorder) when surveyed. In 1993, it was only twice as likely. They also have higher rates of self-harm, bipolar disorder and post-traumatic stress disorder. Such statistics are relevant for the population at university. The same survey showed that one in six of all adults (over 16) met the diagnostic criteria for a common mental health condition in the prior week.

Mature students

Office of National Statistics (2017) figures reveal that 20- to 24-year-old adults in the UK have the lowest levels of mental wellbeing of the whole adult population, although this group is not, of course, limited to students. When caring for, or working with, mature students (defined as being over 21 when commencing an undergraduate degree) it may therefore be helpful to bear in mind some common challenges, and how these may adversely impact on their wellbeing.

For many students, financial pressures are significant, but for mature students they may be even higher if they are also responsible for a family or dependants. They may have caring responsibilities and have to plan their timetables well in advance to allow for child care or other arrangements. They potentially have further to travel, are less likely to live on campus, and may also hold down part-time jobs, which add additional demands on their time while being essential to meet their financial responsibilities. The consequences of debt may be far greater for mature students, and thus the stress associated with earning adequately correspondingly much higher. Mature students report feeling more isolated at university (Newson et al., 2011), having less in common with the traditional undergraduates, and this can lead to loneliness and low mood. Some have skills gaps, having had a different educational pathway, and fewer technical or computer skills, depending on their age and educational level. This can lead to self-doubt and 'imposter syndrome', or guilt that they are trying to do too much and yet not doing anything properly (Shanahan, 2000). They will be working extremely hard with the aim of eventually seeing significant benefits to their career prospects and lifetime achievements, but at a potential cost to their family and home life, as well as wellbeing. Mental ill health may have delayed their entry to higher education, and such problems could recur as their stress or isolation increases. They might be unsure where to seek help as a mature student, or be reluctant to do so when they feel so much time, effort and sacrifice has been invested, in case it is suggested that they pause or stop their studies. They may not realise what support is available to them, and that they should, if they sought help, be able to continue with their studies.

Going to university as a mature student can be a hugely positive and rewarding achievement, an opportunity to redefine oneself in middle life, and a chance to launch a new career, but it can be fraught with challenges, not least of all to one's mental health, and appropriate early support and advice from higher education staff can significantly improve outcomes for such 'lifelong learners'. For university staff, early and regular contact with mature students could pre-empt some of these issues, with open acknowledgement of the additional challenges, and discussion of support services and options should they ever be required.

Some specific conditions

With reference to specific conditions, psychotic disorder has remained stable in the general population for the last 14 years at around 0.5%, and is equal between men and women. Prevalence of bipolar disorder in 2014 was found to be highest in the 16- to 24-year-old age group at 3.4%, but of equal prevalence between men and women, and emotionally unstable (previously known as 'borderline') personality disorder prevalence was 2.4% in all adults. Attention deficit hyperactivity disorder (ADHD) prevalence was high, with 10% of the general population screening positively, though an even higher proportion (14.6%) of the 16- to

24-year-olds screened positively. Almost one in four of those screening positive for ADHD were receiving treatment for anxiety or depression. This illustrates how often mental health diagnoses go hand in hand, one linked with another, and how often students might be managing more than one condition, whether or not they are formally diagnosed.

From this it is evident that national studies increasingly validate the sense of an increasing need for mental health support from university staff over the last few years, which is likely to reflect an increasing prevalence of mental health issues on UK university campuses. In addition to rising demand there has also been an increase in the complexity of mental health issues, with more students disclosing mental health diagnoses as part of their Disabled Students' Allowance (DSA) claims, and a steady rise in the number of student suicides (ONS, 2018), all of which make it increasingly likely that university staff from all departments across higher education institutions will have come into contact with students in distress or requiring additional support.

A basic understanding of common mental health difficulties and mental illness will be of help to all university staff members as they endeavour to support the students towards better outcomes, such as healthier, happier lives, successful graduation and future employment.

Understanding the development of mental health issues in the young brain

When humans are born their brains have enormous potential for change and development. This potential, or 'plasticity', gives people the opportunity to develop in a myriad of ways with regard to learning, memory, personality, risk taking behaviours, control and language. Scientists have discovered that as individuals move from childhood to adulthood their brains change in structure and size, leading to greater numbers and density of connections between brain cells (called synapses), 'pruning' of these connections leading to remodelling of nerve pathways and a differential rate of growth between differing areas of the brain that control specific functions. It has been shown that the higher mental abilities, often referred to as the executive functions, including planning, prioritising and control of impulses, and overseen by the prefrontal cortex, develop later than the more basic functions.

This delayed maturation can persist into adulthood, as the brain is thought to continue significant growth and development until the age of about 25 years. A study at the University of Pennsylvania (Baum et al., 2017) further clarified that the brain networks responsible for executive functions become increasingly well organised and integrated with the rest of the brain from the ages of 8 to 22 years, leading to better self-control for example. This may help to explain how, as people move from teenage years to their mid-twenties, they become gradually less likely to take risks, more organised and better able to focus. It is worth bearing in mind that brain development does not stop but does slow down after the age of 25, and that more mature students can protect their cognitive functions by exercising their bodies as well as their minds, eating well and minimising chronic stress (Mora et al., 2007).

Neuroplasticity, the brain's potential to react and adapt to adverse stimuli, can progress well, allowing humans to respond in a beneficial manner and be resilient, but it can also go wrong. There are several theories about how mental illness develops. The neuroplasticity hypothesis of mental illness holds that depression, for example, is a disorder of the hard wiring of the brain, and that significant pathological stress results in aberrant wiring of the brain pathways which cannot be reversed quickly, leading to long-term depressive symptoms. The part of the brain identified as being much more active and enlarged when this abnormal wiring response occurs, the amygdala, is associated with anxiety and fear responses. Conversely, the areas responsible for executive functions, the prefrontal cortex, and memory, the hippocampus, become reduced in activity (Pittenger and Duman, 2007). So the hypothesis would suggest that depression would lead to heightened fear and anxiety, poor organisation, planning and control, and poor memory.

Much research has also been done into a theory that mental illness is caused partially by an overactive inflammatory response (Raison and Miller, 2011). This theory asserts that stress leads to raised cortisol, adrenaline and noradrenaline, leading in turn to an immune (inflammatory) response that adversely affects brain development. The inflammation interferes with serotonin production. Serotonin is a neurotransmitter that, along with dopamine, is needed for a healthy mind and stable mood. If production is interfered with by the inflammatory process and there is not enough serotonin, then the theory argues that depression will follow. Some studies have shown that early life traumatic events do lead to an increase in inflammatory response, and this may explain why mental illness may then follow many years later (Niwa et al., 2017). Multiple causes of stress to the human brain and its emotional development have been suggested and researched, including maternal stress in pregnancy (suffering from influenza or iron deficiency) and childhood maltreatment, malnutrition or early trauma (Weir, 2012).

Theories about neuroplasticity and inflammatory responses do not however address why some people who survive traumatic or stressful experiences do not develop mental illness or symptoms of mental difficulties when others do. These theories suggest a process, but not what 'switches on' the process in certain individuals. Genetic mechanisms are thought to be involved. Factors which affect gene expression, that activate genetic processes without affecting the DNA sequence, are called epigenetic factors. These genetic triggers may explain the different kinds of depression, or variety of mental disorders, for example schizophrenia, in individuals exposed to stressors. In one study, teenagers who had died by suicide had a 48% higher expression of a gene that adversely affects dopamine activity (Manitt et al., 2013).

In summary, it is becoming apparent that the development of mental illness and disorders in young adults is likely to follow exposure to a stress event in their environment (in the womb, in early childhood, in adolescence) leading to changes of gene expression, causing changes in structural brain development and neurotransmitter activity. These events can have long-lasting effects and be 'hard wired' into the brain. Early experience and environment undoubtedly shape the developing brain and our responses to adverse events later on. Student-specific environmental stressors such as moving away from home and support networks, relationship challenges, parental expectations or social pressures, perfectionism, drugs and alcohol, financial pressures, and academic burden can all interact to potentially trigger mental disorders at a critical time of educational life. Recognition, understanding and intervention by well-placed, well-prepared and knowledgeable university staff can ensure early support and therapy are provided, with better long-term outcomes. University support staff, alongside academic colleagues, have the opportunity to make potentially transformational interventions in their students' lives by listening non-judgementally, being kind, curious, and then normalising emotions where appropriate, whilst picking up on more serious and significant signs. They can prevent a drama becoming a crisis, and can refer early to ensure better outcomes.

To differentiate between mental difficulties and mental illness, and thus intercede before things deteriorate, staff should check for the presence of the following features. The more they are present, the further along the continuum towards illness a person is:

• Persistence and pervasiveness of symptoms
• Their relentless nature
• Their impact on daily life AND the student's ability to function in a normal manner.

Early signposting to appropriate professional support will then lead to better outcomes.

What might university staff notice if students are suffering from mental difficulties?

Students rarely tell people that they are suffering from mental health problems. The likelihood is that university staff, along with other people around them, will notice behaviours that may indicate mental health difficulties or illness. This provides an opportunity for staff to normalise these difficulties, make them part of the conversations to be had at university, and to reassure and signpost to further help.

An academic, for example, might notice that a student's attendance at lectures is erratic. Such behaviour can have many causes. Mental health causes may vary from depressive symptoms causing insomnia or difficulty waking in the mornings, to social phobia or panic disorder, or obsessive-compulsive disorder, for example repeated washing of hands and thus lateness. Students with alcohol, drug or other addictions can also present with erratic attendance, and recent times have seen a rise in students presenting with addictions to social media, gambling, gaming and pornography sites. Being aware of such a variety of causes will allow academic and other staff to be diplomatic and sensitive in their enquiries about the student's wellbeing and attendance. Academic staff are well placed to notice deterioration in work standards or poor engagement in group tutorials. Some risk taking behaviours are, of course, normal in this age group and at university, but at the point where they regularly impact negatively on daily activities, or on academic achievement, it may warrant a supportive enquiry from staff about welfare, or excessive stress or pressure.

CASE STUDY 3.1

Jen spent the summer before starting university going to festivals. Wanting to make the most of her pre-university 'freedom', she decided to try some of the recreational drugs that she was offered. She arrived at her new halls feeling happy and chatty, was an enthusiastic contributor to welcome week, and ran for JCR president. In lectures she responded quickly and amusingly to questions, felt creative and inspired, even going up to the front of the lecture spontaneously to write on the white board. Everyone found her entertaining and fun, but she wasn't sleeping much, or eating, and the posters that she put up for her presidential campaign were incoherent. Some of Jen's sentences were no longer making sense and she seemed distracted and jumpy. Concerned, students and academic staff asked the senior residence staff to intervene. The residential staff made Jen a GP appointment for that day, and she agreed to have an assessment as she was exhausted and becoming anxious. She was diagnosed with hypomania, and referred for an urgent psychiatric assessment within 72 hours. Medication was discussed and started. She consented to her parents being contacted by the GP. With support, therapy and medication, she continued her studies and did not suffer any relapses that year, but she herself realised that avoiding recreational drugs was a sensible precaution in preserving her mental health.

Recreational drug use is a well-recognised trigger for a variety of mental health conditions, including hypomania and mania, and students who already have a history of mental illness should, in particular, be advised to avoid them.

Isolated students may be lonely because of language barriers, social phobia, physical barriers (such as hearing impairments), or may have Asperger's syndrome. No assumptions should be made, but discreetly engaging the student in discussion at the end of a class or lecture may reveal clues as to the cause of the isolation. This could lead to signposting for support, not necessarily after the first conversation, but perhaps when a level of trust has been built between staff member and student. Asperger's syndrome, for example, has become more common in an increasingly diverse student body, and classically presents with social awkwardness, difficulties reading social cues, poor eye contact, difficulty with empathy, and great sensitivity to change, but such students may have a positive academic record. It is a lifelong condition and signs will have been evident from childhood.

CASE STUDY 3.2

Jack was a second year student, doing well at his academic studies, but did not know where to turn for advice. He came to see the GP due to loneliness. In the GP's consulting room, he did not make eye contact, was quietly spoken, brief in his answers, and seemed distracted. When asked what he was thinking he said, 'What angles the walls meet at, and the proportions of the room.' The GP enquired about his interests, how he had found school, about his parents, and about friends he had at home. It became apparent from his answers, his longstanding social difficulties and behaviours, such as poor eye contact, that Jack had undiagnosed Asperger's syndrome, which was causing significant issues now that he was in a university environment. Living independently, having to socialise, getting a girlfriend and 'fitting in' were a challenge. Jack also admitted to anxiety on a day-to-day basis, which commonly coexists in this condition (Farrugia and Hudson, 2006).

Loneliness is surprisingly common in the student population, but fortunately there are significant resources and activities available to help people like Jack. Universities hold events which do not involve immediate direct eye contact or small talk, and these particularly appeal to those with Asperger's, such as pub quizzes, or bowling, or pizza and film nights. There may be local third sector organisations that can offer additional specialist support with regard to life skills and anxiety management. A conversation with a well-informed staff member can make significant change possible for such isolated students, and transform their experience by helping them integrate and find friends at university. The GP was able to offer advice and refer on to the university student support services, as well as to peer-to-peer support with appropriately skilled students.

Eating issues may become apparent to catering or accommodation staff, if for example they see students drinking only water or fizzy low-calorie drinks (to create a sensation of fullness) at meal times, or they notice them developing a new or growing preoccupation with food. Sudden changes in eating behaviours associated with other warning signs such as weight loss, or excessive exercise, can be indicative of an eating disorder. Anorexia nervosa results in avoiding calorie intake, leading to a low weight, whereas bulimia may lead to a normal or slightly high body mass index (BMI) as people binge eat (eating an uncomfortably large amount at one sitting), then purge (vomit) or 'compensate' for the calorie intake with excessive exercise. One cannot tell if a student has an eating disorder by looking at them, but if other signs are present then early intervention is much more likely to lead to better outcomes (NICE, 2017). Male students may also have eating disorders, and the Queer Futures study of 2015 found that gay and bisexual men were more dissatisfied with their bodies and their health than heterosexual men. This was further underlined by the fact that being gay is a risk factor for men developing eating disorders (Russell and Keel, 2002).

When speaking with a concerned member of university staff, a student with depression may admit to feeling tired all the time, suffering 'brain fog', having difficulty concentrating or focusing. Insomnia, loss of appetite, poor motivation, loss of enjoyment, mood swings and irritability are all common. Memory impairment, possibly secondary to poor sleep, is also likely. Depression may be the undiagnosed cause, but they may be worried that they are developing a physical illness, and unsure about what to do next. They are likely to be very relieved to be asked about their issues. This can be a key turning point in many students' mental wellbeing, as they are encouraged to seek professional support from health and welfare services. They may not be aware of what is freely available to them as students, especially if they are young, away from home, or from overseas. They may not feel they 'deserve' help; they may believe themselves to be lazy, and so require encouragement to talk it through with a professional; or they may believe it to be a physical issue, in which case general practice is a good place to signpost to (if they are actively suicidal a same day assessment is warranted).

At the other end of the mood scale some students will develop feelings of excessive happiness, euphoria, irritability, high energy and disinhibited behaviours. They stop sleeping, and become busy at night making outlandish plans and developing grandiose schemes. Their spending may spiral suddenly, to the point that others notice, and they talk at great speed, though not necessarily making sense. Such students are likely to be developing 'hypomania' or 'mania', and need urgent medical assessment, as such manic (with possible psychotic features) illness can lead to dangerous activities ('flying' from heights, or running into traffic), if there is loss of insight on the student's part. Such extreme behaviours can lead to the student feeling very embarrassed and awkward when they return to normal mental health, and so the sooner intervention takes place the better. Any loss of insight should prompt an urgent medical assessment. This situation requires assessment by a medical practitioner on the same day, as there is potential for the student to be an unwitting danger to themselves (or others) and thus, depending on the time of day or day of the week, and according to university protocol for mental health crises/emergencies, the student should be accompanied to either their GP for a psychiatric referral, or to a hospital emergency department for psychiatric assessment. If the student is uncooperative and in immediate risk of danger then the police will need to attend and assess the situation, potentially taking the student to a designated place of safety. It is important to also take into account the potential impact of such behaviour on other students who may be trying to care for their unwell friend or flatmate, or who may be distressed by their symptoms.

Early intervention is also particularly helpful to those students who develop hallucinations, auditory or visual, and delusions (which are both symptoms of psychosis); these are often coexistent with other symptoms such as isolation, or paranoia. Such students may complain to staff that other students are 'spying' on them in their residence, that they can hear others talking about them all the time, that the radio or television is also commenting on them, or they may be noticed talking to themselves as they respond to the voices that they are hallucinating. Clearly, if they present with obvious delusions such as believing they have 'special powers' it becomes much more obvious to those around them that help is urgently required. An urgent assessment by a medical professional is the first step, unless they appear to be in immediate danger, or a danger to others, in which case emergency services should be called without delay. Such conditions can spiral rapidly out of control and these cases of psychosis can lead to harm, especially to the affected individual, as insight is lost completely.

Self-harm is very common among young people, with one in four young women and one in 10 men aged 16–24 having self-harmed (digital.nhs.uk, 2017). One in two of these will never have sought professional help. It is common in those who have suffered emotional trauma, such as childhood abuse (physical, emotional or sexual abuse, or neglect), and the act itself can be a source of significant relief for the person affected, and is a coping strategy which cannot simply be stopped, and they should not be asked to do so. It is far better, and more likely to be successful, to address the underlying issues that led to self-harm in the first place, and to ensure that they receive evidence-based therapy from appropriately trained professionals, such as counsellors, psychologists or psychotherapists.

CASE STUDY 3.3

Roshni joined the hockey team at university, and it was her coach who noticed the razor blade scars on her upper thighs and abdomen, as well as unusual bruises on her underarms. The coach had received training about self-harm, she understood that it was not 'attention seeking', but

(Continued)

(Continued)

associated with a higher risk of suicide or suicide attempts (Carroll et al., 2014), and so gently asked Roshni, away from the other team members, if she was ok, or if there was anything she would like to talk about. She made it clear that Roshni did not have to talk then but could come back any time she wanted to. She did not ask Roshni to stop the self-harm, but encouraged her to seek support from health or wellbeing professionals. Roshni was relieved to be asked about her self-harm and talked to her coach about how she was feeling, explaining that when she was overwhelmed with emotions she would hurt herself physically, to distract herself, and that sometimes she would 'self-medicate' with alcohol to blot out troubling memories. Her coach encouraged her to try to improve her sleep pattern, and keep up her exercise regime, and advised her to avoid the alcohol and recreational drugs that could make her feel worse. Roshni sought help, and was referred to a psychologist to explore her overwhelming emotions, where she slowly started to engage in therapy.

Suicidal thoughts and risk assessment (referral)

With statistics reporting that a person (aged over 10) dies by suicide every two hours in the UK (ONS, 2017), and rates of suicide in students increasing slowly, no-one can afford to ignore suicidal thoughts. Seventy five per cent of suicides are by men (ONS, 2017). Recent statistics showed that of those people who completed suicide between 2002 and 2012, almost three-quarters had not consulted their GP or any health care professional in the year prior to their death (Hewlett and Horner, 2015; OECD, 2017).

Suicidal thoughts can be frightening both to those who are having them and those who are supporting the affected person. Thoughts of suicide, that somehow it would be easier for everyone if the person wasn't here anymore, that they would like to go to sleep and not wake up, are actually quite common. One in five adults reports having had suicidal thoughts at some point in their lives (digital.nhs.uk, 2017). The most common age group is 16–24 years, with thinking about suicide being much more common in females than males. For some people with depression it can be a safety valve, a 'go to' thought that they can retreat to when all else is too difficult. This in itself, although distressing, should not raise the same level of concern as someone who is feeling trapped and considering ending their life, for example by making plans to do so, writing notes, preparing and buying the necessary equipment, researching suicide online, and spending increasing amounts of time thinking about it. Those who are in the former group, who ruminate but have no plans, should be advised to seek professional advice and support, though less urgently. The latter group warrant urgent, same day assessment by a medical professional. During GP opening hours, acutely and actively suicidal students should be accompanied to a same day appointment. In out-of-hours situations, depending on the acuteness of the scenario, the options are to call an out-of-hours GP service, take the student to the emergency department for a psychiatric assessment, or call the police if there is immediate danger and the need to take a student to a place of safety. If a university does not have a clear mental health crisis policy and action plan, then designing one should be made a priority.

The current generation of undergraduate students has grown up in a world where it is possible to buy shoes online at 3 a.m., order takeout delivered to the door 24/7 and video chat with friends across the world at any time of day or night. From such a perspective it must seem perverse if, when they have a psychological crisis, society insists that they wait for help, book an appointment with the correct professional, and have perhaps only 10 minutes in which to explain the issues and sort out solutions. This has created a significant conflict. When the current student generation is distressed, they expect instant relief. This means that they are not very good at waiting, or 'sitting with' difficult feelings. This can lead to impulsive behaviours in challenging situations and, added to a lack of life experience, self-harming or suicidal actions can result. Overwhelming emotions or suicidal thinking can spiral out of control much more quickly, with potentially tragic consequences.

Apart from the heightened impulsivity of many young people, other risk factors for suicidal behaviour should be considered when caring for distressed students. Many studies have reviewed the multiple risk factors for suicidal thoughts and behaviours, and have found that they vary depending on whether the risk is of having suicidal thoughts, attempting to take their own life or actually ending their life. Interestingly the risk factors are not the same for each.

A recent meta-analysis of 365 studies carried out over the last 50 years (Franklin et al., 2017) found the following, which has since shaped assessment processes and advice around suicide and risk:

- Completed suicide is most likely to be preceded by a history of prior psychiatric hospitalisation, prior suicidal attempt, prior suicidal ideation, poor socio-economic status and stressful life events.
- Suicide attempts (such as overdoses) often occur after hospitalisation for psychiatric care, but the highest risk factor is prior non-suicidal self-harm (Franklin et al., 2017). In other words, if they self-harm they are likely to have done so before. They are also more likely to have a personality disorder diagnosis (Black et al., 2004).
- Suicidal thoughts should be taken seriously, listened to and referred to an appropriately trained professional for further assessment. Risk factors that increase the likelihood of such suicidal ideation include previous such thoughts, clinically diagnosed depression or anxiety, hopelessness, and a history of abuse of any kind (Rodgers, 2011).

It is important to remember, of course, that risk factors (above) may indicate that the possibility of suicide is heightened, but they differ from warning signs, which may indicate that it is imminent. Warning signs tend to occur just prior to an event, whereas risk factors raise our awareness that an event is more likely to happen to an individual at some time in the future. Warning signs for imminent suicide may include seeking the means to harm oneself, erratic behaviour, increased drug or alcohol misuse, threatening to harm oneself, and volatile mood changes (Rodgers, 2011).

Protective factors are also worth considering and have been found to include cultural factors, for example religious beliefs, and responsibility to family (Malone et al., 2000). The Reasons for Living Inventory (Linehan et al., 1983) reviews and scores six categories of protective factors: Survival and Coping Beliefs, Responsibility to Family, Moral Objections, Fear of Suicide, Fear of Social Disapproval and Child Related Concerns. Further protective factors have been defined in several studies of adolescents in particular, and include problem-solving-based coping skills ('self-agency', or the feeling of control over one's own actions), participation in sport and healthy physical activity, good relationships with parents (especially in those young adults who have been sexually abused), social support, having strong social values, and, finally, access to medical health professionals (Scottish Government, 2017).

Recent research has shown that young LGBTQ+ people under 26 are more likely to attempt suicide and self-harm than their heterosexual and cisgender (where gender identity matches the gender assigned at birth) peers. Almost twice as many LGBTQ+ people surveyed had made at least one suicide attempt compared with their heterosexual peers. Risk factors were related to negative experiences and bullying specific to their sexuality. Protective factors included a positive reaction from professional and medical staff, as well as feeling part of an LGBTQ+ community, and having a supportive family (Queer Futures, 2015). This clearly demonstrates the importance of university staff being supportive and non-judgemental in working with LGBTQ+ students. The young transgender community in the survey were shown to have particularly high rates of mental distress, with almost half having tried to take their own lives according to research by the charity PACE (Queer Futures, 2015). This compares with 6% of 16- to 24-year-olds in the UK (digital.nhs.uk, 2017). Causes of additional distress may include discrimination, intolerance, abuse, stigma, lack of acceptance, rejection, aggression and violence. Such experiences can lead to anxiety, isolation, self-harm and depression, among other issues. However, acceptance by their community can make a significant positive impact in the lives of our transgender students.

Being aware of symptoms and signs can endow staff with a degree of confidence in asking after mental health and wellbeing, and knowing that suicidal thoughts are common, but suicidal planning is not, will help them to signpost with a reasonably accurate degree of urgency.

Conclusion

The rising demand for support for often complex mental health issues on university campuses reflects the rise in mental health conditions being detected in the general population. Students report lower wellbeing scores than their non-student peers, with some specific demographic groups being further disadvantaged, and the peak age of onset of mental illness is between teenage and early twenties. There can be an assumption that young people, especially students, should be in their prime, but the evidence is clear that, at the age when most students attend university, they are at high risk of developing mental health difficulties which, in the context of transition to new environments, social network upheaval, increased academic, financial and career pressures, could make them more likely to struggle.

University staff are ideally placed to be alert to, normalise and respond to signs of mental distress, over a period of time. If staff are familiar with some of the more common mental health difficulties, and develop a sense of how urgently to refer to professional support services, then they can play a crucial role in the welfare support provided on campus. Multiple factors will play a part in how a student will respond to stresses throughout life: genetics, childhood trauma, and changes to their environment, among others. Young adults, with their 'plastic' and adaptable brains, however, have a significant potential for recovery with appropriate treatments and interventions; the earlier, the better.

Further reading

An Unquiet Mind (2015, Picador) by Kay Redfield Jamison (bipolar disorder)
    Jamison is a Professor of Psychiatry who writes an eloquent and engaging account of her journey into bipolar disorder.

Lighter Than My Shadow (2013, Jonathan Cape,) by Katie Green (eating disorders)
    Green spent five years illustrating this graphic novel of her personal experience of eating disorders, and it formed part of her recovery.

My Body is a Book of Rules (2014, Red Hen Press) by Elissa Washuta (personality and bipolar disorders)
    Washuta, now a university lecturer, describes her transition from 'college kid to adult' in a no holds barred account of her life with mental ill health.

Black Dog Books (2007, Robinson) by Matthew Johnstone (depressive disorders)
    Johnstone describes his beautifully illustrated, witty and moving book as a 'visual articulation of what it is to suffer from depression'.

Reasons to Stay Alive (2015, Canongate Books Ltd) by Matt Haig (depression and suicidality)

Author Haig turns his hand from fiction to reality as he describes his own struggles with depression and suicidal thinking in this accessible and compelling account of mental ill health.

References

Baum, G., Ciric, R., Roalf, D., Betzel, R., Moore, T., Shinohara, R., Kahn, A., Vandekar, S., Rupert, P., Quarmley, M., Cook, P., Elliott, M., Ruparel, K., Gur, R., Gur, R., Bassett, D. and Satterthwaite, T. (2017) Modular segregation of structural brain networks supports the development of executive function in youth. *Current Biology, 27* (11): 1561–72.

Black, D., Blum, N., Pfohl, B. and Hale, N. (2004) Suicidal behavior in borderline personality disorder: Prevalence, risk factors, prediction, and prevention. *Journal of Personality Disorders, 18* (3): 226–39.

Carroll, R., Metcalfe, C. and Gunnell, D. (2014) Hospital presenting self-harm and risk of fatal and non-fatal repetition: Systematic review and meta-analysis. *PLoS ONE, 9* (2): e89944.

Digital.nhs.uk (2017) *Adult Psychiatric Morbidity Survey: Survey of Mental Health and Wellbeing, England, 2014.* www.digital.nhs.uk/catalogue/PUB21748 (accessed 21 September 2017).

Farrugia, S. and Hudson, J. (2006) Anxiety in adolescents with Asperger syndrome: Negative thoughts, behavioral problems, and life interference. *Focus on Autism and Other Developmental Disabilities, 21*(1): 25–35.

Franklin, J., Ribeiro, J., Fox, K., Bentley, K., Kleiman, E., Huang, X., Musacchio, K., Jaroszewski, A., Chang, B. and Nock, M. (2017) Risk factors for suicidal thoughts and behaviors: A meta-analysis of 50 years of research. *Psychological Bulletin, 143* (2): 187–232.

Gask, L., Lester, H., Kendrick, T. and Peveler, R. (2009) *Primary Care Mental Health.* London: Royal College of Psychiatrists.

HEA (2016) The 2016 Student Academic Experience Survey https://www.hepi.ac.uk/wp-content/uploads/2016/06/Student-Academic-Experience-Survey-2016.pdf (accessed 26 April 2019).

Hewlett, E. and Horner, K. (2015) *Mental Health Analysis Profiles (MhAPs): England.* OECD Health Working Papers, No. 81. Paris: OECD Publishing. Available from https://doi.org/10.1787/5jrxr7vj1g9v-en (accessed 11 June 2019).

IPPR (2017) *Not by Degrees Improving Student Mental Health in the UK's Universities.* www.ippr.org/files/2017-09/1504645674_not-by-degrees-170905.pdf (accessed 21 September 2017).

Kessler, R., Amminger, G., Aguilar-Gaxiola, S., Alonso, J., Lee, S. and Ustün, T. (2007) Age of onset of mental disorders: A review of recent literature. *Current Opinion in Psychiatry, 20* (4): 359–64.

Kessler, R., Berglund, P., Demler, O., Jin, R., Merikangas, K. and Walters, E. (2005) Lifetime prevalence and age-of-onset distributions of DSM-IV disorders in the National Comorbidity Survey Replication. *Archives of General Psychiatry*, *62* (6): 593–602.

Linehan, M., Goodstein, J., Nielsen, S. and Chiles, J. (1983) Reasons for staying alive when you are thinking of killing yourself: The Reasons for Living Inventory. *Journal of Consulting and Clinical Psychology*, *51* (2): 276–86.

Macaskill, A. (2013) The mental health of university students in the United Kingdom. *British Journal of Guidance and Counselling*, *41* (4): 426–41.

Malone, K., Oquendo, M., Haas, G., Ellis, S., Li, S. and Mann, J. (2000) Protective factors against suicidal acts in major depression: Reasons for living. *American Journal of Psychiatry*, *157* (7): 1084–8.

Manitt, C., Eng, C., Pokinko, M., Ryan, R., Torres-Berrío, A., Lopez, J., Yogendran, S., Daubaras, M., Grant, A., Schmidt, E., Tronche, F., Krimpenfort, P., Cooper, H., Pasterkamp, R., Kolb, B., Turecki, G., Wong, T., Nestler, E., Giros, B. and Flores, C. (2013) *dcc* orchestrates the development of the prefrontal cortex during adolescence and is altered in psychiatric patients. *Translational Psychiatry*, *3*(12): e338.

Mind (2016) *Better Equipped Better Care*. www.mind.org.uk/media/5063246/find-the-words-report-better-equipped-better-care.pdf (accessed 23 September 2017).

Mora, F., Segovia, G. and del Arco, A. (2007) Aging, plasticity and environmental enrichment: Structural changes and neurotransmitter dynamics in several areas of the brain. *Brain Research Reviews*, *55* (1): 78–88.

Neves, J. and Hillman, N. (2017) *Student Academic Experience Survey 2017*. [ebook] Oxford: Higher Education Policy Institute. www.hepi.ac.uk/wp-content/uploads/2017/06/2017-Student-Academic-Experience-Survey-Final-Report.pdf (accessed 21 September 2017).

Newson, C., McDowall, A. and Saunders, M. (2011) *Understanding the Support Needs of Mature Students*. Guildford: University of Surrey. www.surrey.ac.uk/psychology/files/Mature_student_report_2011.pdf (accessed 21 September 2017).

NICE (National Institute for Health and Care Excellence) (2017) Eating disorders: Recognition and treatment. Guidance and guidelines. www.nice.org.uk/guidance/ng69 (accessed 21 September 2017).

Niwa, M., Jaaro-Peled, H., Tankou, S., Seshadri, S., Hikida, T., Matsumoto, Y., Cascella, N., Kano, S., Ozaki, N., Nabeshima, T. and Sawa, A. (2017) Adolescent stress-induced epigenetic control of dopaminergic neurons via glucocorticoids. *Science*, *339*(6117): 335–9.

NUS (National Union of Students) (2014) *Black Students and Mental Health*. London: NUS.

OECD (2017) *Mental Health Analysis Profiles (MbAPs): England*. OECD Health Working Papers. Paris: OECD Publishing.

ONS (Office for National Statistics) (2017) Total number of deaths by suicide or undetermined intent for students aged 18 and above in England and Wales, 2014. www.ons.gov.uk/peoplepopulationandcommunity/healthandsocialcare/causesofdeath/adhocs/005732totalnumberofdeathsbysuicideorundeterminedint entforstudentsaged18andaboveinenglandandwales2014 (accessed 21 September 2017).

ONS (Office for National Statistics) (2018) Estimating suicide among higher education students, England and Wales: Experimental statistics. www.ons.gov. uk/peoplepopulationandcommunity/birthsdeathsandmarriages/deaths/ articles/estimatingsuicideamonghighereducationstudentsenglandandwalesex perimentalstatistics/2018-06-25 (accessed 24 January 2019).

Pittenger, C. and Duman, R. (2007) Stress, depression, and neuroplasticity: A convergence of mechanisms. *Neuropsychopharmacology, 33* (1): 88–109.

Queer Futures (2015) *LGB&T Mental Health; Risk and Resilience Explored*. www. queerfutures.co.uk/wp-content/uploads/2015/04/RARE_Research_Report_ PACE_2015.pdf (accessed 21 September 2017).

Raison, C. and Miller, A. (2011) Is depression an inflammatory disorder? *Current Psychiatry Reports, 13* (6): 467–75.

Rodgers, P. (2011) *Understanding Risk and Protective Factors for Suicide. A primer for preventing suicide*. Newton, MA: Education Development Center, Inc. (accessed 21 September 2017).

Russell, C. and Keel, P. (2002). Homosexuality as a specific risk factor for eating disorders in men. *International Journal of Eating Disorders, 31* (3): 300–6.

Scottish Government (2017) *Risk and Protective Factors for Suicide and Suicidal Behaviour: A Literature Review*. www.gov.scot/Publications/2008/11/28141444/2 (accessed 21 September 2017).

Shanahan, M. (2000) Being that bit older: Mature students' experience of university and healthcare education. *Occupational Therapy International, 7* (3): 153–62.

University of Nottingham (2011) Investigation into the Mental Health Support Needs of International Students with Particular Reference to Chinese and Malaysian Students. www.nottingham.ac.uk/studentservices/documents/investigation-into-the-mental-health-support--needs-of-international-students-with-particular-refer ence-to-chinese-and-malaysian-students.pdf (accessed 22 December 2017).

Weir, K. (2012) The beginnings of mental illness. www.apa.org/monitor/2012/02/ mental-illness.aspx (accessed 21 September 2017).

Whiteford, H., Degenhardt, L., Rehm, J., Baxter, A., Ferrari, A., Erskine, H., Charlson, F., Norman, R., Flaxman, A., Johns, N., Burstein, R., Murray, C. and Vos, T. (2013) Global burden of disease attributable to mental and substance use disorders: Findings from the Global Burden of Disease Study 2010. *The Lancet, 382* (9904): 1575–86.

4

The Student Lifecycle: Pressure Points and Transitions

Denise Meyer

Objectives

This chapter will:

- Introduce the idea of the student lifecycle and the student identity as, by definition, one of transition
- Discuss the psychology of transition and its application within the student lifecycle, including additional challenges facing particular groups of students
- Identify conflicting discourses affecting the expectations of students, parents and staff
- Establish effective support and a sense of belonging as essential factors for learning and for a successful university experience for all students
- Recommend practical strategies for supporting students' mental wellbeing at each stage of the student lifecycle

---

Introduction

The experience of transition is central to the student experience, and also a significant psychological challenge, recognised as an important factor in student vulnerability to mental health difficulties. An early recommendation for a whole-university approach to student mental health was Stanley et al.'s (2007) in-depth case study analysis of UK student suicide. In two-thirds of the included case studies, the student had been diagnosed with a mental health problem at the time of their death, and in most cases problems had emerged while they were students. The study highlighted the periods of transition at the start and end of the academic year as an important point of vulnerability, with a significant proportion of the students having died during these times. Many of these students were described by friends and family as having disrupted academic histories, with fear of failure a significant pressure for them, and many were experiencing a web of problems, such as relationship difficulties, heavy alcohol and drug use and financial problems, in addition to their academic problems. The study's authors described these difficulties interacting with the students' mental health problems as appearing to have left the students 'feeling trapped at a time of change'.

The study's recommendations included provision of intensive and targeted support at periods of transition and further exploration of students' vulnerability at transitional periods at schools and colleges as well as in higher education. These findings cast a spotlight on periods of transition in the student lifecycle and on the potential for typical student pressures to interact with the pressures of these transitions in significantly detrimental ways. The purpose in citing these findings extensively is not to scaremonger about students' particular fragility or vulnerability, but instead to highlight the importance of acknowledging and addressing the psychological challenges integral to the student experience and to learning.

In particular, this chapter will argue that a better understanding of the psychological impact of transition is important for addressing the needs not only of students with significant difficulties, but for all students and as the foundation for effective teaching and learning. It argues that appropriate support for students' development is essential for effective learning, and that this should not be seen as the exclusive domain of specialised support services but rather a routine consideration for all university staff.

The psychology of transition

Extensive studies of the psychology of transition indicate that 'disruptions to an accustomed way of life ... resulting in changed relationships, routines, assumptions and roles ... trigger a relatively predictable cycle of reactions and feelings' (Sugarman, 2001: 144). One well-known framework (Bridges, 2004) encapsulates the gist of these findings in the distinction made between a change in external circumstances and the emotional transition accompanying the change – the ending and feelings of loss which are the starting point for every change, and the transitional neutral zone, which must both be negotiated before a change is embraced as a new beginning. Even for positive, anticipated changes (such as progression to university) these emotions might include:

- Ending of previous life stage and/or circumstances: loss, grief, resistance, protest, despair, shock, numbness, denial, minimisation, anger, fear, longing, homesickness, doubt, relief, elation
- Neutral zone between two stages: letting go, sadness, uncertainty, disorientation, chaos, self-doubt, discomfort, worry about the future, excitement, grandiosity, tentativeness, caution, vacillation, apathy, experimenting, creativity, feeling overwhelmed, anxiety, fear of failure, frustration, search for meaning
- New beginning: acceptance, readiness, comfort, integration, clarity, commitment, ambition, celebration, but also possibly ongoing fear, resistance, or resignation.

Understanding of these responses as normal (and variable) is an important starting point in ensuring successful negotiation of a transition, promoting endurance and constructive coping as a response to the temporary emotional discomfort. Conversely, a lack of this understanding and/or heightened psychological vulnerability can result instead in attempts at avoidance or a struggle against this discomfort, often causing increased distress and difficulty. Indeed, unhelpful avoidance strategies are central features in the exacerbation of the two most common mental health difficulties, anxiety and depression (Hayes et al., 1996).

How well any individual will cope with a transition depends also on a number of individual and situational variables, making up both assets and liabilities for coping (Schlossberg et al., 1995). Schlossberg's '4S' model identifies four categories of coping factor: situation, self, support and strategies.

Situational factors include triggers such as: whether the change is anticipated or not, and the meaning to the person of the change; the timing of the change and the relationship of the timing to social norms and the person's life stage; the person's actual and perceived level of control over the change; any changes in social role and the person's perceptions of social expectations around the role; whether the change is permanent, temporary, or uncertain; whether previous experiences of transition have been successful/positive or negative; whether there are concurrent stresses, including concurrent transitions; and the person's assessment of the change as positive or negative.

Factors specific to the person's self include their personal and demographic resources, such as socio-economic status, gender, ethnicity, age and life stage and state of health; and their psychological resources, such as personality, maturity, commitment and values.

Support factors include the availability (or lack) of emotional support and nurturance; of affirmational recognition or reassurance from others of the person's worth, competence, skills and value; and of material or cognitive forms of help/aid, such as money, time, advice, and entitlements available from social networks, communities and institutions, and physical environments.

The strategies employed to navigate the transition are the final coping factor, and can be categorised in three broad types: modifying or avoiding/escaping the situation; altering the way the situation is perceived or assessed; and/or developing additional coping strategies or personal resilience.

CASE STUDY 4.1

Michael is a 19-year-old first year student found incapacitated in the corridor one early evening in the second Tuesday of term. While the resident assistant is helping him back to his room a flatmate rolls his eyes, saying Michael is a loser and doesn't really hang out with the rest of the flat. When the halls support manager later checks in on Michael, he is withdrawn, monosyllabic and visibly anxious. Through direct questioning she hears that although he attended induction sessions in the first week he has skipped some of the first timetabled events this week. He says there is a group assignment but he doesn't really know anyone on his course. He thinks he has blown it with his flatmates because he got 'stupidly drunk' each time he went out during freshers' week – now they are pointedly leaving him out of social arrangements. When she suggests making an appointment at the Student Wellbeing Service his face falls and he says, 'That would just prove to everyone here and at home what a complete loser I am. It's happening all over again – I don't know why I'm here.'

Michael is clearly having some difficulty adapting to the 'rules of the game' at university, both socially and academically, and is questioning his ability to settle in and belong. Excessive alcohol consumption is a cliché of student identity, and doubles as a socially accepted strategy for management (suppression) of difficult emotions; but in Michael's case it is possible that heightened distress has led to him overdosing on this self-medication, and/or insufficiently masking his distress to comply with peer expectations. He is giving indications of being socially anxious, and there may be a range of personal and situational factors contributing to his current difficulties. Earlier education experiences may have left him with a static evaluation of his abilities and a focus on performance, a fixed mindset about who he is and what he is capable of. He may be a first-generation student and/or from an international or minority ethnic background, whose family may not have the maps (or cultural capital) to help him plot his route into and through UK higher education.

The flatmate's description of Michael may mirror past experiences contributing to his social expectations and interactions; for example, he may have experienced bullying, prejudice or discrimination due to personal characteristics such as uncertainty about his gender identity or sexual orientation, or rejection due to traits on the autistic spectrum. He is a year older than most traditional first year students, and his reference to it all happening again may indicate a false start last year affecting his expectations this year.

Michael references problems in relation to his use of alcohol primarily in relation to dissonance with peer social norms. He may be less accustomed to alcohol than his peers or he may have an existing substance misuse difficulty affecting his ability to calibrate his consumption against the social norm. The social anxiety (and possible substance abuse problem) may be part of an entrenched mental health difficulty or diagnosed disorder, which may need further monitoring or treatment. Not knowing 'why I'm here' may refer to being at university, or a deeper existential question (indicating possible suicide risk), or both. He may have previous experiences of family and other support, or the lack of it, as well as perceptions about the social norms for his age and stage, affecting his ability to make constructive use of any available support.

As Michael's case study illustrates, the individual factors in the 4S model overlap and interact, with personal and situational factors affecting the strategies employed and the ability to make use of standardised support. Taking this into account, the model offers a useful framework not only for considering the impact of transition on individual students, but also for evaluating effective institutional measures to better support students in general.

Transition and identity

The student identity is, itself, a transitional identity. A student in higher education is traditionally someone who starts from a point of relative ignorance, considered as an apprentice within an academic discipline, in training to master the discipline and become something or someone else – a mathematician, physicist, classicist or geographer, for example. The transitional student identity eventually makes way for the stable identity endowed by the discipline mastered. In the modern world, there is a more obvious vocational angle. Students on vocational courses are working towards qualification into clear vocational identities, such as doctor, lawyer, graphic designer or social worker, and increasingly all degrees are seen (or are required to be seen) as stepping stones either into specific career paths or at least into a certain status of employability.

For students in the traditional age range (18–25), the educational transition and initiation into a vocational identity also overlaps with, and forms an important part of, identity formation within the wider developmental stage of early adulthood – also labelled 'emerging adulthood' (Arnett, 2000) or the 'threshold' stage (Apter, 2001). Most developmental theories recognise this age and stage as one during which key aspects of social identity, psychosocial, moral and cognitive development take place, alongside the epistemological or intellectual development which forms the foundation of university experience for all students (Patton et al., 2016).

Traditional-aged students will be experiencing many of the practical transitions relevant to the growing autonomy and independence which characterise this life stage – leaving home for the first time, with new self-care and other responsibilities. Students of all ages are also likely to experience some aspects of these concurrent transitional challenges related to their wider lives – changes in accommodation, financial status, routines, etc. For some students these changes alone will require significant emotional transition: international students, for example, will need to make substantial adaptations to a new host culture, possibly including use of a second or third language. The considerable transition stress occasioned by such a culture change is well documented (see Berardo and Deardoff 2012) and is often summed up in the phrase 'culture shock'. The phenomenon finds many echoes in Chapter 5.

It can be useful to recognise that all new students are subject to versions of culture shock when starting out as new citizens of an institution, not yet familiar with the institutional culture or rules of the game both socially and academically. Central to their adaptation is the learning of these rules in order to forge and maintain a new identity as a student.

Widening participation policies have opened up this privileged rite of passage experience to a greater proportion of young people, but it is important to recognise that the expectations and social norms which define student identity are still based on 'majoritised' templates of privilege. Students with 'minoritised' (Patton et al., 2016) aspects to their identities – ethnic minority, LGBTQ+, working class, or disabled students – or those from disadvantaged backgrounds, such as carers or care leavers, face additional challenges in this process of adaptation to both the student identity and the graduate identity. Independence and autonomy for students with financial and emotional backup from their families is also very different from the potentially brittle independence and autonomy of those whose family circumstances do not or cannot offer this kind of secure base from which to transition into adulthood (Petch, 2009).

The student lifecycle

There is growing recognition that transitions are not only relevant at the start and end of a university career, and that the student lifecycle is one of ongoing transition (Christie et al., 2016). A course of study entails a process of steps and intermediate identities along a path of becoming, moving through a range of transitional identities, from aspirant student or new recruit through to new employee or otherwise gainfully employed member of society. Alongside each intermediate identity are a range of choices, challenges and concurrent transitions, often including practical changes such as accommodation arrangements. Typical points of identity include:

- Applicant/new recruit – a complex mix between choosing and being chosen, evaluating and being evaluated; qualifying to join the club
- First year student – induction into the rules of the game, socially and academically; new living arrangements (often a first experience of living with peers in university halls); new financial status
- Second year student – stepping up a level, when it starts to count; often experiencing private renting for the first time or new living arrangements; not infrequently experiencing diverging lifestyles and/or conflicts alongside additional responsibilities
- Placement/non-final year student – possibly taking on additional transitional challenges, such as living in a new country or trying out the practicalities of a vocational identity via a work placement
- Final year student – stepping up another level; focus on performance; looking ahead to the next transition into graduate status, often with looming uncertainty over practical arrangements and plans; sometimes returning home to changed family relationships, or needing to establish an adult identity while returning to a dependent position within the family home

- Postgraduate student – new rules of the game, with higher expectations about autonomous learning; fewer peers from a wider diversity of backgrounds, often with differing experiences of taught and research degrees; further financial commitment/debt; often a more complex mix of additional responsibilities alongside study
- Alternative study formats: distance learners, part-time learners and those on degree apprenticeships, two year degrees or other currently minority study formats may experience these and other changes at different times and at differing intensities to other students, with services and support usually geared towards the majority and less accessible or inclusive of their needs
- Recent graduate – labelled via degree classification and institution as well as discipline; entering a new round of evaluations and assessments as part of choosing and being chosen for a job; may involve 'going back home' and a reduction in independence and autonomy
- New employee – may or may not be within 'graduate' employment; unlikely immediately to gain full financial independence.

CASE STUDY 4.2

A course administrator notices that Tariq, a final year student, has missed a February submission deadline without explanation. He has been a middle of the road student who has generally met deadlines and passed his modules, and has not previously been 'on the radar' as a student in need of additional support. When she tries to contact him to follow up, he does not respond at first, then sends a brief email to say that he has been unwell, but doesn't refer to the extenuating circumstances procedure. She books an appointment for him with his personal tutor, in order for him to take things forward. At the tutor meeting, Tariq presents with rather flat mood and says that he has always had problems with his motivation, and a tendency to procrastinate until the pressure of the deadline forces him to get his work done. He does not refer to having been unwell, instead mentioning recent 'girlfriend hassles' causing him to fall behind – but brushes aside any further discussion about this. He says it is clear he is too far behind to complete the third year assignments to the standard required to get a good degree, and that he is now completely stuck. He has no suggestions for how his tutor might be able to help.

Tariq is not alone in finding the performance pressure in the final year stressful and difficult, with the reality that a good degree is more important in a context where a much larger proportion of young people are attending university. Like other final year students, he will also be grappling with the looming uncertainty of life beyond university, and his mention of longstanding motivation problems may indicate ambivalence about the future path laid out by his chosen course.

There may be a number of specific factors contributing to his current predicament, including family expectations or a cultural context for Tariq's feelings about his position or prospects, which may have shaped his choices or may be relevant to his next steps after university. There may be very specific consequences for Tariq's future prospects or financial circumstances, such as visa issues or significant financial losses if he is an international student, which place particularly high pressure on his results. Personal or relationship circumstances may also be playing a role in the current situation, such as an actual or threatened relationship breakdown or possible concerns about changes to relationship status following the end of university. His procrastination might indicate an element of self-sabotage related to a wish to delay next steps, in the light of conscious or unconscious ambivalence about these next steps. Tariq's low mood may be a proportionate response to current stressors or may indicate a more serious underlying mental health issue, such as depression or suicidal ideation.

As Tariq's case study illustrates, an impending transition can have significant emotional impact, affecting current behaviour. For many students, as in Tariq's case, it is possible that the post-study identity towards which they have been travelling since the start of their course is one which they wish to avoid or postpone. This can affect every stage of their student experience as well as their final level of success on the course.

Learning as transformation

Learning transitions are, of course, the central aspect of the student lifecycle, with a modern undergraduate course carefully planned to guide a student through the levels of learning which correspond with its upwardly spiralling stages. Stepwise increases in the complexity of learning outcomes take place from Level 4 (first year) to Level 6 (final year), particularly a transition towards greater criticality of understanding, evaluation and problem solving within contexts of ambiguity and unpredictability (Milsom et al., 2015).

Each step of the lifecycle must be successfully completed, usually via objective assessment against standard learning outcomes, which in turn earns the right to embark on the next step. When all goes well, this series of graded, manageable steps provides intermediary attainments marking steady progress towards achievement of the final goal, the mastery of the discipline and graduation into a newly earned identity and vocational status. However, at each stage in the lifecycle, there is also the potential for failure to meet the standard, and each transition to a new stage requires a new engagement with the uncertainty of eventual success at this new level and thus in the eventual goal.

Indeed, transition and uncertainty are essential elements of the process of deep, transformative learning by which higher education is characterised (Mezirow, 2000) – developmental on a personal level, whatever the age of the student (Patton et al., 2016). This deep learning, by which a discipline is truly mastered, requires the student to step from the safety of the known and familiar over the threshold into the limbo and uncertainty of not knowing, in order to start to grasp new concepts and master higher levels of understanding (Meyer et al., 2010).

Such learning requires experimentation, and the experience of anxiety, doubt, frustration and failure on the path to understanding. Like any transition, learning therefore demands a sufficiency of mental wellbeing and emotional resilience on the part of the student – the capacity to endure the anxiety inevitably provoked by these periods of uncertainty and to persist in the face of frustration or initial failure.

Pressure points

Looking at this combination of emotional challenges facing students raises a fundamental dilemma at the heart of the idea of success as a student – successful students must be prepared to let go of certainty and safe knowledge, yet must also regularly demonstrate mastery and understanding; they are regularly graded and assessed in a manner which fixes their abilities and attainment at measured levels, while being asked to hold faith in their ability to grow and improve.

Indeed, the 'deep performative culture across education' (Stewart and Darwent, 2015: 53) has been found to have a pivotal effect during the second/middle years at university, with a clear motivational shift for students away from mastery towards performative learning goals, contributing to the 'second year slump' phenomenon but, more importantly, interfering with the wider learning process and inhibiting motivation and confidence alongside learning (Stewart and Darwent, 2015).

CASE STUDY 4.3

A member of library staff has noticed a smartly-dressed student Alison, who spends long hours in the library, often not moving from her place for hours at a time. She is there when he opens the doors on the first day back after the Christmas break, but later that day he sees her sitting immobile for some time with tears pouring down her face. He feels very uncomfortable when she breaks down into loud sobs in response to his offer of help, and before he knows it she has started pouring her heart out about how stupid she feels, that she has no idea what is expected of her for both of her current assignments, and that despite spending hours and hours working she is certain she will fail in both of them. She says she has worked very hard to get to university as it wasn't an option for her when she was younger. She gained confidence from getting very good results on her access course and in the first year, but things seem a lot harder in the second year – her marks have dropped for assignments this year, just when she is aware that they start to count towards her degree result, and lecturers have made it clear that they are expected to be independent learners now, so she doesn't want to go and ask for feedback or help. She says she feels exhausted – that she can't go on like this.

Alison seems to be experiencing the second year slump. Her concerns about asking her tutors for help may be realistic or they may be unfounded – it is worth considering whether all students have been given clear guidance about the changed expectations in the second year, clear feedback about what they each need to work on to reach these expectations, and access to support as they adapt to these new expectations.

A number of other factors could also be relevant. Factors related to her background, for example if she is a mature student whose route to university has not followed the traditional path, may be influencing her expectations of herself, her confidence stepping up to the next level of higher education learning, and her sense of belonging. While her study habits on the surface may seem impressively committed, they may indicate a problem with over-work resulting from perfectionism and/or fear of failure. Alternatively, her long hours in the library may reflect issues with her current living arrangements or home study conditions, linked to the quality of her home relationships and/or wider support networks. She may have other commitments affecting her ability to make effective use of the hours she spends in the library. For example, if she is also working long hours in a part-time job, in order to make ends meet, then she may simply be too tired to be working effectively. And there is always the possibility that when she says she 'can't go on like this' Alison may be indicating a more serious underlying mental health issue and/or suicidal ideation.

The central role played by assessment, and therefore by success and failure, within the student lifecycle is an important situational factor adding to the emotional challenge of student transitions and is key to understanding the pressure points for students – the potency of the pressure engendered is the intimate connection between these assessments and their context within a process of core identity formation, together with the raised stakes relating to the significant investment, financial and otherwise, made when embarking upon a university education (Antonucci, 2016). At its heart, success or failure as a student is also success or failure in building a valued and valuable personal and social identity. It is about who you are, and who you can – or can't – be.

Even without taking into account any of the additional stresses and life transitions which might be relevant to individual students, the endings and beginnings of each academic year are the obvious potential pressure points for students, the periods when success or failure are determined, or when adjustments to new levels of challenge are required, respectively. Negotiating these pressure points requires sufficient mental wellbeing to remain resilient to meet these challenges, and this is most likely to take place in an environment where these pressure points are recognised and acknowledged.

Taking students' emotions seriously

What are the implications, for the higher education institution and its staff, of recognising the significant emotional challenges inherent in the life and learning transitions integral to the student experience? Timmermans (2010: 11) has emphasised that recognition of learning as a 'deeply emotional venture' for learners, as well as a cognitive venture, requires educators 'to acknowledge the difficult journey on which we are asking students to embark' and to 'help them live more comfortably with their discomfort'. However, she notes that the 'affective nature of these [learning] transitions is often [instead] minimised, denigrated or altogether ignored' (Timmermans, 2010: 5).

Indeed, alongside media handwringing about a 'snowflake generation' of young people, lacking independence and resilience, the increasing focus on emotion in education has been dubbed 'therapeutic education' and criticised as 'dangerous' (Ecclestone and Hayes, 2009), with so-called 'weaponisation' of emotion seen as a key factor in the 'infantilising' of universities (Furedi, 2017). Ecclestone and Hayes' (2009) thesis is that defining most forms of human experience as a source of 'distress' constructs a 'diminished human subject' and a 'diminished sense of human potential' which 'denies the intellectual and privileges the emotional'.

Furedi's (2017) concern about over-medicalised discourse and scaremongering over student vulnerability and safety is not without foundation, and there is a core of important critique in these arguments which must be addressed in a book about student mental health. It is, indeed, 'reinforce[ing of] misconceptions and counterproductive' when understandable anxiety and other emotional discomfort are presented or experienced as 'disorder' (Brown, 2016). As we have seen, emotional discomfort, challenge and even distress are an integral part of learning and of the student experience. However, identifying emotion as an important factor in learning is not the same as privileging the emotional over the intellectual. Neuroscientists have shown that emotions are inextricably integral to learning and knowledge, finding that 'neither learning nor recall happen in a purely rational domain, divorced from emotion' and 'knowledge and reasoning divorced from emotional implications and learning lack meaning and motivation and are of little use in the real world' (Immordino-Yang and Damasio, 2007: 9).

Likewise, there are very real issues to be untangled when calls start being made for universities to adopt legal duties 'in loco parentis'. However, pathologising calls for increased support for students as 'infantilisation' participates in and further invokes the polarising false dichotomies – dependence/independence and childishness/adulthood – which skew this debate, in the service of an ideological insistence on adulthood at 18, which does not take into account the complex transition into adulthood which is a reality for twenty-first century young people, who have greater freedom and autonomy at earlier stages in some areas of life, while economic and social policies have left them with longer economic dependency on families of origin (Morrow and Richards, 1996). This 'maturity myth' ignores the evidence about 'the conditions in which young people attain more or less satisfactory positions in young adulthood' – conditions which include emotional, practical and financial *support* as they negotiate ongoing developmental challenges (Apter, 2012).

Similarly, the dominant discourses around student distress or psychological difficulty – invoking diagnostic and medical categories as well as equality and disability measures – arguably offer relatively limited and limiting, overly binary positions from which to address these issues and challenges. For example, in some cases where avoidance strategies, such as special arrangements for exams to mitigate anxiety, solidify as 'reasonable adjustments' for disability they may exacerbate symptoms and further disable, rather than offering constructive support.

It is around the key issue of support that the confusion lies. Medical and disability discourses have the disadvantage of linking support for distress with a position of deficit (either illness or disability), rather than addressing the disabling toxicity of a culture which denigrates ordinary emotion and pathologises dependence. Once support can be recognised as a basic human need, and as the foundation for the primary human competence of managing emotions, essential for adults and children alike, then much of this argument becomes redundant.

Compassion and support

The type of support described by Apter and listed in Schlossberg et al.'s (1995) 4S model for considering the management of transitions is not therapeutic or medical support, it is the support which is an essential component of survival and thriving for all human beings. Apter's description of developmental thresholds echoes the earlier discussion regarding the nature of learning, which takes place when crossing the threshold from the place of familiarity and relative security within to that which lies beyond, the unfamiliar, the unknown, the potentially dangerous.

Effective and ethical teaching, in this context, will be interested in establishing the correct conditions for this successful negotiation to take place – and will require a compassionate and emotionally literate stance, respectful of the psychological impact of the challenges of higher education in all its facets. Such a stance recognises that thresholds are successfully crossed from a position of relative security – and that anxiety can only be tolerated and creatively responded to when it can be kept within optimum levels, so that it does not overwhelm and send the person into full threat response. A much more fruitful set of positions and options is made available for students to occupy when this kind of psychological understanding is integrated into standard processes and curricula, via recognition of the psychological and neuroscientific foundations for successful learning and application of institutional strategies to support these foundations. This is discussed further in Chapters 3 and 7.

The work of Gilbert (2009) and others in recognising the central role of compassion for regulating mental states and healthy functioning is a useful source of understanding here. This approach highlights the role of the crucial soothing/calming aspect of brain function located as part of the human drive for affiliation and social connection. This emphasises that psychological security is provided *in relationship* with others, through shared identity within an identifiable community and a sense of acceptance and belonging within that community. In this context, the relative security from which students can risk venturing forth into the unknown territory required for learning should be seen not only as a matter of individual capacity or resilience, but also as one of social support and connection within an inclusive community of learning.

This approach sheds new light on the central finding of the What Works? student retention studies (Thomas, 2012), that the promotion of a sense of belonging is a crucial factor in successful student retention initiatives. It puts the wider challenges of the student lifecycle into context, showing that settling in well, making friends, establishing a secure home base, and then maintaining sufficiently secure personal and social foundations, will have an enormous effect on the student's ability to engage with learning and the curriculum. Social support and connection should therefore be a priority for the institution and for HE staff. Such support cannot be located only in specialist support services, delivered in relation to an individual deficit model, but needs to be an integral part of every student's experience.

As previously discussed, transitional challenges will be magnified for students entering the university as part of the widening participation agenda, or in other ways entering from positions of greater cultural remove and therefore at greater risk of experiencing culture shock in the transition. For students entering university with a history of mental health difficulty, there might be a number of important additional measures to support their transition, including facilitation of the transfer of NHS care from child and adolescent to adult services, and from the home jurisdiction to the new region. Additional efforts to welcome and support such students would be appropriate for HE institutions and staff, recognising the importance of inclusion and a sense of belonging to all student success. A truly inclusive community, which routinely identifies and addresses barriers to inclusion and pays ongoing attention to the quality of relationship and connection between its members, is the environment in which all students can learn and thrive.

Strategies for supporting student transitions

As argued above, and as illustrated in the case study examples, it is not just at the very beginning and end of each academic year that the pressures of transition might be experienced – individual differences and circumstances can contribute to anticipation of transitional pressures and/or delayed responses. While in each case study there is the possibility of a more serious condition, for which specialist mental health support might be helpful, a great deal can be put in place to ensure consistent support for the routine transitional pressures and challenges faced by these exemplar students and students generally, which would in turn be likely to ameliorate the effects of any more serious condition. Indeed, as such pressures are inherent in the process of learning, it follows that the most effective measures will be those embedded within standard processes and within a core curriculum.

The following are suggested as potential strategies for providing support for student transition.

An inclusive and welcoming university community

Actively structuring a university as a community requires a clear vision from senior leadership of what kind of community it wishes to be, with commitment to inclusivity and the promotion of wellbeing, and an emphasis on all members experiencing a sense of affiliation and belonging, at the macro level as well as cascading through the faculty, subject and course sub-communities. To make every student feel personally welcome and valued as a member of the community, the diverse needs and backgrounds of students should be taken into account in all aspects of the university's arrangements and structures, including clear anti-bullying and inclusivity policies, along with practical measures to promote respectful citizenship, such as encouraging staff and students to make proactive interventions when they notice breaches of community values. In particular, such a community requires well-resourced, robust and embedded support services, appropriately equipped to address the full range of students' support needs – especially those of disadvantaged students – and managed to ensure joined up support for all students.

Well-planned, holistic induction activity

Transition and induction activities should be recognised as longer-term and repeated activities designed to help all students feel welcome and at home across all aspects of university life (not just academic) and at every stage in the student lifecycle, including tailored options for students with additional transitional challenges. Students should have a range of opportunities to meet and build relationships with fellow students and staff, with one-to-one personal tutor meetings prioritised. They should be offered a variety of structured settling-in activities making the rules of the game transparent to everyone at each stage, and scaffolding understanding and mastery of the rules of the game around evaluation and assessment in particular. The personal challenges inherent to higher education learning should be named and normalised, alongside routine input within the curriculum on managing stress and anxiety. All students should be proactively introduced to and reminded of the full range of support services, presenting these as basic utilities for university life rather than deficit-based options.

Support for life transitions

While academic skills development is most obviously better embedded routinely within curricula, rather than supplemented on a deficit model, the practical realities of students' wider lives should also be central within initial transition and induction activities, and remain in view throughout. Routine and proactive practical support and opportunities to learn appropriate life skills should be provided to all, so that those from disadvantaged backgrounds have equal access to the basic security supporting successful learning. As well as needs-based access to additional practical resources, all students could, for example, be offered proactive advice and support in managing rental and other financial commitments and contracts, and access to non-patronising opportunities for learning basic self and home care skills, at any stage in their university journey. Proactive development of skills for life beyond graduation – not just job application and interview skills, but also demonstrable employability skills – should also routinely be included within curricula.

Skills for citizenship and community belonging

The key life skill taught to every student should arguably be the conscious development and maintenance of supportive networks, alongside recognition of the value of community citizenship. All students should be supported in forming respectful co-habiting and neighbour relationships, whether in halls or in shared private accommodation, receiving clear expectations about behaviour and responsibilities as tenants, and being encouraged to develop shared agreements about issues like noise, cleaning and use of shared spaces. Mentor or peer supporter roles offer important developmental opportunities for students, and structuring these as a routine feature ensures that students themselves play a role in developing and strengthening a culture of mutual support. Universities can work with their student unions to coordinate and promote wider peer support, ensuring that students are proactively welcomed to join clubs and societies where they can meet likeminded fellow students and make further connections and networks. Students' connections with and citizenship of the wider local community should also be routinely promoted and supported, for example through affiliations with local groups (such as religious groups) or through opportunities to make a contribution through volunteering.

Supportive academic communities

Within the context of wider promotion of community, the vital central locus of belonging for each student should be within the learning community of their academic discipline, with a sense of relationship and connection within the academic discipline promoted and developed throughout the whole course of study, and not just as an introductory measure. Relationships within the learning community should be structured to ensure that at any time each student can feel part of a small enough connecting network to be known personally and individually by some fellow students and at least one member of staff, such as a personal tutor. Proactive measures to develop this learning community could include discipline-based peer mentoring, and should include promotion in the curriculum of ongoing learning about effective group cooperation and team work, including conflict resolution. Early group work tasks could be introduced in structured ways, with students assigned to groups by staff so that all students are fairly included and initial activities structured to help students learn appropriate group work skills during class time. This could include structured frameworks for the formation of study/buddy groups with others on the course, reintroducing and reinforcing these opportunities on a regular basis, not just in the first year, to ensure equitable inclusion for all.

Emotionally literate teaching and learning

Emotionally literate teaching recognises personal development as both a foundation for and central outcome of higher education learning, not an optional extra. Such teaching is undertaken from a growth mindset (Dweck, 2017), recognising the capacity of every student to learn and develop, maintaining teaching focus on mastery rather than performance, and emphasising learning relevant to mastery rather than learning relevant to assessment. Promoting growth mindsets in students includes helping them to evaluate their personal development needs and progress as an integral part of their learning, naming and normalising learning challenges and their accompanying anxieties, and giving students regular opportunities to experience productive failure. Crucially, such teaching also sees resilience as a skill rather than a fixed attribute – and ensures that skills for emotion regulation and the management of uncertainty are embedded within the curriculum.

Supportive institutional processes and values

The emotionally literate teaching and learning that is the foundation for appropriate transition support requires recognition at an institutional level of its importance. It requires both teaching and personal tutoring to be seen as central and valued academic tasks, with workloads and promotion pathways appropriately weighted to reinforce this. It requires staff to be properly supported in offering appropriate support to students, including knowing the limits of their responsibilities. This could include ensuring there are sufficiently robust data systems and processes to allow staff to have easy access to coordinated data about their tutees, and the skills to evaluate and use these data to support students' learning. Such support is enhanced when teaching teams are sufficiently connected with each other to ensure appropriate handover for ongoing relevance of feedback and support.

Conclusion

The compassionate and supportive institution outlined above is one which takes a whole institution approach to mental wellbeing, as outlined in the Universities UK #stepchange framework. It is one where students with mental health difficulties feel welcomed and accepted, along with everyone else, and where they can feel confident that they will be supported collaboratively by teaching and other staff alongside specialist services. It is one where psychological challenges are acknowledged and normalised, and seen as shared challenges, with teachers collaborating with students in addressing them; where anxiety is normalised, and anxiety management skills are built into curricula, along with active group and team working skills; and where learning includes robust challenging of habits of perfectionism with supportive opportunities to experience productive failure as part of learning.

What this chapter argues for is that our discourses around student support move away from the pathologising polarities of mental health or ill health, ability or disability, independence or dependence, adulthood or infantilisation, and instead take up a more emotionally literate and compassionate position which recognises and takes seriously the psychological challenge of the holistic experience of higher education learning, and which makes mental wellbeing for all an institutional strategic priority.

Further reading

Apter, T. (2002) *The Myth of Maturity: What Teenagers Need from Parents to Become Adults*. New York and London: Norton.

The University of Cambridge social psychologist Terri Apter argues for the importance of continuing emotional and practical support as young adults build their independence.

See also updated research in Apter 2012 journal article 'On the threshold' listed below.

Dweck, C. (2017) *Mindset: Changing the Way You Think to Fulfil your Potential*. 6th edition. New York: Ballantine Books.

www.mindsetscholarsnetwork.org

Introduction to the substantial and influential body of research demonstrating the importance of growth mindsets (in both learners and teachers), and a sense of belonging, for positive learning outcomes.

Gilbert, P. (2009) *The Compassionate Mind*. London: Hachette.

Comprehensive explanation of the compassionate mind approach to emotion regulation, offering insight into strategies for ameliorating the threat and drive-focused approaches which dominate modern life, including the modern HE context.

Milsom, C. et al. (eds) (2015) *Stepping up to the Second Year at University*. Abingdon and New York: Routledge.

Detailed focus on the academic, psychological and social dimensions of the second year, with recommendations for appropriate teaching and support which have resonance across the student lifecycle.

References

Antonucci, L. (2016) Student Lives in Crisis: Deepening Inequality in Times of Austerity. Bristol: Policy Press.

Apter, T. (2002) The Myth of Maturity: What Teenagers Need from Parents to Become Adults. New York and London: Norton.

Apter, T. (2012) On the threshold. AUCC (Association for University and College Counselling) September 2012: 4–7.

Arnett, J.J. (2000) Emerging adulthood: A theory of development from the late teens through the twenties. *The American Psychologist, 55* (5): 469–80.

Berardo, K. and Deardoff, D.K. (eds) (2012) *Building Cultural Competence: Innovative Activities and Models*. Sterling, VA: Stylus Publishing.

Bridges, W. (2004) *Transitions: Making Sense of Life's Changes* (2nd edn). Cambridge, MA: Da Capo.

Brown, P. (2016) *The Invisible Problem? Improving Students' Mental Health*. HEPI Report 88. Oxford: Higher Education Policy Institute.

Christie, H., Tett, L., Cree, V.E. and McCune, V. (2016) 'It all just clicked': A longitudinal perspective on transitions within university. *Studies in Higher Education, 41* (3): 478–90.

Dweck, C. (2017) *Mindset: Changing the Way You Think to Fulfil your Potential*. 6th edition. New York: Ballantine Books.

Ecclestone, K. and Hayes, D. (2009) *The Dangerous Rise of Therapeutic Education*. Abingdon and New York: Routledge.

Furedi, F. (2017) What's Happened to the University? *A Sociological Exploration of its Infantilisation*. Abingdon and New York: Routledge.

Gilbert, P. (2009) *The Compassionate Mind*. London: Hachette.

Hayes, S.C., Wilson, K.G., Gifford, E.V., Follette, V.M. and Strosahl, K. (1996) Experiential avoidance and behavioral disorders: A functional dimensional approach to diagnosis and treatment. *Journal of Consulting and Clinical Psychology, 64* (6): 1152–68.

Immordino-Yang, M.H. and Damasio, A. (2007) We feel, therefore we learn: The relevance of affective and social neuroscience to education. *Mind, Brain, and Education, 1* (1): 3–10.

Meyer, J.H.F., Land, R. and Baillie, C. (eds) (2010) *Threshold Concepts and Transformational Learning*. Educational Futures – Rethinking Theory and Practice, Vol. *42*. Rotterdam: Sense Publishers.

Mezirow, J. (2000) *Learning as Transformation: Critical Perspectives on a Theory in Progress*. San Francisco: Jossey-Bass.

Milsom, C., Stewart, M., Yorke, M. and Zaitseva, E. (eds) (2015) *Stepping up to the Second Year at University: Academic, Psychological and Social Dimensions*. Society for Research into Higher Education. Abingdon and New York: Routledge.

Morrow, V. and Richards, M. (1996) *Young People's Transition to Adulthood (summary findings)*. Social Policy Research 98. York: Joseph Rowntree Foundation.

Patton, L.D., Renn, K.A., Guido, F.M. and Quaye, S.J. (2016) *Student Development in College: Theory, Research, and Practice*. San Francisco: Jossey-Bass.

Petch, A. (ed.) (2009) *Managing Transitions: Support for Individuals at Key Points of Change*. Bristol: Policy Press.

Schlossberg, N.K., Water, E.B. and Goodman, J. (1995) *Counseling Adults in Transition: Linking Practice with Theory*. New York: Springer.

Stanley, N., Mallon, S., Bell, J., Hilton, S. and Manthorpe, J. (2007) *Responses and Prevention in Student Suicide: The RAPSS Study (summary)* www.papyrusuk. eu/attachments/PSSsummary.pdf (accessed 31 August 2017).

Stewart, M. and Darwent, S. (eds) (2015) Psychological orientations to learning in the second year. In Milsom, C., Stewart, M., Yorke, M. and Zaitseva, E. (eds) *Stepping up to the Second Year at University: Academic, Psychological and*

Social Dimensions. Society for Research into Higher Education. Abingdon and New York: Routledge.

Sugarman, L. (2001) *Life-span Development: Frameworks, Accounts and Strategies* (2nd edn). Hove: Psychology Press.

Thomas, L. (2012) Building Student Engagement and Belonging in Higher Education at a Time of Change: Final Report from the What Works? *Student Retention and Success Programme*. London: Paul Hamlyn Foundation.

Timmermans, J.A. (2010) Changing our minds: The developmental potential of threshold concepts. In Meyer, J.H.F., Land, R. and Baillie, C. (eds) *Threshold Concepts and Transformational Learning*. Educational Futures – Rethinking Theory and Practice, Vol. *42*. Rotterdam: Sense Publishers.

5

Cultural Approaches to Mental Health Among Migrating Students

Antonio Ventriglio, Gurvinder Kalra and Dinesh Bhugra

Objectives

Cultural factors are at the heart of any individual's functioning. Cultures determine cognitive schema and shape how individuals express and deal with distress. This chapter will address:

- Definition of culture and related terms
- Understanding how culture is impacted upon during the migration experience of students
- How students experience and express distress within the host culture
- How such students can be helped

While the chapter is directed at the experience of students who have moved to a new country in order to study in a new place, it is relevant to the many other cultural changes that take place in the transition to university life, and can be read with these in mind.

Introduction

Every individual, no matter where they are born, is born into a culture. Cultures influence child rearing practices, childhood itself and the subsequent development of a world view. Cultures are, by and large, not absorbed deliberately, but in subtle and unconscious ways. Cultural values and paradigms are carried within the individual no matter where they go, although some of these values and resulting attitudes will change over time. These changes are often in response to other cultures, either directly or indirectly. Attitudes and behaviours respond to new cultures and, in turn, individuals will influence cultures, creating a loop. Cultures can thus affect not only the world view of the individual, but also their cognitive development, how people respond to each other and what their expectations from each other are. Cultural values teach us to recognise what is seen as normal in one place but abnormal or deviant in another. Thus moving across cultures may create problems in adjustment.

Mental health is a highly contextualised concept, all too frequently taken as universal. There are often cultural and religious differences in attitudes to mental health, perception of mental health and in the access to and provision of mental health services in different countries and cultures. Some of this may be particularly relevant for international students who arrive with less exposure to the dominant concepts of mental health in the host country. This can cause confusion in terms of understanding the nature of support services in universities in the United Kingdom, including statutory services such as the National Health Service (NHS). It can lead to services acting inappropriately or misunderstanding certain presentations of mental health, for example the hearing of voices.

This chapter sets out to describe culture, its impact on the mental health of international students in higher education coming from different cultures, ethnicities and religions, and its influence on the processes of seeking help. It will describe how culture has an impact during the migration of students and how students experience and express distress within the host culture. It will discuss the above in the context of students and the study environment that they live in (which may well be markedly different from the cultural environment they have grown up in), particularly focusing on the experience of culturally diverse students. The chapter will address mental health in relation to different cultural approaches which may impact on both how a student communicates their difficulty and how their communication is understood and perceived.

Culture and its impact

Culture is defined as the learned, shared meanings of symbols which are embedded in language, rituals, religion, food and so on (Bhugra and Becker, 2005). The emphasis is on learning these symbols and meanings but not by inheriting them; people are born *into* a culture but not *with* a culture. Cultures are imbibed and constituted of various aspects. They are heterogeneous: not all individuals from the same culture will behave in the same way or have the same values. Cultures are dynamic and continue to evolve and change in response to a number of factors.

An individual's cultural identity is affected by their gender, age, religion, attitudes and knowledge. Many cultures face a rapid transition as a result of globalisation, rapid urbanisation and industrialisation. In addition to broad cultural influences, local institutional cultures also play a role, including places of learning, training and employment. There is little doubt that, for example, although there may be similarities in the curricula of two universities, their cultures and environment will be different, and these symbols and meanings will also be absorbed by the students. Thus, exposure to other cultures, whether through direct contact or indirectly, through social media, the internet, television or cinema, will bring about change.

Mori (2000) proposed that international students experience additional stress due to the demands for cultural adjustments which may include difficulties with language, academic work, interpersonal relationships and the financial challenge of paying fees and managing the cost of living. The ways of teaching and learning in the UK, and the types of examinations and assessments, may prove to be stressful; for example, Chinese children are often taught not to interrupt or engage with their teacher, so it may be challenging for them in the UK where lecturers are frequently called by their first name, interact collegially and expect active engagement in discussion.

Concepts of the self

There is no doubt that concepts of the individual self vary across cultures. Morris (1994) drew attention to the difference between personhood and self-hood, reminding the reader that the concept of self in the Eastern part of the world varies from that of the West. The earlier clear divide between socio-centric Eastern cultures and ego-centric Western cultures has faded over time, and the simplistic concepts of ego-centrism versus socio-centrism have given way to more complex concepts, while still being useful generalisms. A likely contributing factor for this has been globalisation and the increased migration between nations that form the East and the West. Nevertheless, socio-centric individuals from socio-centric societies may find themselves not only isolated but also seen as less sophisticated or more traditional/less modern in ego-centric societies. Thus, a student moving from a socio-centric to an ego-centric culture for their higher education studies is faced with the newness and differentness of the host culture, and has to decide whether to allow ego-centricity to develop in themselves or to continue to be socio-centric, although this process may not be conscious.

Students' attachments to their own culture and the 'attractiveness' of the host culture will be two crucial factors that will determine how much of the new culture is allowed to assimilate in their concept of self. Mauss (1979) argued that over the centuries people have moved from a socio-centric concept of the self to an ego-centric one. He expanded on the argument that there are subtle differences between a sense of the self, the conscious personality and the concept of the self – the latter being attributed to social categories. Shweder and Bourne (1984) pointed out that a concrete, rational way of thinking influences the concept of the self; however, it is difficult to ascertain which comes first. They went on to emphasise that people around the world do not think in the same way or have similar world views; ego-centrism and autonomy on the one hand, and socio-centrism and co-dependence on the other, suggest that human variations are influenced by cultures and in all human interactions these need to be understood.

CASE STUDY 5.1

Gurpreet is a 23-year-old Sikh man who recently moved to Melbourne, Australia. Coming from a devout Sikh family from rural Punjab (India), Gurpreet had always wanted to move abroad and live away from family duties and discipline. He applied for a student visa with a future plan to settle in Melbourne. On arrival, he soon began to adopt the Australian

(Continued)

(Continued)

culture by making local friends, learning the Australian slang expressions and even adopting a more Australian name, Gary. However, within three to four months he started to feel increasingly homesick. He began to miss his family and friends from Punjab and felt increasingly sad. He found it difficult to sleep and he lost his appetite. He felt lethargic and struggled to find motivation to participate in his university activities, including his studies. He refrained from discussing his difficulties with anyone, including his friends, because it was not deemed manly for a man to discuss difficulties with others in the culture that he grew up in. This continued for another month before his contact with the university counsellor that was triggered because of his non-attendance in several classes. The counsellor found it quite difficult to engage with Gary for the first two to three sessions. Gary did not speak much and denied that these difficulties were impacting on his day-to-day functioning. The counsellor suspected that this was not due to a mental illness or a lack of insight but maybe related more to a cultural process. A direct discussion of his cultural norms led to Gary opening up about his adjustment difficulties. Following sessions brought newer insights for the counsellor, including how Gary found it difficult to open up with her because seeking help from a woman was another challenge to his masculinity. Similarly, having individual sessions with a professional counsellor was new to Gary because professional help seeking, in his culture, meant that the patient was accompanied by at least one family member who could speak on behalf of the patient to help him describe his difficulties.

As Gary became increasingly comfortable with the female counsellor, he was able to confide in her about how desperately he had wanted to move to a 'Western' country since childhood because of his sexual orientation. In-depth discussions with the counsellor led to an understanding of Gary's confusion between identities: his self-view as a Sikh man born in a devout Sikh family in rural paternalistic Punjab society, versus a gay man born in a highly masculine Punjabi family, versus a person who has never been out of home and is now living on his own terms in an urban, individualistic society. Moving to Australia helped him in certain ways; for instance, he could now freely live as a gay man without the fear of outright criminal conviction or family rejection. However, this also led to a struggle between his other micro-identities such as a Sikh man, or a man coming from a rural paternalistic background. He remained scared of people finding out about him and the news getting back to his parents, so in many ways he still did not feel free.

Based on his work in various international companies, Dutch sociologist Geert Hofstede (1984/2000) classified cultures into ego-centric/socio-centric, masculine/feminine, long-term orientation, closeness to the centre of power, and uncertainty avoidance. Hofstede defined individualism as referring to societies where the ties between individuals are loose and everyone is expected to look after themselves and their immediate family, whereas in socio-centric or collectivist societies people are integrated into strong, cohesive in-groups from the time of their birth. The expectation in socio-centric, collectivist societies is that the group will look after the individual in exchange for unquestioning loyalty. The focus is on emotional solidarity and sharing duties and responsibilities; justice and institutions are seen as an extension of families. These cultures have different notions of privacy and are much more susceptible to social influences and pressures, and have a feeling of involvement in others' lives. Globalisation has brought many challenges to stable cultures such as these, resulting in the likelihood of an increase in cultural conflict.

According to Hofstede's model, 'masculine' cultures show a clear gender difference: incomes are unequal, and women are expected to stay at home and bring up the family. 'Feminine' cultures show greater equality of sexes, and children are treated as equals. Latin American cultures for example are viewed as masculine while Scandinavian cultures are seen as feminine. Beynon (2002) discussed the difference between 'maleness', based on a physiological difference, and 'masculinity' as a cultural construction, affirming masculinity as shaped by cultural and social factors such as class, ethnicity, sexuality, age and nationality.

Hofstede (1984/2000) has further argued that individuals from ego-centric cultures are good at entering and leaving new social groups, and ego-centric individuals possess great skills in fostering new in-groups and superficially appearing more sociable. Therefore, it is likely that ego-centric individuals, even from socio-centric cultures, will settle down more quickly in individualistic societies, whereas socio-centric individuals may find it difficult.

CASE STUDY 5.2

Corinne is Korean by birth and has come to a university in a small town in Italy to study the violin. On her arrival, she had looked on Facebook and Instagram for any LGBTQ+ groups but had been unable to find one. Several of her peer cohort approached her asking about her interest in Italian men. She therefore decided to hide her own sexual orientation during the period that she would be spending in Italy.

Micro-identities

An individual's cultural identities define them, and the concept of self varies across cultures. Two students from different parts of the same geographical region may well carry different values (Ventriglio and Bhugra, 2019). Micro-identities define an individual and can be related to their place of education and employment.

Identity is both self-defined and externally validated. Sometimes a dissonance may occur between the two because the individual may choose to hide or exaggerate one particular aspect of their identity. In similar vein, local gangs may choose to have their bodies tattooed or pierced in order to belong, but equally they may choose to hide these if faced with other situations. One potential way of managing perceived stigma or rejection is to hide the particular micro-identity that may be the cause (Wachter et al., 2015). The role of micro-identities (race, religion, sexual orientation, political views) in the context of notions and concepts of self needs further detailed exploration, particularly among international students.

Acculturation

Acculturation is the process by which cultural values of individuals, as well as groups, change. Berry (1990) defined acculturation as culture change that happens as a consequence of continuous, first hand contact between two distinct cultural groups (Redfield et al., 1936). More importantly, these authors go on to suggest that acculturation can lead to subsequent changes in the original cultural patterns of either or both groups. They also caution that acculturation should be differentiated from culture change. Assimilation, diffusion and deculturation can be seen as subtypes or results of acculturation. When individuals do not wish to maintain their cultural identity, and seek daily interaction with other cultures, the assimilation strategy is defined, as Case Study 5.1, Gurpreet/Gary, demonstrated. When there is an interest in both maintaining one's original culture and being in daily interaction with other groups, diffusion is the option, as with Corinne, Case Study 5.2. Finally, when there is little possibility or interest in cultural maintenance (often for reasons of enforced cultural loss), and little interest in having relations with others (often for reasons of exclusion or discrimination), then deculturation is defined.

Acculturation applies to both the individual and the group. If the pace of change between the group and the individual is at variance then the likelihood of conflict between the two, based on culture, starts to increase. Individual acculturation, although described as psychological acculturation by Graves (1967), goes beyond the psychological aspect as it affects individuals' social linking and social attitudes and behaviour. According to Berry (1990) acculturation changes may be physical (housing, circumstances of living); biological (related to new diseases, nutritional status); political (loss or gain of autonomy); economic (new environment, upscaling or downscaling of financial status); and cultural (linguistic, educational, religious values). Existing identities and attitudes change, and new ones develop, including alterations in attitudes to self and group. Lifestyle preferences may also alter and develop during and as a result of acculturation. This process may affect the social integration of the migrating students and may greatly influence their learning and student experience. International students may be young or mature and may come as undergraduates or postgraduates. Postgraduates on research degrees in particular have the disadvantage that they may not have the peer group, level of care and support that undergraduates or taught postgraduates are given. Although they may have brought their families with them to their new student life, bringing a familiar context will have its own impact on the process of acculturation.

Berry (1990) described adaptation as a generic term used to refer to both the process of dealing with acculturation as well as the outcome of the acculturative processes. This chapter argues that any adaptation may lead to an adjustment, a reaction or a withdrawal. Individuals in culturally plural societies, or as a result of migration, may refer to maintenance and development of their ethnic distinctiveness in the society, and consider whether it is worth retaining. At the same time there may be an urge to desire inter-cultural or inter-ethnic contact, raising questions about whether and how the connection with larger society is desirable or should be pursued. Some individuals may find themselves biculturally adapted (even if this may lead to some conflict in their own families or communities, whether they are home or international students), whereas others may feel threatened and decultured and may withdraw into themselves. It is likely that students who become biculturally adapted may be seen as odd or foreign by those from different cultures and often seen as trying too hard to fit into either of them.

Four variables emerge in response to acculturation, as Berry (1990) has illustrated: integration, assimilation, separation and marginalisation. These consequences emerge from prolonged contact between cultures so students who move for the temporary purposes of education may well fit in half way. From a language point of view, they are, or certainly should be, reasonably proficient in the language and, to a degree, the cultural values and expectations of the new culture, though they may not be entirely comfortable with it. Settlement and adaptation will take a variable amount of time, depending in part on the level and accuracy of this preparedness, and the institutions need to recognise this and design induction programmes accordingly.

Culture shock

Culture shock reflects the shock experienced by some migrants after their move to a new culture (Oberg, 1960). The entire experience of migration affects various aspects of an individual's functioning where, possibly related to loss and resulting stress, a sense of bewilderment and alienation to the new culture sets in. These feelings of anxiety and helplessness, perhaps added to a sense of impotence, may confirm to the vulnerable individuals that the new culture is not welcoming due to a number of factors, including physical ones such as environment and climate, but also emotional ones. Socio-centric individuals from socio-centric countries may thus feel further isolated and alienated in ego-centric cultures. This may produce an additional sense of anxiety and isolation. It is possible that for many students culture shock may raise specific issues related to bereavement (and cultural bereavement is discussed further below), thereby creating complex responses and possible delays to adjustment and settling down. They may see such a response as validating their alienation or may see it as an essential step in settling down in the new environment. This makes it all the more crucial to ensure that each migrating student is seen as a unique individual who brings their own unique experiences to the new study environment.

CASE STUDY 5.3

Ravi is a 21-year-old student who moved from Mumbai to London to study for an MA in management studies. He grew up in a large household within the Chawl culture of Mumbai where he was always surrounded by neighbours who were treated as if they are part of a large extended family. Calling people in his neighbourhood uncles and aunts was a common part of his growing up and feeling a sense of belonging. Using public transport to go to school and college meant navigating through the heavy crowds where a sense of personal space was almost non-existent and looking at other fellow travellers in the eye was normal. For Ravi, moving to London meant leaving all these experiences behind. He still had to navigate the public transport system to visit his university, but it meant following strict unwritten rules in terms of how he negotiated personal space and eye contact in these public places. This made him feel like he was not welcome and did not belong in this alien country. His anxiety and sadness increased, interfering with his adjustment to his new life in London.

The sense of bereavement can bring with it odd intrusive thoughts and feelings of guilt, anger and loss, leading to depression. Those who experienced trauma previous to or during their relocation may experience a level of post-traumatic stress disorder. The perceived locus of control (the degree to which people believe that they have control over the outcome of events in their lives, as opposed to external forces beyond their control) in managing this grief is important (Bhugra and Becker, 2005), and counselling at university may assist with this.

It also needs to be remembered that students who migrate from English speaking nations to the UK may also experience culture shock: while two countries might use the same words, they can have different meanings, and the cultural values and norms may be very different too. Home students from minority ethnic groups may also feel a sense of discomfort, especially if they have moved from their local areas and find themselves in a quite different environment and social mix. Even the four capital cities of Belfast, Cardiff, Edinburgh and London have very different cultural profiles, within a single United Kingdom.

Cultural bereavement is defined as a feeling of bereavement due to the loss of social structures and support, as well as cultural values and identity, which may be strongly influenced by an almost unnatural attachment to the past (Eisenbruch, 1990, 1991). This may also be related to an idealisation of the past with seeing the culture one has left behind as being perfect. It is likely that the experience of cultural bereavement is more common in cases of forced migration, for example those in the UK with refugee or asylum seeker status, but students may particularly feel this bereavement if they migrated alone, under family pressure. The sense of loss may be exacerbated by personality characteristics or previous life events. It becomes natural in these circumstances for students to want to be in close contact with other students from their own culture rather than integrating with the new culture. Gender roles and gender role expectations may further contribute to a sense of bewilderment and potential alienation, and the confining of social interactions to familiar ethnic or cultural groups even when there are culturally diverse sub-groups and micro-identities. While this should be respected, academic departments can assist in promoting the integration of students of different cultures by mixing cultures for group work and in seating arrangements.

Pantelidou and Craig (2006), from a sample of 133 Greek students in London, found that culture shock was correlated to gender and quality of the support available and it did disappear over time. They found that Greek women experienced higher levels of culture shock and had a greater probability of developing distress (expressed as low mood), which was reduced if the students had a network of friends around them. Social support means access to people to confide in, intensity and reciprocation of contact. High levels of dysphoria (a profound state of unease or dissatisfaction, which may accompany depression, anxiety, or agitation) can occur due to lack of preparation prior to migration, culture shock itself or other unidentified factors. Zhou et al. (2008) suggested that being active in the new settings (learning about the new culture before the migration, attending a university orientation course and joining local groups) may minimise culture shock. However, if the individual student is introverted and has not prepared for their relocation and is experiencing dysphoria, then it may be difficult for them to engage anyway. Knowledge about the new society and culture may help avoid some of the pitfalls: as stated above, a pre-course programme or special orientation course may help as well as mentoring by more experienced international students.

It is important for students to recognise cultural variations, power imbalances, privilege and vulnerabilities of others and micro-identities. First year students have been shown to have higher rates of hopelessness (Poch et al., 2004). Thus, a picture emerges of isolation, lack of social support and culture shock which contribute to alienation (as shown in Figure 5.1).

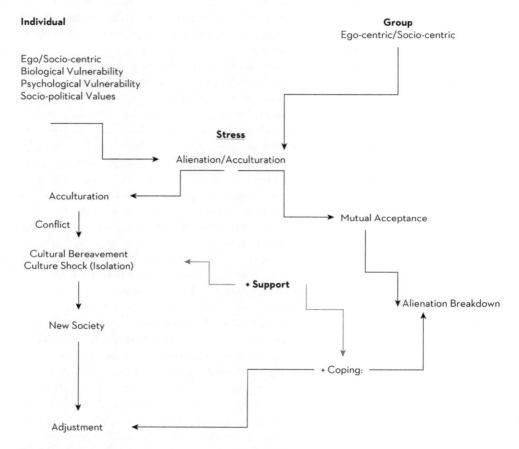

Figure 5.1 Factors leading to acculturation and alienation (among international students, individuals and groups)

Culture conflict

There are two types of culture conflict. One is across cultures due to varying cultural values, attitudes and behaviours, which may create a sense of alienation. The other is related to a degree of discomfort between the two members of the same culture, often across generations. This may arise from various factors. An individual's cultural identity may become more rigid as a result of their migration experiences and they may become more strictly identified with the home culture, but the generation of people born in the new culture may adopt the new values even when these go against those of the older generation, thereby creating a sense of conflict. Such conflict has been shown to be related to high rates of certain mental health difficulties such as deliberate self-harm (Bhugra, 2004; Bhugra et al., 1999a, 1999b). Culture conflict reflects a cognitive and affective dissonance which represents disparity between different and often conflicting beliefs and emotions within the individual. An individual who has spent their early life in one culture tends to develop a certain world view and this is usually challenged during migration into a new culture where they are faced with the new belief system and hence a different world view, leading to emotional incongruence.

Cultural expansion and contraction

The extent of the need for cultural expansion and contraction may depend on the similarities between the home and new cultures and the need for the international student to adjust some aspects of his/her own living on the basis of the host country values, morals and norms. The expansion of their use of the host language is inevitable since language still remains the main barrier to a new culture (Ventriglio et al., 2013). It is likely that the struggle with language and its comprehension may well contribute to stress, which then affects academic performance, which in turn adds to the stress, creating a vicious cycle. Some other cultural aspects such as clothing may require a contraction or an adjustment if not accepted or shared by the host culture; for example, women from the West who decide to study in a Muslim country may decide to wear a burka or a hijab.

The role of culture on distress

Cultures broadly influence how symptoms are generated, how they are expressed and where help is sought from. Cultures also affect the ways in which individuals define illness as well as wellbeing. Idioms of distress (terms people use to express distress) are very strongly influenced by cultural values, and often these do not fit into the culturally dominant diagnostic criteria, which are largely Westernised. These idioms are in keeping with cultural beliefs and traditions and are shared within the culture. For example, mental distress may be expressed in physical symptoms or the use of physical metaphors. Whereas Punjabi women may use the term 'my heart is sinking' to express depression or distress, English men may use 'feeling gutted' and others may use 'butterflies in my stomach'. The expressions thus differ but the underlying distress is similar: university staff and students need to be helped to understand these expressions according to the originating cultural concept of distress (Kohrt et al., 2014). Staff awareness of the range of ways that individuals from different cultures experience and express distress is key to beginning to help students who find adjustment in the new environment difficult. Training and case discussion facilitated by a mental health professional for staff dealing with student distress can better equip them to know how to deal with it as well as how and when to refer the student for more specialist professional help.

Although studies have shown that some migrant groups are more likely to develop some types of psychiatric disorders (for example post-traumatic disorders, adjustment disorders or psychoses; see Ventriglio et al., 2013), it is worth remembering that students who move country for educational reasons may be emotionally vulnerable, though they may be fit physically, creating an inner tension. It must also be noted that all cultures have both strengths and challenges. It would be totally inappropriate to blame the cultural values of the individual for any difficulties that they may encounter.

Generational differences

The attitudes to work–life balance and ways of learning vary across generations. Bernstein and Bhugra (2011) have shown that the younger generations (also called Millennials and Generation X) tend to learn in a more technologically proficient manner. They point out that this generation has a different work ethic and their view of authority varies from that of 'baby boomers', or the older generation. Their views of relationships and work–life balance differ, as does their outlook. This means that engaging them requires a different set of rules. This is the case for students even when not migrating, as the culture of the university may be defined by the norms and expectations of older academics and professional staff, boards of governors, and even government policy. Social media are currently a powerful way of creating an alternative and more student-run cultural environment, and for students who have migrated (even temporarily) can also be an important tool for keeping in contact with loved ones back home – thus adding to the complexity of the cultures that are having to be negotiated at any one time. When comparing immigrant and later generation college students, Mena et al. (1987) highlighted the differences in a number of ways and attributed these differences to acculturation. They found that earlier immigrant students experienced greater acculturation stress but they coped with it by taking a direct planned action (individualistic approach), whereas second and third generations coped by talking to others (using social capital and their social contacts).

University and community support

With the constant movement of students between countries and cultures, it is crucial that institutions and universities understand the importance of how best to deal with the impact of the migration experience on students and to help them (and, where appropriate, their accompanying families) feel welcome in the new studying environment. Acknowledging that moving country can be a difficult and overwhelming experience can be the first step in helping students feel supported. However, acknowledgement alone is not enough – validation of their experiences should be followed by channelling them to appropriate resources or support groups within or outside the university. Specialist international officers and an international student society can be helpful in identifying students experiencing cultural difficulties and providing support and further signposting if required, though the opportunity to share their experiences with other international students can be supportive in itself. It is important that tutors are sensitive to the mental health needs of their students, acknowledging both stigma and reluctance in seeking help. It is also important to ascertain the individual's strengths so that these can be utilised for managing current and preventing future distress. The access to services that are culturally sensitive and flexible but most importantly, easily accessible, is of paramount importance.

Psychological understanding of distress and its resulting problems will vary across cultures, and the concept of accepting psychological interventions may play a role in engagement and therapeutic interactions. Stigma related to mental distress and illness may stop people from seeking help in the first place (Dollery and Yu, 2011). Mori (2000) pointed out that in some cases family honour may stop people from seeking help. Not knowing the health care system and pathway to professional health care may also delay help seeking and, when help is eventually sought, help may be quickly terminated (Mori, 2000).

Using idioms of distress which may not be applicable in the new country may create confusion in clinical settings. Presenting with physical or somatic symptoms may be a clearly understood way of expressing mental distress in a culture of origin, but it is likely that in a Western culture it will result in numerous physical investigations, thereby creating further additional stress. Thus stress related to adjustment may well manifest in ways that clinicians may not be able to recognise and therefore treat, and university student services may struggle to understand and therefore support.

Accepting psychotherapeutic interventions when they happen may create additional problems. Although it has been argued that counsellors take a proactive approach (Mori, 2000; Sandhu, 1995), the perceived power hierarchy within therapeutic relationships may prove to be unhelpful and viewed negatively in many cultures, as in the case of Gary discussed earlier in this chapter. Individuals from certain cultures may see the counsellors and others providing treatment as all powerful, and may do things to please them. Feeling outside the system in several ways will also affect functioning and recovery. International students may appear to be mentally and physically fit, but due to the transitions and the age group, more vulnerable to psychiatric disorders. Thus, it is crucial that student health care systems are firstly and most importantly culturally flexible and sensitive. Culture and its values and responses to the new culture provide a way of engaging students, according to previous models by Berry: integration, assimilation, separation, marginalization (1990).

Cheng et al. (1993) observed that there were clear cultural differences in psychological stress between Asian and Caucasian American college students. They pointed out that international students have been found to differ from American students in the magnitude of their needs, the importance they allocate to these needs and their preferences for seeking help. They also rightly cautioned that any group of students should not be seen as homogeneous. Tracey et al. (1986) had previously reported that Caucasian American students were more likely to present emotional and interpersonal problems when seeking counselling, whereas Asian (in the American context Asian refers to those of Chinese, Japanese and Malay Chinese origins) were more likely to present academic and career problems when seeking help and counselling. It is obvious that poor mental health will affect educational abilities and in view of the stigma faced by students they may see academic activities as a way into help seeking. However, this may point them in the wrong direction in that they may seek help from academic staff in the first instance, rather than student services or health care professionals. This indicates that it is important for academic staff to be aware of the cultural differences and related health problems that international students may experience.

An understanding across all services of the composition of students in the institution in terms of geographical and cultural background is a good starting point. This could be followed by ensuring that university academic and professional staff are offered training in cultural diversity so that they develop an understanding of the range of cultures at the institution, and how their students might benefit from support in order to receive the best possible learning and social experience. Students who enjoy their student life could then pass on the baton by providing peer support to others who are in a similar situation. Booklets and internet pages on student support may increase awareness about care available for such students. Institutions also need to ensure that they offer dedicated induction or orientation programmes to give students an understanding of the host culture, issues that these young people from different cultures can face in the host culture, avenues of support available within the institution and externally if required.

There may be challenges to international students in the UK in terms of employment, which careers services need to address and be prepared for. Students often move with short-term goals in mind, namely to study and then return to their country of origin. On occasion they may choose to stay on, if given the opportunity, and then their stress types and levels may be different. Uncertainty about future job prospects or possible return to the country of origin may play a major role in contributing to ongoing difficulties and distress. It is also important to note that, at the time of writing, the UK government policy Tier 4 requirements (Home

Office, 2018) can limit the access to job opportunities for international students and restrict the time they can take away from their studies in the event of illness or personal problems. This could negatively impact students with mental health difficulties.

The key factors for those working with students with mental distress or illness are illustrated in Table 5.1.

Table 5.1 Pointers for academic and other staff

1	Not all students are the same. Heterogeneity within the same group needs to be remembered
2	Be aware of linguistic problems – ascertain acculturation
3	Be trained in using interpreters when indicated, especially when corroborative information is needed
4	Services to be accessible and flexible
5	Services to be non-stigmatising
6	Services to be culturally competent and sensitive
7	Role of culture, family and friends
8	Idioms of distress will vary across cultures
9	Check pathways into care
10	Psychotherapy/counselling to be tailored
11	Academic staff need to ensure that any skills gap is filled in by training

Conclusion

As more students are moving around the world to access higher education, it is critical that universities and colleges keep their mental health and wellbeing in mind. There is little doubt that all students will face social, psychological and academic adjustments to varying degrees, and educationalists, teachers and professional staff must ensure that the mental health care needs of these groups are met, even if there may be cultural conflict in attitudes, behaviours and help-seeking methods. University student services and statutory health care services need to be both culturally sensitive and easily accessible. There is an urgent need to explore cultural values and beliefs and modify services to understand and work effectively with cultural differences in order to improve students' access to counselling and mental health services.

Further reading

Dollery, R. and Yu, H. (2011) *Investigations into the Mental Health Support Needs of International Students with Particular Reference to Chinese and Malaysian Students.* University of Nottingham (report).
  This report outlines cross-cultural issues affecting Chinese and Malaysian students studying in the UK.

Kurré, J., Scholl, J., Bullinger, M. and Petersen-Ewert, C. (2011) Integration and health-related quality of life of undergraduate medical students with migration backgrounds: Results of a survey. *Psychosocial Medicine,* 8.
  This article outlines a survey conducted among international students regarding their integration and health-related quality of life.

UKCISA (UK Council for International Student Affairs). www.ukcisa.org.uk
  This website offers information and advice to support international students in UK higher education institutions, and resources for the institutions themselves.

References

Bernstein, C. and Bhugra, D. (2011) Next generation of psychiatrists: What is needed in training? *Asian Journal of Psychiatry, 4*(2): 88–91.

Berry, J. (1990) Acculturation and adaptation: A general framework. In Holtzmann, W.H. and Bornemann, T.H. (eds) *Mental Health of Immigrants and Refugees.* Austin, TX: Hogg Foundation.

Beynon, J. (2002) *Masculinities and Culture.* Buckingham and Philadelphia: Open University Press.

Bhugra, D. (2004) *Culture and Self-harm: Attempted Suicide in South Asians in London.* Maudsley Monographs 46. Hove: Psychology Press.

Bhugra, D. and Becker, M. (2005) Migration, cultural bereavement and cultural identity. *World Psychiatry, 4* (1): 18–24.

Bhugra, D., Baldwin D.S., Desai M. and Jacob K.S. (1999a) Attempted suicide in West London, II. Inter-group comparisons. *Psychological Medicine, 29*(5): 1131–9.

Bhugra, D., Desai, M. and Baldwin, D.S. (1999b) Attempted suicide in West London, I. Rates across ethnic communities. *Psychological Medicine, 29*(5): 1125–30.

Cheng, D., Leong, F.T.L. and Geist, R. (1993) Cultural differences in psychological distress between Asian and Caucasian American college students. *Journal of Multicultural Counselling and Development, 21*(3): 182–90.

Dollery, R. and Yu, H. (2011) Investigations into the Mental Health Support Needs of International Students with Particular Reference to Chinese and Malaysian Students. Nottingham: University of Nottingham.

Eisenbruch, M. (1990) The cultural bereavement interview: A new clinical research approach to refugees. *Psychiatric Clinics of North America, 13* (4): 715–35.

Eisenbruch, M. (1991) From post-traumatic stress disorder to cultural bereavement: Diagnosis of Southeast Asian refugees. *Social Science and Medicine, 33* (6): 673–80.

Graves, T.D. (1967) *Southwestern Journal of Anthropology,23,* (4) (Winter):337–50.

Hofstede, G. (1984/2000) *Culture's Consequences.* Thousand Oaks, CA: Sage.

Home Office (2018) *Tier 4 Guidance for Sponsors, Document 3: Tier 4 Compliance.* https://assets.publishing.service.gov.uk/government/uploads/system/uploads/attachment_data/file/725667/Tier_4_Sponsor_Guidance_-_Doc_3_-_Compliance_2018-07-16_FINAL.pdf (accessed 21 November 2018).

Kohrt, B.A., Rasmussen, A., Kaiser, B.N., Haroz, E.E., Maharjan, S.M., Mutamba, B.B., de Jong, J.T. and Hinton, D.E. (2014) Cultural concepts of distress and psychiatric disorders: Literature review and research recommendations for global mental health epidemiology. *International Journal of Epidemiology, 43* (2): 365–406.

Mauss, M. (1979) *Sociology and Psychology* (translator B. Brewster). London: Routledge and Kegan Paul.

Mena, F.J., Padilla, A.M. and Maldonado, M. (1987) Acculturative stress and specific coping strategies among immigrant and later generation college students. *Hispanic Journal of Behavioural Science, 9* (2): 207–25.

Mori, S.C. (2000) Addressing the mental health concerns of international students. *Journal of Counselling and Development, 78* (2): 137–44.

Morris, B. (1994) *Anthropology of the Self.* Cambridge: Pluto.

Oberg, K. (1960) Cultural shock: Adjustment to new cultural environments. *Missiology: An International Review, 7* (4): 177–82.

Pantelidou, S. and Craig, T. (2006) Culture shock and social support: A survey of Greek migrant students. *Social Psychiatry and Psychiatric Epidemiology, 41*(10): 771–81.

Poch, F.V., Villar, E., Caparro, B., Juan, J., Cornella, M. and Perez, I. (2004) Feelings of hopelessness in a Spanish university population. *Social Psychiatry and Psychiatric Epidemiology, 39* (4): 326–34.

Redfield, R., Linton, R. and Herskovits, M. (1936) Memorandum on the study of acculturation. *American Anthropologist, 38*: 149–52.

Sandhu, D.S. (1995) An examination of the psychological needs of the international students: Implications for counselling and psychotherapy. *International Journal for Advancement of Counselling, 17* (4): 229–39.

Shweder, R. and Bourne, E. (1984) Does the concept of the person vary cross-culturally? In Shweder, E. and LeVine, E. (eds) *Culture Theory: Essays on Mind, Self and Emotion.* Cambridge: Cambridge University Press.

Tracey, T., Leong, F.T.L. and Glidden, C. (1986) Help-seeking and problem perception among Asian Americans. *Journal of Counselling Psychology, 33* (3): 331–6.

Ventriglio, A. and Bhugra, D. (2019) Micro-identities and acculturation in migrants. In Moussaoui, D., Ventriglio, A. and Bhugra, D. (eds) *Migration and Mental Health*. Singapore: Springer.

Ventriglio, A., Baldessarini, R.J., Iuso, S., La Torre, A., D'Onghia, A., La Salandra, M., Mazza, M. and Bellomo, A. (2013) Language-proficiency among hospitalized immigrant psychiatric patients in Italy. *International Journal of Social Psychiatry, 60* (3): 299–303.

Wachter M., Ventriglio, A. and Bhugra, D. (2015) Micro-identities, adjustment and stigma. *International Journal of Social Psychiatry, 61* (5): 436–7.

Zhou, Y., Jindal-Snape, D., Topping, K. and Todman, J. (2008) Theoretical models of culture shock and adaptation in international students in higher education. *Studies in Higher Education, 33* (1): 63–75.

PART III

POLICY AND PRACTICE

6

From Strategy to Policy and Procedure: Making Mental Health Policies Work

Ruth Caleb

Objectives

This chapter will examine:

- The development of a whole-university mental health strategy
- The requirement for supportive policies and procedures that will address mental wellbeing and mental ill health
- What to include in a staff guide to supporting students who are troubled or distressed, and how to use it effectively to enhance the student experience and ability to live harmoniously in a university community
- What is meant by 'duty of care' towards other students and staff; in particular, reflecting on where it might begin and end
- How a mental health policy and its procedures can be developed and disseminated for maximum impact

---

Introduction

In recent years, higher education institutions (HEIs) have had to consider the mental health of students at a strategic level. Today, most universities have a mental health policy. However, there is a danger that it will reside on a dusty internet shelf, without being regularly reviewed and lacking cohesion with existing procedures for student care.

This chapter will look at the need for and development of a mental health strategy involving the whole institution to support mental wellbeing, for all the university community, in order to offer robust and supportive policies and procedures to create a healthy institution. It will explore the need for a range of procedures that will guide intervention and decision making. These will include fitness to study, mitigating circumstances, crisis intervention, temporary absence and subsequent return to study.

The development of a university mental health strategy

As student mental health and wellbeing has become high profile in relation to retention and progression, universities have worked increasingly towards the improvement of support services that can respond effectively to mental health needs. The rise in the HE student population, with its increased diversity, has created a challenge that requires the adoption of a strategic approach to meet changed needs, offer an excellent learning and personal experience and maximise potential both academically and in terms of future employability.

Widening participation groups include in particular students with little or no family history of higher education, from a low income or participation area, who have attended schools with low statistics of progression to university, disabled students, minority ethnic students, those who have been looked after by a local authority, those estranged from their families, and mature students and young carers. Students from widening participation groups are not necessarily vulnerable as individuals but may experience particular challenges at university.

The need to attend to mental wellbeing has created an enormous challenge and requires a creative response. Previously, in many universities mental health and wellbeing were believed to be the responsibility of student services alone. This included counselling, disability, welfare and wellbeing services which were left to manage the increasing numbers of students who declared a mental health disability on enrolment, or who developed mental health problems during their time as university students. However, the publication of the *Student Mental Wellbeing in Higher Education: Good Practice Guide* (MWBHE/UUK, 2015) suggested that there was a need for a far wider university approach to address the issue of student mental wellbeing, from pre-admission and throughout the student journey, including the transition into employment. The Guide encouraged senior management and executive boards to facilitate the integration and embedding of student mental wellbeing across the institution and to take a major role in monitoring mental wellbeing throughout the entire university community. It outlined what needed to be taken into consideration when developing a mental health framework, outlining the context and legal framework, from pre-admission to graduation and beyond. Each institution is different and has a unique student and staff profile that needs to be taken into account. What is clear for all universities is the requirement for the entire organisation to support good mental health, and that senior management need to not only take part in the development of mental health policy and practice, but to lead it.

In 2017 Universities UK (UUK) published its #stepchange framework for mental health in HE, building on the *Good Practice Guide* and aiming to encourage and support vice-chancellors, senior teams and executive boards to adopt the 'whole-university approach'. It was acknowledged that each institution would need to consider how to adapt it to its own context. However, there were pointers that every university should adhere to, whether small or large, campus or city, ancient or new.

There were two overriding recommendations. First, the HE sector should collectively adopt student mental health and wellbeing as a priority issue, with individual institutions developing their own whole-university approaches. Second, HE institutions should increase the funding dedicated to services which promote and support the mental health and wellbeing of students. UUK strongly advised all universities to develop their strategy together with the student voice, working together to ensure legal compliance and to minimise the risks of increased student attrition, poor progression and suicide.

The creation of a mental health policy

The Institute for Public Policy Research (IPPR) in its report *Not by Degrees: Improving Student Mental Health in the UK's Universities* (Thorley 2017) stated that fewer than one in three (29%) HEIs described having designed an explicit mental health and wellbeing strategy, though many had a stand-alone student mental health policy.

A mental health strategy often begins the process of acknowledging the importance of supporting mental wellbeing in the institution. It is a statement of good intent that speaks for the whole university. For this reason its progression should be a consultative activity, taken on by an internal task group which will take responsibility for its development and the implementation of procedures and other policies linked to the support of good mental health, taking into consideration the duty of care for students and staff. The task group may also take responsibility for monitoring the policy and its attached procedures.

A whole-institution student mental health policy should include:

- The commitment to mental wellbeing for the whole community
- The support that can be implemented for students with mental health issues
- The commitment to raising staff and student awareness about mental health issues
- The commitment to challenging stigma towards mental health issues
- The commitment to developing supportive partnerships with statutory and voluntary agencies in the community, including relationships with GPs and mental health trusts that hold responsibility towards student patients.

The policy and its related procedures should be the starting point for the development of procedural frameworks to guide prevention, intervention and decision making when mental ill health becomes problematic. In terms of student mental wellbeing and mental health, the policy will need to address holistic support for the student's academic (and, where required, professional) progress, the student's enjoyment of life, their ability to live and study in a community and, just as importantly, the challenge that there may be for other students' abilities to study and enjoy their student life as a result of another student's mental health difficulties. There is a need to balance the support of students with mental health difficulties against the duty of care to the wider student and staff community.

The development of a mental health strategy may best be moved forward by the task group being led where possible by senior management, with membership including delegates from student services, academic departments, the student union, residence staff and staff from other areas of the university with front-line responsibilities.

Creating procedures to make mental health policies effective

A mental health policy needs to be supported by a range of procedures that will ensure its worthy aims and commitments are actually put into practice and effectively support those with mental health challenges. Policies and their accompanying procedures may include fitness to study, fitness to practise, mitigating circumstances, fit to sit, returning to study and crisis intervention.

Fitness to study

The term 'fitness to study' is generally understood in the sector to refer to the procedure put into place when there is a serious welfare concern about a student that is impacting on their and/or others' ability to engage with being a student. This may be because of a physical or mental health condition, or some other problem that is causing challenging behaviour. There may be other names for the procedure, such as 'supported study', but the underlying principles are the same.

Most universities use fitness to study policies if there are current concerns, or on return to study after a period of absence for medical, psychological, or emotional problems or due to life events impacting on the student. The way fitness to study policies are used differs between institutions. In some universities the student welfare services will take the lead in beginning the process, and in others it is the responsibility of the faculty or department.

In most cases there will be an initial gathering of information from the academic department, student services and, where appropriate, the security service, the counselling service, the disability service and any other student or staff member who has been concerned about or involved closely with the student. The timing of the process will depend on the urgency of the concern, either for the student or for others.

The policy could take account of the following steps:

- The clarification of the welfare concern that has arisen should be considered and the decision taken as to whether a less formal welfare meeting would suffice or whether a fitness to study meeting is appropriate in these particular circumstances. The reasons why it might be escalated to a fitness to study meeting may include a duty of care responsibility to the student or others, or a raised level of concern, or a concern that has arisen from several sources.
- If it is decided that the fitness to study process needs to be implemented, a panel or case meeting may be convened that will set out the timing and description of the process.
- A welfare meeting or more formal fitness to study meeting may be arranged with the student to explore the concerns, and enquire into any support that

may be advised for his/her physical and/or mental health and wellbeing. The student should be entitled to be accompanied if they wish.

- If the meeting is to be part of the fitness to study process, perhaps because a previous welfare meeting did not achieve the required outcome in terms of improvement or because the situation is deemed to be more serious, this will need to be outlined clearly and a copy of the policy and process sent to the student.
- The policy will need to contain the power to proceed with meetings in the absence of the student if all attempts to engage the student to participate have failed, or if the student refuses to attend and there are concerns about the health and wellbeing of the student and/or that of other students or staff.
- After a fitness to study meeting the panel will need to discuss the outcome with the student.

  o The meeting may have answered current concerns and no further action is required.
  o There may be the need for a further future meeting to review how any support package is progressing.
  o There may be the indication that suspension or expulsion may be required as an outcome.

- The student should be entitled to appeal a decision.
- In most cases the student should be enabled to return to study after any enforced or voluntary period of abeyance (also known as intercalation or study break), once evidence has been received at that point that indicates that they are fit to return. However it is important to note that no evidence will ever be able to give a future surety that a student will be able to complete their course successfully or live harmoniously with others.

The role of a fitness to study process is therefore to examine all the elements above and consider how to best support a student to progress academically, while enjoying life and not impacting excessively on the lives or experience of other students or staff. Taking an inclusive view of the student's experience, academic progress and impact on others, it assists in assessing risks, ensuring that the student is aware of all appropriate support services available both within the university and externally and, where necessary, takes action to ensure that any risks are minimised. It also enables the start of a process in which support and engagement with support can be tried and tested, with any repercussions planned and agreed clearly as part of the process.

The fitness to study meeting must be held with a supportive and non-judgemental attitude in which the facts can be ascertained and the support needs of the student explored. When the facts are examined and the student explains their circumstances, an incident that initially presented as deeply problematic may lead to solutions that are positive for the student, their peers and staff members.

It is worth noting that fitness to study policies often contain the capacity for the meeting to be held at different levels of impact, ranging from a meeting between the student and one or two other people to the full round table discussion outlined above. This has the advantage that where the initial discussion does not work there is a framework for escalation that is already known to all. Other places will separate these functions out into welfare meetings and fitness to study meetings. Either can work well: the important thing is to have a process that is clear.

CASE STUDY 6.1

Theo is a first year international undergraduate student in the third week of his first term at university. He was found to be inebriated and incapable of making his own way back to his hall of residence three times since his arrival at university. On the first occasion he was taken back to his room by the security officer, and was later contacted with the offer of a talk with a residence mentor, which he did not take up. On the second occasion he was offered an appointment with a student wellbeing officer, which he failed to attend. On the third occasion, Theo's drunken behaviour caused serious concern in the university nightclub. A security officer escorted him back to his hall of residence, made sure he was in the care of his friends and helped him to his bedroom (1). A welfare visit by security officers an hour later to check his condition (2) found Theo asleep on the floor of the hall kitchen, surrounded by debris including a damaged kitchen table and chair, and smashed crockery. The security officers were aware that Theo might have a problem with alcohol and anger control, and were concerned about the impact of Theo's behaviour on his flatmates, who had said that they felt threatened and did not want the responsibility of looking after him while he was drunk. The security officers informed the student support service about the student (3). Photographic evidence was sent to the student welfare officer, who asked Theo to attend the following week for a fitness to study meeting (4).

At the meeting Theo took full responsibility for his behaviour. He said that he had experienced a problem with alcohol in the past and felt he had had a wake-up call after the events of the night in question. He acknowledged the need to consider others but challenged being blamed for the state of the kitchen, saying that the table and chair were already known to be damaged and when he sat down the chair broke

(Continued)

(Continued)

and he fell on the table, causing it to collapse, smashing the crockery. The poor condition of the furniture was later substantiated by the residence manager (5). Theo accepted his disciplinary warning, and said that he was grateful to be informed about the counselling service, residence mentors, and the local NHS alcohol support service (6). He never came to notice again in terms of problematic behaviour during his ultimately successful university career (7).

In this case study, initiatives were taken to ensure his own wellbeing as well as that of others.

1. Security service officers recognised Theo's name on the incident reports and realised that he had been escorted back to his hall of residence on several occasions.
2. There was a need to check that his condition had not reached the point where an ambulance was required, and ensure that his friends were still looking out for him.
3. The security officers realised that there might be a duty of care issue for Theo's flatmates, if he was behaving violently in the kitchen and the students living with him were feeling responsible for his recovery.
4. The student welfare officer was concerned that Theo might have an alcohol problem and that he had twice resisted the offer of support. It was decided to institute a formal fitness to study meeting due to the originally perceived seriousness of the damage, the fact that Theo had been spoken to about his condition twice previously, had failed to attend a meeting with a student welfare officer set up for his support, and the possible duty of care issue in terms of the care and safety of his flatmates.
5. While there may have been an assumption that Theo had been responsible for the damage from the photographic evidence, the welfare officer kept an open mind and checked with the residence manager.
6. Theo was informed about the services available to him but left free to decide if or when he would like to use them. He therefore felt in control of his own situation and made his own decision whether or when he would find them of value.
7. Maybe Theo used the services available, or maybe he did not, but either way there was a successful outcome.

A comprehensive fitness to study policy should be widely accessible and embedded into the wellbeing culture of the institution. It will address holistic support needs and aims to be a transparent, fair and robust process which is compliant with legal requirements (see Chapter 2). It should be linked with other relevant institutional processes.

Fitness to practise

Fitness to practise frameworks are applicable for courses that lead to particular professional qualifications and eligibility to register with a relevant professional, statutory or regulatory body upon successful completion. For professional eligibility, students are required to ensure that they are fit to practise within and as defined by their profession and are not likely to put clients or patients at risk. On some of these courses there will be routine occupational health assessments prior to enrolment. The responsibility to monitor fitness to practise is usually taken by the academic department, as the requirements are so specific to the particular professional programme.

Due to the pressure on students on these courses to appear to be fit to practise it is likely that some may be reticent to engage with student services at times of stress, or avoid medical consultation when suffering from symptoms that may indicate mental ill health. It is important that departmental staff remain vigilant in order to notice those students who may be struggling or who would benefit from support. In particular they should be informed about the confidentiality policies of available services such as GPs and the university counselling service, which will normally keep confidentiality unless there is a serious concern.

Professional organisations have their own procedures which are specific to their profession's requirements and some may have particular indicators around mental health concerns. The General Medical Council, for example, states 'Medical schools should explain that mental health conditions are common in medical students and that support is available. In almost every case, a mental health condition does not prevent a student from completing his or her course and continuing a career in medicine' (GMC, 2017: 4). Prospective students of relevant professional courses are encouraged to look at the particular advice for students and universities given by their repetitive profession's regulatory body and by their chosen HE institution for guidance on the fitness to practise requirements.

Mitigating circumstances

Mitigating circumstances policies and procedures refer to circumstances, health issues and events which are generally unexpected and out of the student's control and that negatively impact on their academic performance in examinations, assessments, assignments or ability to study.

Students with mental health difficulties may have particular problems negotiating the requirements for mitigating circumstances, as they may not be fully aware of their condition. The National Alliance on Mental Illness website describes how someone experiencing an acute episode of mental illness may not be thinking clearly and may have a lack of insight into their condition. These students, or those who develop symptoms that may fluctuate, may be unable or unwilling to access support, sometimes denying their need for it. Therefore they may be unable to properly judge their need for mitigation, evidence their condition or engage usefully with the mitigating circumstances process at the time that it is required.

University staff need to be aware that mitigating circumstances policies should be designed with these conditions in mind, with each situation reviewed on a case by case basis, in a humane and non-judgemental way. While it is important to require evidence where it is reasonable, there will be cases for which evidence is unlikely or impossible. The Office of the Independent Adjudicator states that while students with an acknowledged mental health disability should already have adjustments that take their condition into consideration, they may need to make a claim for mitigating circumstances, if, for example, 'They experience an acute episode or worsening of their condition which means that the reasonable adjustments in place are no longer sufficient' (OIA, 2017: 21).

It is also necessary to impart to students early in their student life the importance of alerting their department to any major problem that arises during their course. They will benefit from explicit advice in their student handbook and during their induction as to the institutional and external support available (see Chapter 8) as well as the procedures required to put in for mitigating circumstances in as timely and compliant way as possible. Policies themselves need to be easily available in terms of access, simple language and a clear explanation as to what is acceptable as evidence.

In the event that a student asks repeatedly for their mitigation to be taken into consideration, this should trigger a concern as to how best to support that student, for example, by offering an appointment with student services or with their personal tutor.

'Fit to sit'

'Fit to sit' policies assume that a student who submits coursework, undergoes an assessment or attends an examination is declaring him or herself to be fit for that activity and therefore the grade achieved cannot be changed. However, this policy does not take into consideration that mental health problems can be fluctuating conditions. It may be unreasonable to expect a student to assess their own condition as fit to sit throughout an examination before it even begins. For example, a student may develop a panic attack during an examination or presentation, having felt well before and at the beginning of the activity, and students experiencing conditions such as depression may only realise in retrospect that they were unable to work to their best ability. It can therefore be seen that the student is not always in the best situation to assess his or her own ability to undertake an activity.

The *Student Mental Health and Wellbeing Good Practice Guide* (MWBHE/ UUK, 2015: 23) states: 'A blanket implementation of this kind of policy might be considered to be unfair and in some instances individual cases may need to be considered on their merits. It is therefore advisable to build provision into academic appeals frameworks to respond appropriately to such circumstances.' Rather than having a fit to sit policy, it may be more appropriate to incorporate clear guidelines in the event of problems before or during examinations and presentations into the institution's mitigating circumstances policy and procedures.

Returning to study

Students with mental health issues who return to study may have needed to take abeyance (also known as interruption, intermitting or intercalating). They may have been suspended due to concerns about severe self-harm or suicidal ideation, or as a result of duty of care to others, for example due to threatening behaviour. Or they may have decided on their own behalf to take some time away due to life events or a deterioration in their mental health condition. A return to study policy will need to commit to easing the return of any student who needs or is required to take time out. It will outline the process towards the return to study, including the rights of students to access and use any University support services during their time away.

On the return itself, students need to feel welcomed and supported by their personal tutor or supervisor, as well as being reminded about the student services that can help the adjustment back to university. Whatever the reason for the break from study, students are likely to benefit from pastoral support and monitoring which in some cases may begin before the return.

For those students who were on abeyance due to fitness to study requirements, evidence may be required of their condition and current fitness to return, to ensure that the student is well enough to take up the challenges of study. In terms of mental health difficulties, the appropriate evidence may be acceptable from a psychiatrist, GP or other mental health professional who has been involved in the student's treatment. However it is important to note that no evidence can ever attest that a student will be able to complete their course successfully.

Crisis intervention

Crisis intervention frameworks outline ways to respond to urgent situations. They offer appropriate guidance in terms of how to react appropriately to circumstances in which evidence of mental health difficulties, or psychological, personality or emotional disorders may have a disturbing impact on the functioning of individual students and/or on the wellbeing of others around them.

Crisis intervention procedures outline the responsibilities and actions that would apply in the event that a student with mental health difficulties requires an emergency or urgent response. They should not only outline the internal processes and support services in the event of a crisis, but also emphasise the importance of procedures that incorporate external agencies. This will require the development of an effective working relationship with the NHS and other relevant local and national statutory and voluntary organisations that might be appropriate for referral in the event of a mental health emergency.

CASE STUDY 6.2

Jamal is a second year undergraduate student who obtained good results at the end of his first year. He did not have a close relationship with his personal tutor, though he had always attended group tutorials. After the mid-semester assessments, his tutor noticed that his grades had fallen and that one assignment had not been completed, with no mitigating circumstances requested (1).

The tutor contacted the student and suggested that he came to see him for a chat. On his arrival, the tutor noticed that Jamal, who had previously looked clean and well dressed, was in a dishevelled state (2). Jamal could not make eye contact and when the tutor enquired how he was, he looked down and shook his head. The tutor explained that he could see the difference and that Jamal did not look well or happy.

Jamal then told him that he had been struggling enormously not only with his studies but with life itself. There were days when he was unable to get out of bed. The tutor asked how he was feeling right now (3). Jamal said that he did not want to be alive, and had taken handfuls of pills an hour previously. The tutor asked if he could help him by asking the security service to call an ambulance to ensure that he goes to hospital immediately for a check-up; Jamal reluctantly agreed (4). He made an appointment with Jamal for the following week and alerted the student welfare office to the situation (5).

The security service came to the tutor's office to collect Jamal and accompany him to the local hospital's accident and emergency department where Jamal was treated for an overdose and subsequently seen by the psychiatric liaison officer. He was discharged from hospital the following day, collected and returned to university by a security officer. The security service checked on him at intervals through the next day and night until the early intervention service team began daily visits (6).

In Case Study 6.2 there were several critical moments that required the tutor to act so that he could enable Jamal to be cared for appropriately:

1. Though the tutor did not have a strong relationship with Jamal, he knew him well enough to have noticed that he was not working to his potential, and called him in for a chat.
2. He noticed that Jamal had changed physically.
3. The tutor became aware that Jamal was possibly depressed, having observed his body language, and decided to probe how Jamal was feeling.
4. The tutor acted immediately when he realised that Jamal was at risk of suicidal behaviour. He was aware of the procedure in his university, to care for a student who needed urgent intervention. He followed this by calling the security service who were trained in supporting distressed students and who were the first response to call for an ambulance. He recognised his own limits to the support he could offer at this moment.
5. The tutor made a future appointment for Jamal so that he could return for further support when the tutor would encourage the student to make full use of the university's counselling and mental health services and, if appropriate, discuss the possible option of taking time out to recover.
6. There need to be appropriate safeguards to support a student who could be deemed to be at risk, including on their return from hospital or time at home.

All these steps were critical to ensure that Jamal did not drop through the net and was offered immediate and appropriate help.

Guide for staff to support students who are troubled or distressed

Without the assistance of a guide as part of a procedure to support troubled or distressed students, with its concomitant training, the tutor in Case Study 6.2 may have missed or avoided the need to act. Jamal might have taken his own life or dropped off the radar and just disappeared from the university, which may not have noticed his absence until the end of the academic year, when it was realised that the student had not handed in assignments or sat examinations. He may then have failed his course or, if appropriate, offered to repeat the year.

It is important to consider how to train all staff to recognise and respond to students in distress, including those that work in recruitment, teaching, research, student services, registry, finance, accommodation, security and estate such as cleaners, gardeners and maintenance staff. In fact these last three categories of staff are perhaps the most likely to come across students who are distressed or troubled. Training in mental health and supporting distressed students could include dedicated workshops, seminars, online courses, and, regular space could be made at staff meetings to discuss the procedures and cases of concern.

Staff members benefit enormously from being given confidence in how to proceed with students who have mental health issues. A guide to supporting those who are suffering in any way, including those who have been victims of sexual violence or any event or disturbance that may impact their mental well-being, is of great value. The guide should support the policy, aiming to identify, support and signpost students so that they can achieve the best possible academic results and maximum enjoyment of their experience at university. A guide should contain:

a.   Identifying a problem. This requires getting to know a student, observing how s/he is behaving, looking for example at weight changes, hygiene issues, tearfulness, unpredictability, study problems, and responding to any other signs that all is not well. It may be necessary to gather more information from friends, family or staff, and may result in a consultation with student services.
b.   Recognising if the situation is urgent. The situation is not necessarily urgent even though the student may be stressed, anxious, depressed, homesick or not studying well, if there is no immediate risk to the student or others. However, it is urgent if it is believed that the student may be at risk of serious self-harm or suicide, behaving in a way that may put others at risk, has stopped functioning, or is abusive or threatening.
c.   Signposting. The guide should outline how to signpost, list the available internal and external services, and how to proceed in the event that the student will not accept help, as well as if she/he is in agreement with support that can be put in place.
d.   Who to contact. The guide should outline the internal, external and emergency services that may be of use, both in and out of normal office hours. The staff members who have taken part in an incident should log it with their line manager and debrief by sharing their experience with a colleague, head of department or student services.
e.   Keeping boundaries. It will be important for the staff member talking to a troubled or distressed student to remain mindful of their boundaries. If, for example, they are approached in the corridor on their way to give a lecture, they are unlikely to be able to concentrate on the student's needs and would be best advised to make a time for after the lecture unless there was reason to believe that the student was in urgent need of support. The staff member will have to consider whether they have the time and private space to discuss personal issues with a student. They will need to outline to the student how they can help, how long they can offer and the limits of their professional role, referring on if required.

The guide should be made widely available online (with the recommendation that it is downloaded onto the PC desktop so that it is readily accessible). Training should be offered so that staff are confident in how to use it effectively and reminded of the need to ensure a duty of care for the whole community.

Duty of care

There can be considerable tension between the duty of care to a vulnerable student and the duty of care to other members of the university community. While supporting a student experiencing mental health difficulties, it must be remembered that their care needs to be weighed against the impact of their condition on other students' experience and academic progression. Case Study 6.3 illustrates this tension.

CASE STUDY 6.3

Maria is a PhD student hoping to complete her course at the end of the current academic year. She had received excellent results in her first two years' study, had shown no previous problems and had worked very hard on her studies, being keen to finish her PhD in the shortest possible time. However as she came to what she had hoped was her final semester, she developed symptoms including tearfulness, panic attacks and insomnia. She was diagnosed by her GP with depression and anxiety. Maria came to the notice of the student wellbeing service when three of her flatmates went to see the residence mentor, as they were concerned to have discovered her self-harming and were equally worried that their own studies were suffering due to Maria needing a great deal of attention (1). They had not felt able to speak to Maria about their concerns (2).

After initial reluctance, Maria attended a welfare meeting with a student wellbeing officer, where it was explained to her that other students were being affected by her state of mind as they were trying to care for her due to her mental ill health. She was told about all the services available to her including counselling and disability services. An appointment was made for her to visit both services but she did not attend. When the residence manager checked a month later the situation had deteriorated, with several of Maria's flatmates having formed a rota to stay overnight with Maria in her room as they were so concerned by her level of distress and threat to self-harm (3).

At this point it was made clear that the impact that Maria was having on her flatmates was negative enough for the situation to have to change. She was asked to attend a fitness to study meeting as there was a concern for her own wellbeing and also a duty of care for other

(Continued)

(Continued)

students. She was invited to bring a friend to the meeting. Maria said at the meeting that she was clearly fit to study as she had met all her previous deadlines. It was explained to her that the situation was affecting not only her own mental health but also impacting on the study and student experience of others. Her accompanying friend agreed that she herself had indeed been affected (4).

Maria was adamant that she did not want to use the university counselling service. She was asked to consider taking time out of her course voluntarily, in order to engage in treatment to help her to recover and return to university, or to come up with a plan that would improve the situation for herself and her flatmates. It was made clear to her that the situation could not continue and if she did not take time out, or have treatment that bought about a speedy positive change in her condition, the head of student services may need to consider what further steps would need to be taken (5). After a period of consideration, Maria agreed to voluntary abeyance, and returned the following academic year, after medical treatment, having agreed to take up the offer of sessions with the university counselling service to support her during the stressful weeks before she submitted her thesis and sat her Viva examination.

1. Maria's case clearly outlines the issue that being able to study is only one of the aspects that needs to be considered in cases where a student's behaviour impacts on others. It must be remembered that even though a student obtains good results they may still be struggling and eventually this could impact their positive progression and retention.
2. It is important that students in halls of residences or university flats are aware that they can turn to their student services and residence mentors where available, if they have a problem with the behaviour of another student.
3. It is difficult for flatmates to share with a student if their behaviour or state of mind is impacting them detrimentally, as they frequently fear making the situation worse.
4. Students will often go out of their way to support others and need to be supported themselves to understand that there should be limits to this, and there are times that it is important for professional services such as counselling and GPs to intervene.
5. It was made clear to Maria that the initial suggestions of support at the earlier meeting with the residence manager had not had a positive impact on

her condition, and that the situation could not continue for the sake of other students. After all other paths have been rejected or unsuccessful, it may be that sanctions including suspension may have to be considered.

There is sometimes a reluctance to challenge the behaviour of a student who is known or suspected to have mental health problems. However, the impact of a student's behaviour will need to be weighed up with the duty of care for others, as in Case Study 6.3 above, or if, for example, a student's disruptive behaviour in a lecture is seriously impeding the learning or safety of other students. In that case it will be critical to deal with the disruption, for example by calling security to remove the student from the teaching space.

Dissemination of mental health strategy, policy and procedures

Policies and procedures are of little or no use without effective dissemination and training for both staff and students. The *Student Mental Wellbeing in Higher Education: Good Practice Guide* advises that all policies are easily accessible to all staff and students and 'should be drafted in clear, student-friendly language' (MWBHE/UUK, 2015: 51). Both of these aims are laudable but challenging to achieve. The open availability of policies and procedures is important of course, but if staff and students do not know that these even exist, they will be useless. Therefore it is critical to raise awareness about the need to encourage staff and students to talk about mental health problems, train staff to respond appropriately and ensure that there is a clear structure that can be used with confidence in the event of concern for a student's wellbeing.

This is made clear in the Universities UK *Minding our Future* report, which points out that the 2.3 million students studying at UK universities are an important mental health population, with distinctive characteristics and vulnerabilities. 'While the young adult population enjoys good physical health compared to the general population, the same cannot be said for their mental health and wellbeing. In the wider young adult population, there is a rise in common mental disorders, driven particularly by increased depression and anxiety in young women.' (UUK, 2018: 7) It is therefore of great importance to make close partnerships with the NHS, including the local mental health trust, as well as voluntary support agencies in the area, to ensure that the needs of students are met in timely and flexible ways that incorporate an understanding not only of the pressures of university life but also take into consideration the shape of the student's year.

The *Minding our Future* report points out that the higher education context offers an excellent environment in which to encourage positive attitudes and behaviours towards good mental health and wellbeing. 'This provides the perfect setting for universities and health services to embed positive mental health, strengthen protective factors, work to reduce risk factors, and take opportunities to intervene early in mental illness or distress' (UUK, 2018: 10).

Raising awareness

Stigma must be challenged at every level. In particular it is critical for senior managers to make their support clear and visible for mental wellbeing by attending and speaking at awareness-raising events, ensuring that resources are available not only for student services which support students who are experiencing mental health difficulties but also wellbeing initiatives that engage the university community in positive experiences such as volunteering, charitable events and events to celebrate successes. They can ensure that mental wellbeing is brought to notice in committees and meetings, and emphasise its importance in newsletters and messages.

Events to support World Mental Health Day, and in particular University Mental Health Day, offer excellent opportunities to welcome onto campus partners in the community, including the Samaritans, Mind, local GPs and NHS mental health trusts. However, perhaps even more important are fairs, stalls, events and meetings that keep mental health and wellbeing at the forefront of university life.

It is essential to develop a culture of care for the whole higher education community. Alongside student support services, all staff and students should be helped to be aware of their responsibility to care for their own mental health and to keep an eye out to care for others. Senior managers have a critical role in laying the foundations for a positive culture by owning, championing and celebrating a whole-university approach to a mental wellbeing strategy that will encompass all aspects of university life.

Conclusion

In this chapter a whole-university approach to student mental health and wellbeing has been explored. The university mental health strategy needs to be made active through policies and procedures that not only support students who are experiencing mental health difficulties but also support the wellbeing of the whole university community.

Clearly this indicates the need to raise awareness about the importance of good mental health and the support services available to enable staff and students to work and study effectively. But more than this, it requires a culture within universities in which mental health and wellbeing are constantly borne in mind within all administrative and academic aspects of university life. This culture will encourage speaking out about mental health, embracing positive wellbeing and supporting students throughout their university career from their open day experience, through pre-admission, right up to graduation.

Further reading

MWBHE/UUK (Mental Wellbeing in Higher Education and Universities UK) (2015) *Student Mental Health and Wellbeing: Good Practice Guide*. www. universitiesuk.ac.uk/policy-and-analysis/reports/Documents/2015/student-mental-wellbeing-in-he.pdf (accessed 26 January 2019).

This guide supports strategic thinking on the whole university approach to mental wellbeing and discusses policy development, legal requirements, the provision of training and awareness raising and the development of partnerships to support mental health.

Thorley, C. (2017) *Not by Degrees: Improving Student Mental Health in the UK's Universities*. London: IPPR. www.ippr.org/files/2017-09/1504645674_not-by-degrees-170905.pdf (accessed 3 March 2019).

This report outlines available research on student mental wellbeing, exploring mental health among HE students, compared with young adults in wider society, the rise in demand for student services, prevention and promotion and accessing support, with examples of good practice.

Universities UK #stepchange framework (2017) www.universitiesuk.ac.uk/stepchange

This framework shows the way an all-encompassing mental wellbeing strategy can be incorporated into a whole university approach to student mental health and wellbeing, and the requirement for it to be led by senior management.

Universities UK (2018) *Minding our Future*. www.universitiesuk.ac.uk/policy-and-analysis/reports/Documents/2018/minding-our-future-starting-conversation-student-mental-health.pdf (accessed 4 March 2019).

This report looks forward to new models of student care and suggests a platform to create partnerships between universities and the NHS.

References

GMC (General Medical Council) (2017) The responsibilities of medical schools to support students with mental health conditions. www.gmc-uk.org/education/undergraduate/26585.asp (accessed 26 January 2019).

MWBHE/UUK (Mental Wellbeing in Higher Education and Universities UK) (2015) *Student Mental Health and Wellbeing: Good Practice Guide*. www.universitiesuk.ac.uk/policy-and-analysis/reports/Documents/2015/student-mental-wellbeing-in-he.pdf (accessed 26 January 2019).

National Alliance on Mental Illness (NAMI) Know the warning signs. www.nami.org/Learn-More/Know-the-Warning-Signs (accessed 26 January 2019).

OIA (Office of the Independent Adjudicator) (2017) *The Good Practice Framework: Supporting Disabled Students*. www.oiahe.org.uk/media/117373/oia-good-practice-framework-supporting-disabled-students.pdf (accessed 26 January 2019).

Thorley, C. (2017) Not by Degrees: Improving Student Mental Health in the UK's Universities. *London: IPPR*. www.ippr.org/files/2017-09/1504645674_not-by-degrees-170905.pdf (accessed 3 March 2019).

UUK (Universities UK) (2017) #stepchange: Mental health in higher education. www.universitiesuk.ac.uk/policy-and-analysis/stepchange (accessed 26 January 2019).

UUK (Universities UK) (2018) *Minding our Future*. www.universitiesuk.ac.uk/policy-and-analysis/reports/Documents/2018/minding-our-future-starting-conversation-student-mental-health.pdf (accessed 26 January 2019).

7

Academic and Departmental Support

Ann-Marie Houghton

Objectives

This chapter explores how to provide academic and pastoral support in ways that foster and nurture the wellbeing of all students, including those who experience mental health difficulties. Academic and departmental staff have distinct and complementary roles and responsibilities regarding curriculum design, teaching, learning and assessment and pastoral support.
The chapter covers:

- Inclusive approaches to issues of mental health by staff working within a departmental context
- Inclusive curriculum design and curriculum design principles
- How both formal and informal pastoral support may be provided within a departmental context
- The individual and collective responsibility of both academic and departmental staff to create a culture that promotes staff and student wellbeing

The departmental context

Two broad groups of staff, academic and departmental, contribute to the academic and pastoral support provided within a department. Academic staff include lecturers, teaching fellows, graduate teaching assistants and practice mentors. They have primary responsibility for teaching, learning and assessment and often have pastoral responsibilities, with many staff having a formal role as a personal tutor. Departmental staff include administrators, technicians, placement organisers and learning technologists. They contribute to administrative arrangements of a course of study relating to timetabling, alternative assessment arrangements and student placements. They can play an important and sometimes unrecognised role in providing pastoral support, acting as an approachable point of contact within the departmental context. Typical comments from students are: 'The administrator was great, she listened and helped me move tutorial group when I told her I was struggling with getting up in the morning because of my medication'; or, 'If I'm worried, I'll talk to [our administrator], it's easier to ask her things without people knowing'. It is worth remembering that these umbrella categories of academic and departmental staff are used inconsistently across the sector, and new roles are continually evolving at the boundary between academic and administrative domains (HEFCE, 2015; Whitchurch and Gordon, 2010).

Departments exist within a broader landscape of higher education policy and practice. Individual members of staff are expected to engage with, and assume responsibility for, issues of student wellbeing and mental health that are shaped by institutional policy, departmental culture and practice as well as by their job description. The depth of their commitment to this agenda is likely to reflect their personal and professional experience.

Students bring with them a unique combination of previous personal, social, cultural and educational experiences which will influence their engagement with the curriculum (Thomas and May, 2010: 5). Regardless of whether a student chooses to disclose if they have mental health difficulties this will only be one aspect of their identity that may influence their student experience. One of the unintended outcomes of equality legislation is that it can isolate characteristics rather than recognise points of intersectionality.

As well as diversity amongst a group of students, there is also change over time regarding students' mental health and wellbeing. Students may arrive with or develop mental health difficulties during their studies and will have a fluctuating sense of wellbeing arising from specific life events, which will require changes in the help they require. For instance, the HEFCE report describes a student who arrived at the university with 'autistic and visual impairment and mental health and psychotic [episodes] … but their needs changed in a three week [period], to go from three hours to 30 hours a week' (HEFCE, 2015: 49). Figure 7.1 shows the four positions in the quadrant created by the Canadian Minister for National Health and Wellbeing's (MNHW) two continua model. For a discussion see Houghton and Anderson (2017: 7). When thinking about an inclusive approach to curriculum design, teaching, learning and assessment or pastoral support, it is important to remember that within a group of students there are likely to be some in each quadrant, and that their positioning may change over time.

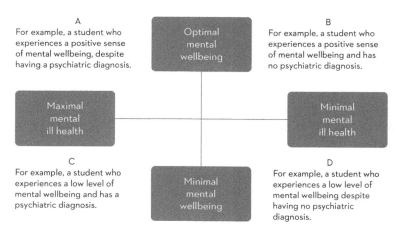

Figure 7.1 The four quadrants in the two continua model.

Source: Mental Health for Canadians (MNHW, 1988) adapted by Houghton and Anderson, 2017: 7.

Birnie and Grant (2001: 2) state, 'it is important to recognise that for some people, some of the time, their mental state creates a barrier that impedes effective learning'. The challenge facing academic departments is how to tackle these barriers, particularly as they fluctuate over time. Thirty-eight per cent of higher education institutions in England now report that they provide slides ahead of lectures as standard (HEFCE, 2017: 72). Originally students with Specific Learning Differences had requested this reasonable adjustment and inclusive measure. Changes in practice for a specific group of learners are now recognised as good practice that can benefit all students. Removing barriers for students with a diagnosed condition, such as severe anxiety or depression, may also reduce many more small impediments that are felt across the student population but are never revealed (Birnie and Grant, 2001).

Inclusive curriculum design

Embedding wellbeing in the curriculum

If the wellbeing of all students is to be supported, it is important to consider it in relation to both the content of curricula and the process of teaching, learning and assessment activities.

In terms of content, embedding wellbeing into the curriculum will depend on the discipline. By using wellbeing topics as a content focus, it is possible to embed it in a range of subjects. Curriculum infusion, originating in America and typified by the Engelhard Project, seeks 'to raise students' awareness of and reflection on wellness and mental health issues in a manner that enhances and reinforces the intellectual content of their course' (Olson and Riley, 2009: 28). Curriculum infusion adopts a holistic, often multi- or interdisciplinary approach to the curriculum that encourages students to see connections with societal concerns in their everyday life: for instance, mathematicians using statistical analysis of eating disorders, historians examining 'madness' over time and in different cultures, or architects designing spaces to minimise stress (see Further reading).

Embedding wellbeing into the process of the teaching and learning experience may be achieved by using the New Economics Foundation's five 'ways to wellbeing' – *connect, be active, keep learning, take notice* and *give* (Steuer and Marks, 2008). Whilst the call to keep learning has an obvious link with higher education, the other ways to wellbeing can be incorporated too, enabling students to be more engaged in the learning process. Greater engagement in turn is likely to enhance their wellbeing and thus help create a virtuous circle.

Curriculum design principles

A commitment to inclusive curriculum design (or universal design, a term more familiar within a US context) can help reduce the need for reasonable adjustments

(DfE, 2017; HEFCE, 2015, 2017). Furthermore, it can enhance student engagement, reducing the need to single students out by making individual adjustments and saving academic and departmental staff time.

The six Inclusive Curriculum Design (ICD) principles are intended to encourage a proactive approach that is anticipatory, flexible, accountable, collaborative, transparent and equitable (Morgan and Houghton, 2011). A course or programme of learning is likely to be more equitable when learning needs are anticipated and student diversity is valued through a process of collaboration that leads to flexible solutions, which are communicated in a transparent manner so that everyone recognises their role in supporting equality of opportunity. These six ICD principles offer a simple and practical alternative to principles of universal design (UD) and universal design for learning (UDL) which are currently more common within a US context. The DfE (2017) report outlines inclusive practice for HE and refers to an Erasmus UDLL project, 'Universal Design for Learning in Higher Education: License to Learn', which focuses on student characteristics which may influence engagement in learning such as: age, culture, experience, language, learning styles, perspectives, physical abilities, preferences, religion, senses, skills and strengths (see Further reading).

The ICD principles support all stages of the course design process, even prior to validation. They are relevant for all aspects of the curriculum, including aims, learning outcomes, teaching, learning and assessment, the learning environment (face-to-face and virtual) or content and learning resources. Academic and department staff can use the ICD principles to minimise the need for reasonable adjustment, avoid unnecessary drop out due to poor curriculum design, and foster a positive learning environment that supports mental wellbeing and enables students to gain the most from their degree studies.

Each principle is now discussed, beginning first with a definition, followed by some frequently asked questions and comments, which shape the practical examples and ideas outlined. Further questions for the reader conclude each principle.

1. Anticipatory

Taking an anticipatory approach means thinking ahead and considering what factors might restrict students from participating in different aspects of the course, ideally removing the barriers before they become an obstacle. Some questions include:

- How can I take an anticipatory approach when I don't know my students?
- With hidden disabilities such as mental health difficulties what anticipatory changes would make a difference?

For many, anticipating or becoming aware of their own reactions and fears about difference, including the topic of mental health, is only beginning to be demystified by initiatives such as the UK social movement Time to Change that challenges how people think about mental health (www.time-to-change.org.uk/). Burstow (2003: 9) explains how, 'It is important to work on ourselves here – to accept that there are different ways of being in the world. It is important to see the strengths and the soundness in ways of thinking and in behaviour that might initially seem strange or frightening.' Most teaching involves anticipating ordinary human experiences relating to fear and anxiety; specialist support services can help to provide information regarding less familiar student behaviours. Students may also be willing to share what would work best, especially when staff have signalled their willingness to be inclusive. Thinking ahead, networking with central and departmental colleagues who can assist, if required, is more important than trying to become an expert with detailed knowledge about all possible diagnoses.

Another effective approach is to review recent requests for reasonable adjustments to identify aspects of the curriculum that can make a difference. Often these proactive inclusive approaches such as advance copies of slides, lecture capture and captioned videos can support many students. These approaches benefit all students, including those with mental health difficulties affecting concentration or attendance, allowing them to read material before a session and/or view material for sessions they have missed.

Anticipating barriers to students' participation in class discussion

There are many reasons why students may not want to talk in seminars and share their ideas with peers. These may include fear of failure, embarrassment at speaking in public, difficulties concentrating due to levels of anxiety, stammering, English as an additional language, being on the autistic spectrum or simply being quiet. Teachers' and students' behaviour within a learning environment can influence participation and may lead students to become stressed. For example, how long teachers wait for students to answer a question or asking named individuals to answer a question without giving them thinking time can cause individuals to feel uncomfortable. Wellbeing may also be affected when students become confrontational or critical of their peers, making racist, sexist, homophobic or discriminatory comments about another student.

Before engaging students in class discussion, it is worth reviewing the learning outcomes and considering if a verbal contribution is always required, or whether there are alternative ways students can *be active* in the learning process. It can be useful for academics to share with students their own challenges in speaking publicly to normalise fears and make explicit that even people who appear to have confidence might find it difficult. Other ideas for increasing participation include:

- Personal thinking time: for students to think and possibly prepare their answer to a question either before or during the session.
- Pair and share: building in opportunities to talk through ideas with another person, initially maybe someone they know, but gradually with others so that they all get to know the group. Feedback then comes from the pair and not the individual. A similar approach may be used in debates when students present ideas for their group as it is sometimes easier to talk when not presenting a personal view.
- Feedforward and feedback: with notice, asking students to summarise aspects of a session they have found useful, or things that remain unclear. Time permitting, allowing two people to do this can enable you to demonstrate that everyone gets something different from a discussion and that is to be expected.
- Question time and minute papers: do not involve public speaking but still allow students to share their ideas in writing and retain anonymity.
- Virtual learning environment: using an online forum as another way of involving students in discussion, while recognising that for some students writing ideas may cause anxiety.

Anticipatory needs for fieldwork, placements and year abroad

Courses delivered in unfamiliar places or involving new and different people or routines are all likely to benefit from adopting an anticipatory approach. Uncertainty and unfamiliarity will engender questions from all students; however, for some the novelty of the situation poses specific challenges. Fieldtrips, placements and year abroad experiences may present particular threats for students who on a day-to-day basis manage their mental health difficulty very well without others being aware of it, for example, students with obsessive-compulsive disorder (OCD) or students with eating disorders. Thinking through the different requirements students may have can help inform the details to include in guidance material.

A useful set of guides developed by the Geography Development Network (Inclusive Curriculum Guides, http://gdn.glos.ac.uk/icp/) illustrate the level of detail students appreciate before a fieldwork trip (Leach and Birnie, 2006: 44–8). Taking an anticipatory approach offers advantages for students and staff. For the students, it avoids unnecessary surprises and anxiety. For academics, it can save time answering individual questions. The preparation of pre-trip information can be valuably informed by student feedback from previous trips and by explicitly asking for ideas about how to improve future guidance materials. The organisation Student Minds is currently collating helpful resources for students planning to study abroad, and these offer ideas for staff to think about when preparing guidance materials (Student Minds, 2017).

Questions to consider

- How do you and colleagues encourage students to engage in discussion; is this scaffolded across a programme so that students develop skills over time?

- Does your institution have standard guidelines for fieldwork and placements; how might students help you review what additional information needs to be included?

- What other activities might benefit from similar anticipatory action, e.g. working in a group, visiting speakers and learning in a new setting?

- How might peer support help students to anticipate and address the challenges associated with different types of learning: for example, students returning from a year abroad sharing their experiences with those who will go the following year?

2. Flexible

Flexibility involves thinking about how to enable all students to have opportunities to engage with the course and demonstrate the learning outcomes through assessment. It is a willingness to be open and consider alternatives. When linked to adopting an anticipatory approach it includes trying to build in options and choice from the beginning. Some educators may have concerns regarding flexibility, as expressed by the following comments:

- I'd like to be flexible but am not sure how can I achieve this when the numbers on my course are so big.
- I think it is important to help students to prepare for when they graduate and worry that too much flexibility is unrealistic.

However, being flexible is not about giving up control of the curriculum or granting students complete freedom, as this form of flexibility is questionable in terms of equity. Flexibility without transparency can also be a source of resentment for students who may not appreciate the reasons for providing alternative options. From the perspective of assessment, building in some element of choice in either the focus or mode of assessment is more flexible.

Flexibility also benefits from transparency in the course design (see below) and from clear communication in a course handbook and/or virtual learning environment (VLE). For some students, it is important to have a sense of the whole course and teaching timetable as this allows them to know what is required and feel in control. For example, a student on medication which makes them drowsy in the morning could negotiate to attend an afternoon seminar. Use of digital resources is often effective for building in flexibility. For instance, students struggling with concentration, finding attendance difficult, or those on the autistic spectrum who like to know in advance what to expect can use such resources to revisit materials, identify what they have missed and how they will catch up or what support they may need.

Transition and induction

Transition into university involves changes; students losing their previous support network can find this unsettling. Including the five ways to wellbeing by encouraging students to *give* can help tackle isolation and support problem solving. Peer assisted learning schemes such as PASS (Peer Assisted Study Sessions, www.pass. manchester.ac.uk/) whereby second year students work with first year students, or less formal peer learning, can provide an ideal opportunity for students to *give, connect* and *keep learning* by sharing ideas with one another. However, it is important to remember that learning with peers can create tensions for some students. This is where the ICD principles of transparency and flexibility may be useful.

Induction should enable students to *take notice* of the similarities and differences between their previous and new learning context. One tutor explained, 'I build in opportunities for students to share how they approach different learning tasks; we talk about where, when and how they liked to study before university and the factors that help or hinder them. Later in the course we reflect on similar questions relating to studying at university. Although these activities do not take long, I find there is often a pressure to cover content, rather than helping students to *make connections* that will help them to *keep learning*.' Another spoke about students being overwhelmed by the number of new systems: 'I had one student who struggled to manage the multiple ways of accessing the VLE, and finding materials. As a personal tutor I tried to help them, but to be honest even I found it confusing! I think it would be helpful to have some standardised features, certainly for first year modules, and/or modules in the same programme.' This observation highlights the importance of academic and departmental staff and students collaborating in the development of infrastructures such as VLE (Virtual Learning Environment).

Questions to consider

- How much choice does the assessment strategy of a degree programme provide?

- How often does your department review the systems surrounding teaching and learning?

- How do you involve students in this process?

- Where flexibility isn't possible, how do you communicate these messages to students?

3. Accountable

Both staff and students are responsible for progress made against equality objectives, in this context staff are accountable for embedding wellbeing into the curriculum that helps to achieve an inclusive learning experience that enables all students to achieve their potential. An inclusive approach that responds to students' wellbeing needs does not mean anything goes. Academic regulations may limit changes to assessment; it is therefore important to consider if there are alternatives and to be explicit when a competence standard exists. (See ECU, 2015 for explanation and further examples of competence standards.)

Most courses contribute to a wider programme of learning, which moves accountability from an individual to a collective responsibility that should involve departmental staff, students, university colleagues and external stakeholders. Departmental culture heavily influences the extent to which staff feel there is an individual or collective responsibility for courses. In response to changes to the Disabled Students' Allowance (DSA), many universities are appointing inclusive teaching and learning advisers, and outside the department these staff are likely to become a valuable source for ideas about good practice. Other institutions will have specialists with inclusive approaches, for instance librarians supporting the integration of academic and digital literacy skills (see SCONUL, 2011).

Course design to ensure accountability and shared responsibility

Giving students control over and responsibility for their own learning by, for example, setting the ground rules for sessions, works to the benefit of all. It serves as a point of reference if difficulties arise later, as well as allowing teachers to demonstrate they have a duty of care. Developing ground rules encourages students to *take notice*, become self-aware and enables them to consider their preferences for learning. In turn, this leads them to *take notice* of their learning environment and possibly *connect* with others who express similar preferences. Encouraging students to *be active* in shaping their learning environment can engender a sense of belonging; however, when students do not know each other well they may find it difficult to share their ideas. It is thus worth exploring different ways for students to share their views without revealing their identity.

It is easy to assume that students can work effectively in a group; however, as one student commented, 'I only know students in this class because you asked us to share contact details; I would never ask someone for their details, it's like saying you are "billy no mates".' Providing structured activities can ensure students exchange basic contact information and agree their individual and collective responsibilities, such as how they will communicate or deal with any difficulties should they arise. Providing a structure and outlining academic expectations can benefit students who find more informal and unstructured 'getting to know you' type activities threatening and confusing.

For some courses, there are accountability considerations relating to external stakeholders, e.g. professional bodies. Where a course has legitimate competence standards then these should be transparent and applied equitably. (For a discussion of competence standards and useful guidance with practical examples, see ECU, 2015.)

Questions to consider

- When asking students to undertake group work does the course design include enough time and guided activities for students?

- Where group work is not a competence standard is there flexibility for students to complete tasks alone, or if this isn't practical is this clear in course information?

- What are the implications of offering greater flexibility for staff workloads and wellbeing?

4. Collaborative

A collaborative approach involves staff, students and other stakeholders working together to design a programme or course. Stakeholders can include professional bodies, the local community, employers or organisations interested in the output of students' work. Stakeholders' multiple perspectives enrich the final design and increase a sense of ownership. Questions include:

- I'm a new member of staff, who should I collaborate with when designing my courses?
- How can I manage multiple perspectives and use collaboration to help me evaluate and develop my current or new course?

Finding time and people willing to collaborate on course design can be difficult; however, the benefits of gaining multiple perspectives and ideas from collaboration are invaluable. Collaboration with students before a new course generates insight into what is helpful or not and it enriches the evaluation of existing courses. Often students have solutions to possible problems. A focus on collaboration creates opportunities to embed the five ways to wellbeing, allowing students to make an active contribution, to *give* something back to the course, and thereby *connect* with their peers and departmental staff and gain a sense of belonging.

Collaboration with the student union or guild regarding institutional considerations such as future teaching spaces, new assessment arrangements, or course regulations can save time and ensure consideration of the student perspective. Meanwhile, direct collaboration or review of the guidance provided by a student-led organisation like Student Minds (www.studentminds.org.uk/) helps to raise awareness and demonstrates a commitment to an anticipatory approach.

Collaborating to design inclusive options for student presentations

Giving a presentation is a common concern. It can be especially troublesome for some students with anxiety, panic attacks, social communication difficulties or if a student stammers, is on the autistic spectrum, or has an Obsessive Compulsive Disorder (OCD) involving multiple pre-task rituals. Collaborating with students about the alternative ways to give presentations helps embed options at the design stage: for instance, presenting to a smaller group of peers, creating a video or an audio for a PowerPoint presentation. Each of these options would allow the student to meet a learning outcome related to presentations, and would provide additional opportunities to develop and demonstrate other communication skills which they could offer to a future employer.

Collaboration with students at the course design and evaluation stage helps identify obstacles to learning and generate possible solutions. Learning technologists can increase staff and student awareness of the institutional resources and support available (e.g. video equipment for recording presentations, or centrally delivered presentation courses using technology) and careers specialists can help embed employability skills and sometimes access to employers' advice regarding presentations during interviews. Admittedly, collaboration takes time, and moving from a course with one mode of presentation to several may be easier to manage if implemented more incrementally.

Questions to consider

- How do students provide feedback on their learning experience and how does this inform future decisions about teaching, learning and assessment?

- How might future accreditation and revalidation processes promote collaboration across the institution?

- Are there ways to incorporate guidance from sources such as Student Minds, Nightline or the National Union of Students who share good practice relating to students with mental health difficulties?

5. Transparent

Investing time to anticipate issues, consider flexibility, accountability and collaboration in the curriculum design is often wasted if the reasons for decisions are not communicated clearly. If decisions are transparent staff and students have more opportunities to *take notice* and *make connections*. During the curriculum design stage the ICD principles support transparency about pedagogical decisions and administrative processes. This approach saves time and confusion because course requirements and taken for granted ways of behaving, which can cause students distress, are clearly communicated. Staff questions include:

- How can students be encouraged to engage with course handbooks and other guidance material that would inform them about the course and expectations?
- How can a Virtual Learning Environment (VLE) help to increase transparency about teaching, learning and assessment or promote student mental wellbeing?
- How do staff help students to appreciate that learning is not always easy and that new ideas can feel threatening and unsettling, especially if they challenge previous knowledge?

Transparency is a key curriculum design principle that relies on effective communication; regrettably, there is no single way of ensuring students receive the intended message. For instance, at the start of a course students may feel overwhelmed, which prevents them from fully engaging with course expectations and documentation. Life events such as a bereavement, or a dip in mental health and wellbeing may affect concentration and engagement with carefully prepared materials. Receiving feedback on coursework or having to process new ideas can also cause students to feel uncertain, doubt themselves, worry or feel anxious.

The learning process is not always easy. In their 'darkness of learning' article Bengtsen and Barnett (2017: 125) suggest that learning processes are often 'highly messy, deeply confusing and exhausting, and at times downright unpleasant'. A commitment to transparency allows staff and students to confront some of the challenges, and discuss and normalise the challenges associated with the complex emotional and cognitive learning journey students are undertaking. Trying to offer clear signposts and reassurance if students need to take a break along the way or decide that a degree is not for them can be very important. Peelo and Wareham's (2002) edited collection, ambiguously and provocatively entitled *Failing Students*, explores the concept of failure and highlights the importance of acknowledging and communicating in a transparent manner that failing is an important part of the learning process.

Supporting students with learning challenges

Although we learn in different ways, students may become anxious if they assume there is a right or wrong way to undertake a specific learning task. Activities that encourage students to share how they approach note taking, planning essays or reports are valuable because they enable students to appreciate the different ways to learn. Similarly, how individuals manage their time and stress around learning varies. Giving students opportunities to discuss different approaches, and for staff to acknowledge that learning is a challenge, can help to normalise coping strategies.

Another normalising and influential approach is for academics to endorse and publicise centrally organised activities such as mindfulness, revision, or wellbeing workshops. Being transparent about the links between learning and life can be approached either within the curriculum by embedding activities into core teaching sessions or by inviting colleagues from student services to facilitate the sessions. Similarly, staff can endorse institutional initiatives that happen outside the classroom which encourage students to *be active* and engage in physical activity or other wellbeing activities that help students to look after themselves so they move towards their or ideally reach optimal mental wellbeing (Houghton and Anderson, 2017: 7).

Using technology to increase course design transparency and communication

Using a VLE as a repository of useful course information demonstrates a commitment to transparency. Using a discussion forum as a single place for frequently asked questions, especially where these can be anonymous, is also helpful. It helps students appreciate that you expect and welcome questions because they are a natural part of the learning process. It can enable students to *be active* in accessing essential and additional resources independently. Clear communication about VLE use is vital: this might include explanations about what students need to do with resources, how much time they should spend, and if documents are for information or action. Being explicit about what to do helps to signal the type of commitment expected from students and reduces their uncertainty that can lead to unnecessary anxiety.

Skill-based resources that help students manage their wellbeing can usefully be provided or signposted via the course VLE and help students to *be active* and *make connections* between wellbeing and learning. These might include activities about time management, or action planning. Similarly, links to wellbeing resources or sessions organised by the institution's student services, counselling or wellbeing colleagues relating to mindfulness, stress management, networking or public speaking can be promoted via the VLE. As a student service colleague noted, 'students often take more notice of the lecturers, so it helps if they give things a push, it kind of gives their stamp of approval'.

Questions to consider

- How comfortable would staff feel about sharing their own learning challenges?

- What institutional resources exist to support wellbeing; could these or those listed below in the Further reading be included in the VLE?

- How might departmental colleagues collaborate with student services, study tutors and wellbeing colleagues to support an institutional approach to embedding wellbeing within the curriculum and university life?

6. Equitable

Being equitable is about fairness and ultimately influences the overall approach to the ICD principles. It is necessary to challenge assumptions that certain behaviours are the norm to avoid disadvantaging individual students.

Many factors shape course design, including the institutional and departmental context. If there is an assumption that all students should be treated the same, then the design might be transparent, but it may not be flexible. Although it may initially sound inclusive and equitable to treat everyone the same, the reality is that students arrive with diverse experiences, learning preferences and fluctuating states of mental wellbeing and mental health. Whilst it may be obvious to start with the course content, it is also helpful to think about the wider learning culture. The learning environment can influence a student's sense of belonging and wellbeing as well as their learning experience and willingness to disclose both formal diagnosis and other undiagnosed mental health difficulties which would entitle them to reasonable adjustment.

The increasing number of students disclosing a mental health condition suggests a greater willingness to disclose than in the past (see Chapter 1). Although many students are diagnosed for the first time at university, there remain students who choose not to disclose, fail to see any benefit in disclosing or do not realise they are entitled to disclose. As the eligibility criteria for DSA change and there is greater emphasis on inclusion, it becomes vital to ensure courses are equitable. Creating a safe learning environment where student and staff wellbeing is valued is likely to be mutually beneficial.

Pastoral support

The creation of a positive and enabling academic environment is central to student retention and success, as the sector-wide What Works? programme has identified (Thomas et al., 2017). Although the departmental context is the focus in this chapter, a cross-institutional collaborative approach provides a more holistic experience. Inevitably, pastoral support reflects the origins of existing departmental practices. It might for instance represent the adoption of an institutional policy or reflect a department's response to a critical incident. Increasingly, student data showing differences in student retention or attainment help to inform decisions about where to target pastoral support. Student feedback also leads to new academic and pastoral support related to employability, academic literacy and wellbeing.

The origins of an institutional pastoral support framework shape the expectations placed on staff by departmental and institutional colleagues, whereas publicity about the various sources of pastoral support will influence students' expectations. Informal interactions and previous encounters with individual members of staff are likely to influence who students choose to approach and their expectations of the support that will be provided. Students' willingness to be referred, or follow up recommendations about where, and from whom, they can access further help, will depend on past experiences and how staff respond to the initial request for help.

Regardless of whether a university has a centralised resource or service staffed by colleagues with specific counselling or mental health training, it is vital for academic and departmental staff to be clear about the boundaries of any pastoral support they can offer. This is because of the centrality of the academic department in students' studies (HEFCE, 2015). Factors for staff consideration include the planned or ad hoc nature of pastoral support, issues of confidentiality and staff training (see Chapter 2).

Planned pastoral and tutorial support

Students may access pastoral support on an ad hoc basis from a course tutor or from a named departmental tutor during a proactive pastoral tutorial programme. The latter is likely to have a clear purpose and may be a departmental response to student feedback via the National Student Survey or a university requirement. Planned tutorials may offer students time to discuss assignment feedback, reflect on their current academic practices, identify their goals and talk about their dissertation action plan or revision schedule. These discussions help communicate and legitimate the benefits of planning and time management. It is evident that planned pastoral support, even where the focus is on employability or academic literacy and not explicitly about wellbeing, can provide an ideal opportunity for enabling students to take ownership of their situation. Such targeted activities can also inform the academic about how a student is managing and provide a space for students to raise other issues.

Using opportunities for future employability

Planned pastoral support with a focus on employability provides an ideal opportunity for students to meet with academic staff with whom they are less familiar, and present ideas, discuss a CV (curriculam vitae), or raise questions they feel unable to ask in other contexts. Encouraging students to identify their achievements and areas for development based on self-reflection benefits many students. Some students find it increases their confidence and helps overcome a fear of talking to unfamiliar people. For others, the scheduled meeting with a member of staff can make all the difference as it gives students permission to meet and discuss their work or the topic of the timetabled activity. Although many academics will schedule office hours or have an open-door policy, for some students there remains uncertainty about knocking on the door and taking advantage of this opportunity. From an academic wellbeing perspective, an open-door policy is also often problematic.

Barriers, boundaries and bridges

There are obvious barriers to successful pastoral support, for instance, not being transparent about the support available, or from whom one should seek support. In addition, there are less obvious signs that communicate inflexibility, such as when staff appear to be too busy or important to interrupt. These barriers may be real or imagined, which is why making things explicit is important. Conversely, it is equally important to be transparent about boundaries on staff time and the limits of their expertise. This can be particularly difficult for staff in certain disciplines (or with certain temperaments) who may have the expertise and may therefore find themselves offering support that is available from others within their institution (see Chapters 6 and 10). Whilst it may be supportive to respond to all requests for help, it is not necessarily practical and certainly not sustainable. Having connections and building bridges of communication based on collaboration with other staff across the university is vital. Collaboration requires academic and departmental staff to gain awareness about who to refer students to and when such referrals are appropriate. Signposting students to access support from centralised services can be as important to staff wellbeing as it is to students' wellbeing.

The department is where students should feel safe and develop a positive sense of wellbeing. Departments often provide a home base, especially for students living off campus. From a departmental perspective, it is useful to have staff connected to central networks that provide a source of information and a forum to discuss issues better addressed institutionally. There is a wide range of possible networks, including those with a specific equality agenda such as Athena Swan (relating to gender), disability, race, sexuality and diversity and inclusion. Other networks relate to specific services such as academic developers, careers, chaplaincy, IT and digital learning or the library where academic and departmental staff connect with institutional initiatives that underpin many of the ideas in this chapter.

Questions to consider

- What institutional networks exist where departments can access further information to enable staff to support students' wellbeing?
- How connected are departmental staff with centralised university student services and are there clear referral routes?
- Given the sector-wide encouragement to promote a more inclusive approach, how can students and staff contribute to institutional discussions about pastoral support or inclusive teaching and learning?

Conclusion

This chapter has outlined some ways in which academic and department staff can think about mental health and wellbeing during course design, teaching, learning and assessment, and the provision of pastoral support. An inclusive approach does not require everyone to become experts in different mental health conditions; it should however encourage us to question our assumptions and expectations regarding what we do and what we ask of our students.

Finally, there are many ways to think about students' wellbeing. An important message for both academic and departmental staff who support student wellbeing, adopt inclusive curriculum design principles and integrate the five ways to wellbeing within their practice, is to ensure that they also take account of their own and colleagues' wellbeing. A focus on staff wellbeing is important in and of itself but it is also vital in enabling staff to offer effective and sustainable support to their students.

Further reading

Erasmus UDLL project, 'Universal Design for Learning in Higher Education: License to Learn' https://udlleurope.wordpress.com/ (accessed 18 June 2019).

A resource based on principles of universal design which complement many of the Inclusive Curriculum Design principles discussed in this chapter and drawing on four perspectives: students, staff in academic departments, student-based services and institutional policy makers.

The Engelhard Project provides examples of curriculum infusion which seek to encourage students to link study with their lived experiences. https://cndls.georgetown.edu/project/engelhard/ (accessed 18 June 2019).

Houghton, A. and Anderson, J. (2017) *Embedding Mental Wellbeing in the Curriculum: Maximising Success in Higher Education*. York: Higher Education Academy. www.heacademy.ac.uk/knowledge-hub/embedding-mental-wellbeing-curriculum-maximising-success-higher-education (accessed 18 June 2019).

For a list of discipline-specific resources, see pp. 18–19, and for a set of reflective questions for individuals and programme teams to reflect on how to embed wellbeing into the curriculum, see pp. 26–9.

The Self-Help INspiring E-learning (SHINE). www.plymouth.ac.uk/student-life/services/learning-gateway/shine (accessed 18 June 2019).

Developed by the University of Plymouth, SHINE contains a range of self-help videos and resources developed by and for students with mental health difficulties.

References

Bengtsen, S.S.E. and Barnett, R. (2017) Confronting the dark side of higher education. *Journal of the Philosophy of Education*, *51*(1): 114–31.

Birnie, J. and Grant, A. (2001) Providing Learning Support for Students with Mental Health Difficulties Undertaking Fieldwork and Related Activities. London: Higher Education Funding Council for England.

Burstow, B. (2003) From pills to praxis: Psychiatric survivors and adult education. *The Canadian Journal for the Study of Adult Education*, *17* (1): 1–18.

DfE (Department for Education) (2017) *Inclusive Teaching and Learning in Higher Education* (independent report by the Disabled Student Sector Leadership Group) www.gov.uk/government/publications/inclusive-teaching-and-learning-in-higher-education (accessed 3 March 2019).

ECU (Equality Challenge Unit) (2015) *Understanding the Interaction of Competence Standards and Reasonable Adjustments*. Prepared by BLS Associates. https://www.ecu.ac.uk/publications/understanding-the-interaction-of-competence-standards-and-reasonable-adjustments/ (accessed 3 March 2019).

HEFCE (Higher Education Funding Council for England) (2015) *Understanding Provision for Students with Mental Health Problems and Intensive Support Needs*. Report to HEFCE by the Institute for Employment Studies (IES) and Researching Equity, Access and Participation (REAP). London: Higher Education Funding Council for England. www.employment-studies.co.uk/resource/understanding-provision-students-mental-health-problems-and-intensive-support-needs (accessed 8 March 2019).

HEFCE (Higher Education Funding Council for England) (2017) *Models of support for students with disabilities*. Report to HEFCE by the Institute for Employment

Studies (IES) and Researching Equity, Access and Participation (REAP). London: Higher Education Funding Council for England https://www.employment-studies.co.uk/resource/models-support-students-disabilities (accessed 8 March 2019).

Houghton, A. and Anderson, J. (2017) *Embedding Mental Wellbeing in the Curriculum: Maximising Success in Higher Education*. York: Higher Education Academy. www.heacademy.ac.uk/knowledge-hub/embedding-mental-well-being-curriculum-maximising-success-higher-education (accessed 1 March 2019).

Leach, J. and Birnie, J. (2006) Developing an Inclusive Curriculum for a) Students with Mental Health Issues b) Students with Asperger Syndrome. *Geography Discipline Network* http://gdn.glos.ac.uk/icp/imental.pdf (accessed 18 June 2019).

Morgan, H. and Houghton, A. (2011) *Inclusive Curriculum Design in Higher Education: Considerations for Effective Practice Across and Within Subject Areas.* York: Higher Education Academy. https://www.heacademy.ac.uk/knowledge-hub/inclusive-curriculum-design-higher-education (accessed 18 June 2019)

Olson, T.A. and Riley, J.B. (2009) Weaving the campus safety net by integrating student health issues into the curriculum. *About Campus, 14* (2): 27–9.

Peelo, M. and Wareham, T. (eds) (2002) *Failing Students in Higher Education*. Buckingham: SRHE and Open University Press.

SCONUL (Society of College, National and University Libraries) (2011) *The SCONUL Seven Pillars of Information Literacy Core Model For Higher Education*. SCONUL Working Group. https://www.sconul.ac.uk/sites/default/files/documents/coremodel.pdf (accessed 18 June 2019).

Steuer, N. and Marks, N. (2008) University Challenge: Towards a Well-being Approach to Quality in Higher Education. London: New Economics Foundation.

Student Minds (2017) Uni Wellbeing: Year abroad. www.studentminds.org.uk/yearabroad.html (accessed 8 March 2019).

Thomas, L. and May, H. (2010) *Inclusive Learning and Teaching in Higher Education*. York: Higher Education Academy www.heacademy.ac.uk/system/files/inclusivelearningandteaching_finalreport.pdf (accessed 18 June 2019).

Thomas, L., Hill, M., O'Mahony, J. and Yorke, M. (2017) *Supporting Student Success: Strategies for Institutional Change. What Works?* Student Retention and Success Programme. York: Higher Education Academy. https://www.heacademy.ac.uk/system/files/hub/download/what_works_2_-_full_report.pdf (accessed 18 June 2019).

Whitchurch, C. and Gordon, G. (2010) Academic and Professional Identities in Higher Education: The Challenges of a Diversifying Workforce. New York: Routledge.

8

Professional Support in Higher Education

Nic Streatfield

Objectives

This chapter will discuss:

- A brief history of professional support in higher education
- Professional support today: the wide range of professional support available to students, including peer support programmes, and the challenges these services face
- Working with external providers, particularly the NHS and voluntary sector services
- Virtual support and how it can be used to support students

Introduction

Who do university students seek support from for their wellbeing and mental health needs? Usually it is friends and family (NUS, 2013) or from a trusted professional, but the transition to university can put a distance, both physically and mentally, between a student and their established support network. The university environment is unique in many important ways that are relevant to good mental health as work (study), accommodation, leisure facilities, social life, social support and professional support are all provided in a single environment. As Malleson wrote in 1963, 'It is because student life demands such a continuously high standard of intellectual efficiency, not because students are psychiatric weaklings, that the incidence of those attending for psychological help are high, and their treatment important' (cited in Mair, 2016: 15). This holds true even for the significantly changed higher education environment of the twenty-first century.

Universities are educational institutions, but it has long been part of university life that some staff have pastoral responsibilities, for example personal tutors or wardens working in university residences. As the academic and pastoral co-mmingled, so academics interested in understanding those aspects of student life that made learning difficult began to focus on specific student support. University College at Leicester began what we would now recognise as a counselling service in 1948, set up by an academic. In 1967 the University of London's Central Institution's health service began running a course called 'The Management of Student Problems' specifically for staff who were in dual academic and pastoral roles, which led in 1972 to the introduction of a Diploma in Student Counselling. The influence of North American universities' guidance and counselling services models precipitated the establishment of 'a single unit to deal with the educational, vocational, social, personal and emotional problems' at Keele University (Bell, 1996). What is interesting is that all these streams emerged through the focus of an academic or careers guidance lens. The professionalisation of university counselling services began in earnest in 1970 with the creation of the Association for Student Counselling which, after several transformations, became the British Association for Counselling and Psychotherapy's University and Colleges division (BACP, 2018a).

Another channel to consider in the development of professional psychological support in higher education is the student health service. Edinburgh University was the first to establish an integral health centre in 1930 and many universities had followed suit by the 1950s. The introduction of the National Health Service (NHS) in 1948 could have stemmed the flow of student health as a specialism but, influenced by the use of psychiatrists in prominent American universities and reports of psychiatric illness detrimentally impacting upon university students (Bell, 1996), in 1951 several medical practitioners established the British Student Health Officers' Association which is now the Student Health Association (2018).

A further tributary of specialist staff are disability advisers, a profession that flowed into universities much later than student health and student counselling. As far back as 1974 a small government grant for disabled students was introduced to help pay for extra costs to support their learning. Subsequent legislation (Special Educational Needs and Disability Act 2001; Disability Discrimination Act 1995; Equality Act 2010) further strengthened the need for universities to ensure that disabled students were not disadvantaged in their education. Disability advisers have a focus on equality and inclusivity, and they advocate for reasonable adjustments for disabled students. It was the introduction of the Disabled Students' Allowances (DSA) in England and Wales in 1990 that saw the expansion of disability advisers as a professional service in universities (DSA-QAG, 2017a; NADP, 2018).

Over time, as need, expectation and funding grew, mental health support became additionally addressed through the development of the now common mental health adviser role. This was initially developed as part of an HEFCE-funded project at the University of Northampton in 1997–2000, and a decade later around 80% of institutions had at least one adviser (Royal College of Psychiatrists, 2011). The University Mental Health Advisers Network (UMHAN, 2018a) was formed in 2001 and now also represents the interests of specialist mentors. In 2016 the Disabled Students' Allowances Quality Assurance Group (DSA-QAG), responsible for quality assurance of DSA-funded support, introduced a specialist mentor (mental health conditions) and specialist mentor (autistic spectrum) category of study skills support that require professional qualifications to be eligible to perform the role (DSA-QAG, 2017b).

Universities also invest in a broad range of services and facilities that that are known to positively affect the five ways to wellbeing – *connect, be active, take notice, keep learning* and *give* (New Economics Foundation, 2008) – even though they may not necessarily be characterised as such. For example providing comfortable accommodation helps good sleep; accommodation with social spaces aids community building; sporting facilities mean there are lots of opportunities to keep active; chaplaincy and multi-faith provision provide spiritual guidance; security teams enhance student safety; funding and finance teams help students manage debt concerns; volunteering opportunities help students undertake purposeful lives; the libraries, academic talks and cultural events help students to keep learning; and the abundance of Student Union clubs and societies help students to connect. There are growing calls for universities to adopt a holistic 'whole university approach' (Seldon and Martin, 2017; Thorley, 2017; UUK, 2017) that is proactive, positive and preventative, with wellbeing recommended to become an institutional strategic imperative with strong leadership from senior management.

Before moving to look at professional services today, it is worth reflecting that while it may be much more difficult for academics to take on pastoral roles in the same way as they used to, due to increased pressure on student/staff ratios, academics are often at the forefront of supporting their students (Hughes et al., 2018). As was stated at the beginning of the chapter, friends and family are the support network that most university students turn to and professional support, both in universities and externally, needs to be seen in this wider context.

Professional support

What will work for one university may not be appropriate for another as the sector has institutions of varying sizes, cultures and locations. This chapter discusses some useful structures, but local factors – strategic priority, student needs, internal and external resources – will be the dominant drivers for what will work in a particular institution. Universities themselves are educational not therapeutic establishments and they invest in professional services primarily to support students to achieve their academic potential. This educational aim is an important one to hold in mind as each of the professional services discussed in this chapter has evolved their practice within this specific context of higher education to create a specialist professional area. It might help to look more closely at what each profession does.

Counselling

Talking therapies such as counselling, psychotherapy and cognitive behavioural therapy have many names and theoretical approaches and a long and rich history. According to the British Association for Counselling and Psychotherapy (BACP), 'Therapists will not give you advice or solve your problems for you. They will listen to your story, helping you to understand yourself better and make positive changes in your life' (BACP, 2018b). University counsellors must usually facilitate this empowering process within a short time-frame: 'Three to six sessions is becoming the norm in most student counselling services' (Mair, 2016: 20).

Counsellors working in higher education are distinguished by their understanding of the connections between psychological and academic difficulties, their knowledge of the educational context and their integration with the wider institution (R Psych, 2011). This integration is particularly important during the assessment process, as Dufour writes:

> Assessment is key to the practice of counselling ... because it helps clarify the nature of a problem and the severity of symptoms. It also helps with triage distinguishing between those students who can be helped within the context of a university counselling service and those who need to be seen by specialist mental health services outside the university, their GP, or other colleagues within the institution. Assessing a student helps to identify those whose needs are most urgent. Students approach services for many reasons: assessment helps to clarify the problem they are facing, and the sort of help they require – are their needs psychological, academic, or both? (Dufour, 2016: 70)

Student counselling is a specialist area with its own set of competencies (BACP, 2017) and it can only be those professionals embedded in a higher education institution who are aware of the full exigencies of university life. The benefits of in-house counselling include helping psychological issues to be understood and addressed, a seamless ability to provide consultation to academics and professional staff, a shared institutional purpose and the dexterity to recognise, respond to and prevent emerging student issues, additionally protecting institutional reputation (Wallace, 2014). This in-house knowledge shapes the integrative short-term contextualised work counsellors provide.

Mental health support

Mental health advisers in universities are often trained social workers, mental health nurses, occupational therapists or psychology graduates whose role is to 'support students who may be experiencing emotional or psychological distress or personal difficulties. Whilst the job title and remit of their role may differ across each University, typically, a Mental Health Adviser will be able to co-ordinate support for students with mental health difficulties and act as a point of contact for the duration of [their] studies' (UMHAN, 2018b). The University Mental Health Advisers Network has a capability framework (2018c) reflecting the specialism required for a university setting. In theory, mental health advisers will be the ones to work with students who have a diagnosis of a moderate to severe and enduring mental health problem and those more at risk of suicide and self-harm; but as counsellors will attest, these issues are regularly raised in counselling sessions too. Mental health advisers provide more practical, planning-based support for students, which is a different intervention to the therapeutic self-exploratory space that counsellors facilitate. Mental health advisers can be situated in disability or counselling teams or, increasingly, in multidisciplinary teams. As they have a case coordinator role it is vital that the communication between these professional services is excellent.

Specialist mentoring

The specialist mentor (mental health conditions) and specialist mentor (autistic spectrum) are new roles that are increasingly present on campus as they are funded through DSA. Mentors as non-medical helpers (NMH) have been working in universities for several years, but it was only in 2016 and the introduction of the Non-Medical Helpers Quality Assurance Framework (DSA-QAG, 2017b) that mentors required a professional qualification. It is important to remember that these roles are study support roles which are being delivered by professionals with an expertise in mental health and/or the autistic spectrum. Managers need to ensure that these staff do not enter into a psychotherapeutic relationship with their students. Some institutions will provide their own in-house DSA-funded specialist mentors while others will recommend private NMH providers. It is the student's funding body that chooses which NMH organisation will deliver their specialist mentoring based on the two cheapest quotes provided to them by their independent DSA needs assessor. The delivery of study support by psychological professionals employed by an external provider to students – who may also be supported by university counselling or mental health adviser teams – raises the issue of communication and potentially complicates managing risk.

University health centres

Many universities host GP practices but, at the time of writing, only two directly employ the medical staff in an arrangement with the NHS. Many patients with common mental health disorders, such as anxiety and depression, are treated exclusively in GP clinics without referral to more specialist mental health services. Those GP practices, with a significant cohort of students on their patient lists, have an involvement in the management of mental disorders which is usually considerably greater than that provided in routine GP settings. It is worrying that GP practices with large student populations are facing financial disadvantage because of the withdrawal of the minimum practice income guarantee as a result of the student population being seen as relatively physically healthy; they will therefore generate a lower income, meaning the long-term future of student health centres may be threatened (Royal College of Psychiatrists, 2011). Collaboration and communication between universities and local primary care

are vital as the university-provided support is not intended to replicate or replace mental health support provided by the NHS.

It is worth considering here the differences in approaches of the different professions as this can impact on how services communicate with each other. NHS treatment continues to develop as new research and evidence emerges, but it remains largely based on a medical model approach (Iacobucci, 2018) focused on the physical and biological aspects of specific diseases and conditions located within the individual. The social model, in contrast, would see that the environment the individual is in may contribute to their mental health. As DSA applications require the student to produce medical evidence to prove their mental health condition is a disability, the medical model narrative is predominant in determining access to DSA-funded social interventions such as a specialist mentor or reasonable adjustments (Scarfe, 2013).

Services from different professional backgrounds intrinsically have their own language, acronyms and culture of practice that is not always easily distinguishable by the other groups. What unites these professions is recognition that supporting students is a specialist area. The work of AMOSSHE (2018), the student services organisation, is important in representing members from a broad range of student support specialisms to best design and deliver excellent support for students. These different ways of working can make it challenging for university managers to decide upon the best structure for their institution to provide appropriate and accessible mental health support.

Models of support

One model, influenced by the government's 2007 Improving Access to Psychological Therapies (IAPT) programme, has been stepped care. This seeks to provide the least intrusive, most effective intervention first and has clear criteria for the thresholds determining access to and movement between the different levels of the pathway (NICE, 2011). Research done by the Institute for Public Policy Research (Thorley, 2017) states that the stepped care model is widespread in how university support services are structured. This model can be delivered via different teams, as it is in the NHS, but in the past decade the development of multidisciplinary teams within universities has proliferated. Often called a Wellbeing Team, this model generally has introduced a single point of access for mental health and wellbeing support, where a single assessment process is carried out by a range of different professionals who can refer on to a broader range of support interventions. Such a team may comprise counsellors, mental health advisers, cognitive behavioural therapists, social workers, psychologists, and perhaps welfare advisers, funding advisers, widening participation support advisers and vulnerable students' advisers. The purpose, composition and place in the student support structure for wellbeing teams will vary across universities. Case Study 8.1 considers the creation of one such team.

CASE STUDY 8.1

Having discovered that a student had been receiving support from the counselling team, disability team, the GP, Community Mental Health Team (CMHT) and academics, the Director of Student Services was concerned at the duplication of resources and the lack of communication between the teams. She sought to implement a new structure bringing together her different professional staff into a single multidisciplinary team that would work better together and more effectively with external services. This Wellbeing Team included the mental health advisers from the disability team, the counsellors and the welfare advisers.

The new team, mindful of the need to be accessible, created a daily Wellbeing Drop-In, meaning that a student could be assessed by a psychological professional the same day. The multidisciplinary team developed a wider range of interventions for students based on the question, 'What does the student need right now to best help them get back on track?' Crucially, the team prioritised the option of a supportive referral to a more appropriate external agency if that was what the student needed to best help them.

As with any new team there were tensions between professional identities and it took time and training for staff to understand each other's skills and develop ways of working together. The issue of confidentiality between professionals was discussed and a broader definition within the Wellbeing Team was established. The team more actively sought greater permission from students to be able to discuss support both internally and externally using a simple 'transitions passport'.

Such a multidisciplinary team working together reduces the possibility of duplicating institutional support and means making the important links with doctors and other NHS services can be simplified. However, the different professional backgrounds within one team and the variation in knowledge about mental health interventions can make finding a shared team way of working challenging (Streatfield and Prance, 2016). It is not difficult to see that a staff member from a social work background will work through the prism of their social work training which will be different to someone from a counselling background. The idea of the stepped care model is to provide the student with support at the lowest level of the model that will benefit them right now. A poor assessment, though, may mean a student is given an inadequate or inappropriate intervention and must return to get what they need, which delays effective treatment, or worse still they never return because the first support offered was insufficient. The absence of appropriately funded and accessible local NHS services will also put pressure upon this model as students have their referral routes delayed or blocked because of inadequate NHS investment in services. Having a range of interventions available gives the student choice but also allows the support service, as a component of an educational establishment, to offer appropriate mental wellbeing support to help students succeed at university, while referring properly into NHS provision.

A multidisciplinary team or formal stepped care models are not the only structures that can deliver effective support. Distinct teams with clear remits have been successful, particularly those which have clear referral and communication protocols. As has been discussed, counselling services in universities have a long and rich history and for many decades have been the recognised support for students struggling with emotional and psychological issues. They have always provided a range of interventions aside from one-to-one sessions, such as group work, targeted workshops and self-help materials, and have continued to adapt to the needs of the student population, for instance by providing coaching interventions, mindfulness sessions and training for staff.

The issue of stigma is one that universities need to challenge, and to try and reduce this some universities have introduced student hubs or one-stop shops which students can approach for a wide range of information, advice and guidance. Others have gone further and have self-service technology available that initially provides self-help materials for students experiencing psychological difficulties. This approach relies on the student recognising they have a problem, understanding what the problem is and, crucially, understanding what they need to do to best address the problem. As human beings are complex creatures, having professional support staff embedded in the purpose of higher education allows for appropriate identification of a problem and a solution. For example, a student may say 'I need counselling for my anxiety', when in fact the student is stressed because of an upcoming exam and the most effective intervention for them at that time would be a study skills session. It is imperative, though, that the staff member establishes whether anxiety or exam stress is the major issue so that the student can address any long-term as well as short-term challenges.

Managing demand

There are many reasons why student demand for psychological support has increased (MWBHE/UUK, 2015; R Psych, 2011; Yeung et al., 2016). National campaigns to tackle mental health stigma such as Time to Change (2018) have had a positive impact. Students are under more pressure as a degree now incurs greater debt, life is more pressurised for young people (Prince's Trust, 2018) and there are concerns about how normal human development is being characterised as vulnerability necessitating emotional support (Ecclestone and Hayes, 2009). Terminology, particularly self-diagnosis, can pose a problem: 'People know mental illness can be a problem – but many people do not understand what mental illnesses actually are. Nor do they know how to distinguish between the symptoms of a mental illness and the expected emotional and cognitive challenges that come with being a human being and being exposed to the ups and downs of life' (Student Minds, 2018).

This 'explosion in demand' (Mair, 2016: 14) has put pressure on student services at a time when NHS mental health services remain underfunded (Thorley, 2017). All service managers must make decisions on how to balance the competing demands of accessibility, managing risk, providing an equitable and effective service and supporting students to access the specialist support they need from the NHS mental health teams. Often it is the waiting time for support that students, academics and the media focus on, yet waiting times for university psychological support services are considerably better than in local mental health services (Wallace, 2012). As such it is not unusual for GPs to refer students back into university counselling services because they know their patient will be seen more quickly than a referral elsewhere in the NHS, or to a voluntary organisation. This puts more pressure on university services and requires the institution to take on a duty of care that would not be expected of it should the student have a physical health issue. One of the challenges facing a manager in higher education is how to manage demand when NHS support remains insufficient. This has meant that universities have been adapting the provision of their psychological interventions, as Case Study 8.2 illustrates.

CASE STUDY 8.2

Once again, despite the hard work of his staff, a university counselling service manager is constructing an email of self-help resources to send to those students who he knows will not be seen by a counsellor before term ends. He has already capped the number of sessions offered, developed self-help materials and introduced workshops, but the demand for individual counselling continues to outstrip available sessions. Upon looking at the statistics the manager can see that 30% of counselling service clients occupy 50% of all appointments. The manager recognises that this as an equity issue. He also looks at the waiting list and worries that he might be missing risk in waiting students. His team are not supposed to be a mental health crisis team, as this is what the NHS is for, but due to the NHS funding crisis the burden of responsibility seems to have fallen upon the counsellors.

To improve accessibility and the management of risk, an online self-referral form with a patient completed questionnaire was developed. Importantly, the self-referral form was written to be solution focused and designed to help students recognise their own resilience and coping strategies. The self-referral forms were triaged every morning to assess risk and students were responded to quickly. If no risk was identified a therapeutic consultation was offered for about two weeks later and students were asked to access targeted online self-help resources to help them prepare for their session. As expected some students used their own resilience and support networks and found the online resources helpful and sufficient, which meant they did not need the therapeutic consultation. For those who attended the 90-minute consultation the counsellors adopted a solution-focused approach and the student left with understanding, resources and actions to do before returning for a short follow-up four weeks later. Should progress be limited at this point, other options, such as short-term counselling, could be offered. The manager achieved his goal of eradicating the waiting list, managing risk and providing an empowering model for students to use.

Case Study 8.2 shows one way of addressing the complex demands of providing students with quick access to support, equitable provision and the management of risk. In reducing the waiting list it certainly is a more equitable model, but it will not be a model that works for everyone. As students often delay asking for help until they are in crisis, a two-week wait to see someone face-to-face may be unbearable. The use of an online assessment fits in with the generation of students who easily engage in a digital environment, but might be difficult for a student not so technologically minded or who finds it difficult to express themselves in the written word, for example if writing in a second language. Some students may need to engage in longer term therapy to help them be successful at university. There are clear resource issues here: if the local NHS cannot provide appropriate mental health support it falls upon the university to deliver something, even though it does not have the same treatment remit or resources.

As numbers increase the issue of equity becomes harder to balance, particularly when risk is considered. Any student suicide is a tragic event and impacts upon the whole community. Student suicide rates have been rising over the last decade but remain lower than in the general population (ONS, 2018). Professional support in universities is not designed to be a crisis response as this is the role of the NHS and Police; however professional support teams in universities are well placed to identify, support and refer those students who are at risk. As such most support services have introduced some form of triage system. This is often a duty practitioner who reviews emails, online registration forms, security reports, tutor referrals and makes a judgement on how immediately the student needs to be seen. Risk of serious harm to self or others is usually the precipitating factor. Others have removed the need for students to book ahead and offer daily drop-ins at times where a student can come and be assessed by a psychological professional. This is a very accessible system for students who come when they recognise they need help, but it is very intensive for support staff to manage.

Individual face-to-face work is not the only way to provide mental health and wellbeing support. Other ways of providing psychological support include delivering psycho-educational workshops or therapeutic groups for students to access. There are universities that have a very comprehensive group work programme that students are encouraged to utilise. Other ways of providing wellbeing support for students include mindfulness sessions, bibliotherapy, prescribed exercise (in conjunction with the university sports centre), guided self-help and eco-therapy. Regardless of the range of support universities provide they should be ensuring they continuously evaluate impact, particularly by regularly gathering student feedback. Many support services use patient-reported outcome measures – a validated psychological questionnaire – which is completed by the student before and after an intervention. Being able to articulate the rationale for, and evidence behind, an intervention will help frame the expectations of students, who often ask, or are told to go, for counselling when there may be other interventions that could also support them.

Peer support

As was stated in the introduction, students will tend to seek help in the first instance from their friends and family. In some cases this can leave the supporters feeling overwhelmed or unsure of how to help. Increasingly, professional support staff are providing resources to help support the supporters (see Chapter 10). Many universities provide resources and training for students and staff worried about others (Student Minds, 2018; University of Oxford, 2018). Professional support staff have a key role to support students, and other university staff as supporters, and are helped by the development of external training resources tailored for universities, such as an e-learning programme from the Charlie Waller Memorial Trust (2017) designed to give non-specialists the skills and confidence to offer support to students who may have mental health issues, and a higher education version of Mental Health First Aid (MHFA, 2017). These 'supporting the supporter' models are not new as many universities have professionally run peer supporter programmes.

CASE STUDY 8.3

The University Accommodation Manager approaches the Head of Student Services concerned about how their student residential assistants are coping with supporting student difficulties in halls. The residential assistants are approaching accommodation staff upset, saying they are not qualified to deal with the high levels of student distress. The accommodation manager is unsure of what to do. The Student Union have also approached Student Services concerned that Student Union sabbatical officers and staff are also finding it hard to manage boundaries in their role, as students approach them with personal problems. To respond to this the counselling team (because of their knowledge of students' emotional needs, active listening skills, understanding of group dynamics and the importance of self-care) are tasked with designing and delivering a peer support programme. Suspecting that the need to better support the supporters is not isolated to university halls and the Student Union, the Head of Student Services approaches an academic who is keen for her school to take part in a peer support pilot. Training consists of 10 structured three-hour sessions and takes an academic term to complete. Students receive training on healthy relationships, how to manage people in distress, mental health awareness, how to make appropriate referrals and the importance and limits of confidentiality. Once trained, peer supporters are expected to run drop-in sessions within their own area for other students. These peer support sessions are also a way to raise awareness of the wide range of support available for students at university and, where appropriate, peer supporters refer students to the relevant university professional support service.

Providing peer-to-peer support can be empowering for students and helps them develop valuable skills. Serendipitously, learning how to help others look after their wellbeing is likely to help the peer supporter positively reflect on their own wellbeing. These schemes are not without risk as for them to be effective and to protect both sets of students they need to be properly organised, with the peer supporters supervised, ideally by a psychological professional, and provided with clear and accessible referral pathways into professional support. Institutions also need to be mindful to provide a range of peer supporters so groups such as LGBTQ+, Black, Asian and Minority Ethnic (BAME) and male students feel they have someone who they identify with that they are comfortable talking to. Done well, these programmes can be accredited to be part of the student's Higher Education Achievement Record. Peer support however may not be appropriate for all students or institutions. Some students worry about the confidentiality of peer-to-peer support programmes, particularly in small communities. There are also external organisations that universities work with which promote peer support. One of these is Nightline (2018), which currently has around 40 listening services serving over 100 universities. This charity provides extensive training for their student listeners, who often receive support or supervision from university professional services.

Working with student unions in student mental health and wellbeing is also important as students will often speak to student union staff and sabbatical officers. Professional service staff recognise how vital a role student unions play in student wellbeing and most seek to establish strong working relationships with them. University support staff will often provide training to student union representatives on managing wellbeing issues. As the NUS has been vocal in recent years about student mental health, so student unions are an important partner in getting out key messages to promote positive mental health and wellbeing.

The partnership working exemplified in this chapter has shown that the responsibility for supporting student mental health and wellbeing is not limited to student support professionals, but is everyone's responsibility.

Working with external providers

NHS primary and secondary care services are a vital part of the support of students' mental health. Some universities have an on-campus doctors' surgery and most work closely with local GPs. Yet as Case Study 8.4 shows, the different thresholds, systems and protocols of the NHS can make accessing specialist support and providing continuity of care difficult.

CASE STUDY 8.4

A student is brought to the university's psychological support service by her flatmates who are concerned about her suicidal ideation and self-harming behaviour. She is asked questions as part of the service's standard mental health assessment and, because she is presenting with a high degree of risk, the staff member organises an emergency appointment with the on-campus doctors' surgery to link her into local NHS specialist mental health support. The student is seen quickly by the GP, who undertakes an assessment, asking many of the same questions originally asked by the university service. The GP, who is also concerned about the student's suicidal ideation, telephones the mental health crisis team. The crisis team member asks the doctor a similar set of questions about the student, which the student sits and listens to. At the end of the call the GP is pleased that the crisis team will accept the referral. The student attends the crisis team appointment and the staff member carries out a further, similar, mental health assessment. Each professional carries out these structured assessments as each is looking for particular information – medical, psychological or social – to help them decide which treatment will best suit the student. However, aside from the time it takes for the student to have these three assessments it is also frustrating for them to have to repeat themselves. The student agrees a voluntary admission as an in-patient under the Mental Health Act. Three nights later the student is discharged back to her university halls of residence in the middle of the night and told to present back to the university support services if she needs further help. The university was not informed about her discharge from hospital as there is no obligation for the NHS to do so, and they are bound by patient confidentiality. As the student's self-harming behaviour continued the university received phone calls from the parents of the flatmates blaming the university that their children's wellbeing and ability to study were being detrimentally affected by having to care for a suicidal flatmate. The university has a duty of care to the flatmates as well as the suicidal student, yet it was not involved in communications about that student's care.

The continued under-investment in NHS mental health services (Thorley, 2017) leaves universities little choice but to provide some mental health support that should be provided by the NHS. This case study shows how the structural separation of support can create worrying situations. Often local university/NHS initiatives have relied on the goodwill of individuals and the determination of professional staff to develop closer relationships. Partnership working offers the opportunity for timely cross-referrals, the establishment of joint care plans for students (avoiding duplicating support), better coordinated management of risk, and is likely to ease the transition of care for students moving from home to university or from Child and Adolescent Mental Health Services to Adult Mental Health Services, as well as increasing mutual understanding and awareness of student mental health and wellbeing issues. Universities have a part to play in influencing local NHS systems including Clinical Commissioning Groups (CCGs) and specialist psychiatry teams, local authorities and third sector organisations to consider the appropriate provision of support to students.

On-campus facilities or formal agreements with local doctors' surgeries may make it easier to create those strong relationships to enable appropriate collaborative working and referral of students into NHS specialist services. This type of liaison can also include joint training events, establishing service level agreements for specific inputs such as psychiatrist or psychologist sessions, running joint health and wellbeing campaigns and hosting NHS staff on university premises. Some universities have taken this further and have part funded NHS mental health posts to make access easier for students and to improve links into NHS services. A different view taken by some is to keep NHS services off campus to deliberately set a boundary between what mental health support an educational establishment can offer and what is a health issue most appropriately treated by the NHS.

To influence local policy and provision senior figures in universities are best placed, alongside professional staff, to represent the health needs of the student body by having input, or ideally representation, on the local Health and Wellbeing Board or similar. Some universities are making representations to, or seeking a student health champion on, local Clinical Commissioning Groups (CCGs). Inviting the local mental health clinical commissioner, or the CCG's lead GP for mental health, onto campus to detail the specific health needs of students and their difficulties in accessing local NHS provision is a good starting point for any university wishing to raise the profile of the health needs of their students. This invitation was the starting point for the city of York, which in 2017 published the findings of their comprehensive Student Health Needs Assessment (City of York Council, 2017) which showed mental health to be the biggest health concern for students in the city. Universities UK Minding our Future (2018) recommends all universities should encourage the development of local student health needs assessments. Professional service staff should be contributing to these strategic reviews while senior management should be reminding the local commissioners and service providers that health provision is their responsibility. Local NHS services also have finite amounts of money and will have many competing demands for these resources, but as students contribute a huge amount to their local community their health needs deserve to be advocated for.

The NHS is not the only external service universities have to work with for the benefit of student care. Many areas have developed more informal networks which meet to share good local practice and work together to influence local provision. These groups often involve student union representation, university professional service staff as well as counterparts in local further education colleges and then a range of local voluntary sector services which support mental health. This could include the local Mind, Samaritans, Nightline, sexual assault centres, domestic violence services, LGBTQ+ services, drug and alcohol teams and any young people's counselling services. Professional service staff should have good knowledge and awareness of local referral pathways into these services, so students receive the support they most need at that time. University professional services often will provide rooms and space for local services to promote and deliver their specialist intervention.

Another way of strengthening relationships between university staff and external providers is to share expertise and put both sets of staff on the same training programme. Examples of this have included a range of staff across multiple organisations being trained on established commercial programmes such as Applied Suicide Intervention Skills Training (ASIST) and SafeTalk (LivingWorks, 2018). The training can be delivered by university professional staff or by other organisations. The benefit of such joint training events, aside from interpersonal networking, is that shared training can lead to shared language and a greater consistency in how support is delivered across a local area. These events can also lead to further discussions and create an impetus for a local area approach to shared concerns, for example York, in 2015, held a city-wide conference on young people's mental health (Higher York, 2015) and Worcester's Suicide Safer initiative is a city-wide collaboration (Smith, 2016).

The development of close ties to local external services is vital for universities so that they can provide the support students need to help them flourish academically but be clear that there are accessible pathways to external specialist services so the student receives the appropriate help.

Virtual support

External support is no longer only available as a face-to-face intervention. Through the internet students can access a wide range of mental health and wellbeing apps, videos, webpages, self-help materials as well as peer-to-peer forums. There are commercial products that include 24/7 provision for online chats with psychological professionals, support forums and online resources which some NHS areas have purchased, just as other CCGs have invested in computerised cognitive behavioural therapy (cCBT) programmes for their patients.

As there is a plethora of choice online for mental health and wellbeing support, universities need to consider the options that they promote on their own websites, as linking to another product is often seen as an implicit recommendation from the institution. It is important that professional support staff monitor and evaluate the use of the online programmes they recommend, but the concern is that this does not happen consistently (Thorley, 2017). It is good practice for support staff to understand how the digital products they recommend work so that they can use them in conjunction with any face-to-face work. Using virtual tools should be carefully considered as part of the wider service strategy.

Some institutions have developed their own digital resources drawing on the expertise of professional service staff and academics, while others have purchased products that promote a range of student mental health and wellbeing multi-media self-help resources and programmes. An additional benefit of an effective digital mental health and wellbeing strategy is the ability to learn from the aggregated data these online programmes can provide on the state of wellbeing in the student population. As more institutions invest in learning analytic systems to help them aid retention by being more proactive in supporting students, so it is important that professional support staff can influence the composition of the algorithms such a system would use to include data about wellbeing indicators. Identifying through data who may benefit from a support intervention is seen as controversial by some, as university students are adults and have autonomy over whether they want to seek help or not. Yet as students with poorer mental health are more likely to be considering dropping out of university (McIntosh and Shaw, 2017), the institutional priority of retaining students may see learning analytics systems become more common.

Virtual support is not only internet based. National charities such as Samaritans (2018) and Papyrus (2018) offer email and text support as well as telephone support, and university professional services have also been expanding their offer with some providing e-counselling, telephone counselling or video-link counselling. These areas require particular skills and competencies (Anthony and Merz Nagel, 2010; Worley-James, 2017) and services need to carefully consider the security of the technology, their data protection obligations and their duty of care position if using these media. For example, if a risk of harm to self emerges during a virtual conversation how will the university professional effectively respond to this? A student on a virtual medium may not be near their university, or indeed be in the same country. Should a student in mental health distress be relying on their university for support when they are not physically present at university? Or does the responsibility for providing treatment rest with NHS services, as it would if the student was in physical distress?

Conclusion

Professional support services for student mental health and wellbeing have adapted and expanded over the years based on student demand and complexity. Services to deal with student crisis, emotional distress and mental health needs have never been more in demand. Universities already invest a lot in support services for student mental health and wellbeing that, particularly when compared to NHS provision, offer an accessible, professional service that helps students stay and succeed at university and excel in their future employment (Wallace, 2012).

Supporting student mental health and wellbeing is not just the preserve of the professional support teams. All the areas discussed in this chapter have a responsibility for student mental health and wellbeing, as does the individual student. A theme throughout has been the move to multidisciplinary and partnership working – within professional services, with external providers, with a broader cross-section of university staff and with students. A more holistic approach requires strategic leadership and enhanced collaboration, particularly with students, so that they recognise their own responsibility for their wellbeing, and with NHS services so universities can be confident that the NHS will be accessible to treat those students who have a mental illness. Universities can then structure support for students to help them reach their academic potential and fulfil the institution's primary role as an educational establishment.

Further reading

MWBHE/UUK (2015) *Student Mental Wellbeing in Higher Education: Good Practice Guide.*
  This is an excellent pragmatic guide to good practice focused in a university setting.

Mair, D. (ed.) (2016) *Short-term Counselling in Higher Education: Context, Theory and Practice.* Abingdon and New York: Routledge.
  Focused on counselling but discusses the issues relevant to mental health and wellbeing support in universities

Thorley, C. (2017) *Not by Degrees: Improving the Student Mental Health in the UK's Universities.* London: Institute for Public Policy Research. Available at: www.ippr.org/files/2017-09/1504645674_not-by-degrees-170905.pdf (accessed 8 September 2017).
  A good and current overview of the mental health challenges in higher education

Universities UK (2017) #stepchange. www.universitiesuk.ac.uk/stepchange (accessed 7 September 2017).
  A proposed framework for a whole university approach to mental health and wellbeing.

Student Minds (2018). *Transitions. Helping You to Navigate University Life.* Available at: www.studentminds.org.uk/uploads/3/7/8/4/3784584/180531_transitions_interactive.pdf (accessed 14 June 2018).
  An excellent and balanced practical guide for students going to university.

References

AMOSSHE (2018) The student services organisation. www.amosshe.org.uk/ (accessed 1 July 2018).

Anthony, K. & Merz Nagel, D. (2010) *Therapy Online: A Practical Guide.* London: Sage.

BACP (British Association for Counselling and Psychotherapy) (2017) *BACP Competencies for Working in Further and Higher Education.* www.bacp.co.uk/media/2042/bacp-competences-working-in-further-higher-education.pdf (accessed 2 July 2018).

BACP (British Association for Counselling and Psychotherapy) (2018a) BACP Universities and Colleges division. www.bacp.co.uk/bacp-divisions/bacpuc/ (accessed 1 July 2018).

BACP (British Association for Counselling and Psychotherapy) (2018b) Thinking about therapy. www.bacp.co.uk/about-therapy/we-can-help/ (accessed 1 July 2018).

Bell, E. (1996) *Counselling in Further and Higher Education*. Buckingham: Open University Press.

Charlie Waller Memorial Trust (2017) E-learning. http://learning.cwmt.org.uk/ (accessed 4 June 2018).

City of York Council (2017) *York Student Health Needs Assessment*. http://democracy.york.gov.uk/documents/s115873/Annexpercent20Bpercent20-percent20ONLINEpercent20ONLYpercent20-percent20Yorkpercent20SHNApercent20fullpercent20reportpercent20FINALpercent2026-06.pdf (accessed 28 June 2017).

DSA-QAG (Disabled Students' Allowances Quality Assurance Group) (2017a) History of DSA-QAG. https://dsa-qag.org.uk/about-us/history-dsa-qag (accessed 14 June 2018).

DSA-QAG (Disabled Students' Allowances Quality Assurance Group) (2017b) *Non-medical Helper Providers: Quality Assurance Framework*. https://dsa-qag.org.uk/application/files/7215/1213/6252/NMH_Quality_Assurance_Framework_V2.0.pdf (accessed 14 June 2018).

Dufour, G. (2016) Assessment in student counselling. In Mair, D. (ed.) *Short-term Counselling in Higher Education: Context, Theory and Practice*. Abingdon and New York: Routledge. pp. 70–86.

Ecclestone, K. and Hayes, D. (2009) *The Dangerous Rise of Therapeutic Education*. Abingdon and New York: Routledge.

Higher York (2015) Everybody's business.Exploring current issues around mental health for young people aged 0–25. www.higheryork.org/eb/ (accessed 24 September 2017).

Hughes, G., Panjwanu, M., Tulcidas, P. and Byrom, N. (2018) *Student Mental Health: The Role and Experiences of Academics*. www.studentminds.org.uk/uploads/3/7/8/4/3784584/180129_student_mental_health__the_role_and_experience_of_academics__student_minds_pdf.pdf (accessed 4 June 2018).

Iacobucci, G. (2018) Medical model of care needs updating, say experts. www.bmj.com/content/360/bmj.k1034 (accessed 1 July 2018).

LivingWorks (2018) The world leader in suicide prevention training. www.livingworks.net/ (accessed 14 June 2018).

Mair, D. (2016) The rise and rise of higher education and therapeutic culture. In Mair, D. (ed.) *Short-term Counselling in Higher Education: Context, Theory and Practice*. Abingdon and New York: Routledge. pp. 7–24.

McIntosh, E. and Shaw, J. (2017) *Student Resilience. Exploring the Positive Case for Resilience*. www.unite-group.co.uk/sites/default/files/2017-05/student-resilience.pdf (accessed 4 June 2017).

MHFA (Mental Health First Aid) (2017) Higher education mental health first aid courses. https://mhfaengland.org/individuals/higher-education/ (accessed 4 June 2018).

MWBHE/UUK (Mental Wellbeing in Higher Education Group and Universities UK) (2015) *Student Mental Wellbeing in Higher Education: Good Practice Guide*. www.universitiesuk.ac.uk/policy-and-analysis/reports/Documents/2015/student-mental-wellbeing-in-he.pdf (accessed 10 July 2017).

NADP (National Association of Disability Practitioners) (2018) About NADP. https://nadp-uk.org/about-nadp/ (accessed 14 June 2018).

New Economics Foundation (2008) *Five Ways to Wellbeing*. http://b.3cdn.net/nefoundation/8984c5089d5c2285ee_t4m6bhqq5.pdf (accessed 24 September 2017).

NICE (National Institute for Health and Care Excellence) (2011) Common mental health problems: Identification and pathways to care. www.nice.org.uk/guidance/cg123/chapter/1-guidance (accessed 24 September 2017).

Nightline (2018) Nightline Association. www.nightline.ac.uk/ (accessed 4 June 2018).

NUS (2013) Mental Distress Overview. https://www.nus.org.uk/Global/Campaigns/20130517%20Mental%20Distress%20Survey%20%20Overview.pdf slide (accessed 3 July 2019).

ONS (Office for National Statistics) (2018) Estimating suicide among higher education students, England and Wales: Experimental statistics. www.ons.gov.uk/peoplepopulationandcommunity/birthsdeathsandmarriages/deaths/articles/estimatingsuicideamonghighereducationstudentsenglandandwalesexperimentalstatistics/2018-06-25 (accessed 14 June 2018).

Papyrus (2018) Papyrus. www.papyrus-uk.org/ (accessed 1 July 2018).

Prince's Trust (2018) *Princes Trust Macquarie Youth Index*. www.princes-trust.org.uk/about-the-trust/news-views/macquarie-youth-index-2018-annual-report (accessed 4 June 2017).

Royal College of Psychiatrists (2011) *Mental Health of Students in HE*. Royal College of Psychiatrists' Council Report CR166. www.rcpsych.ac.uk/files/pdfversion/cr166.pdf (accessed 24 September 2017).

Samaritans (2018) Samaritans. www.samaritans.org/ (accessed 1 July 2018).

Scarfe, P. (2013) *Considering the Needs of Students with a Mental Health Condition: Resource for DSA Needs Assessors*. https://dsa-qag.org.uk/application/files/3314/8705/6016/Resource_for_study_needs_assessors_-_mental_health_conditions_September_2013.pdf (accessed 14 June 2018).

Seldon, A. and Martin, M. (2017) *The Positive and Mindful University*. HEPI Occasional Paper 18. www.hepi.ac.uk/wp-content/uploads/2017/09/Hepi-The-Positive-and-Mindful-University-Paper-18-Embargoed-until-21st-Sept-1.pdf (accessed 22 September 2017).

Smith, J. (2016) Student mental health: A new model for universities. *The Guardian*. 2 March. www.theguardian.com/higher-education-network/2016/mar/02/student-mental-health-a-new-model-for-universities (accessed 1 July 2018).

Streatfield, N. and Prance, L. (2016) Managing a multidisciplinary wellbeing team. *University and College Counselling*, 4 (1). www.bacp.co.uk/bacp-journals/university-and-college-counselling/march-2016/managing-a-multidisciplinary-wellbeing-team/ (accessed 1 July 2018).

Student Health Association (2018) About us. www.studenthealthassociation.co.uk/about-the-sha/ (accessed 1 July 2018).

Student Minds (2016) Looking after a mate. www.studentminds.org.uk/lookingafteramate.html (accessed 14 July 2017).

Student Minds (2018) *Transitions. Helping you to Navigate University Life*. www.studentminds.org.uk/uploads/3/7/8/4/3784584/180531_transitions_interactive.pdf (accessed 14 June 2018).

Thorley, C. (2017) *Not by Degrees: Improving the Student Mental Health in the UK's Universities*. London: Institute for Public Policy Research. www.ippr.org/files/2017-09/1504645674_not-by-degrees-170905.pdf (accessed 8 September 2017).

Time to Change (2018) Time to change. www.time-to-change.org.uk/ (accessed 24 September 2017).

UMHAN (University Mental Health Advisers Network) (2018a) About us. www.umhan.com/about-umhan.html (accessed 4 June 2018).

UMHAN (University Mental Health Advisers Network) (2018b) What is a mental health adviser? www.umhan.com/mental-health-advisers.html (accessed 4 June 2018).

UMHAN (University Mental Health Advisers Network) (2018c) UMHAN capability framework. www.umhan.com/capability-framework.html (accessed 4 June 2018).

University of Oxford (2018) Peer supporters programme. www.ox.ac.uk/students/welfare/counselling/peersupport?wssl=1 (accessed 4 June 2018).

UUK (Universities UK) (2017) #stepchange. www.universitiesuk.ac.uk/stepchange (accessed 7 September 2017).

UUK (Universities UK) (2018) Minding our future. www.universitiesuk.ac.uk/minding-our-future (accessed 14 September 2018).

Wallace, P. (2012) The impact of counselling on academic outcomes: The student perspective. *Association of University and College Counselling (AUCC)*. November. www.bacp.co.uk/bacp-journals/university-and-college-counselling/november-2012/the-impact-of-counselling-on-academic-outcomes/ (accessed 14 July 2017).

Wallace, P. (2014) The positive wider impact of counselling provision in colleges and universities. *Association of University and College Counselling (AUCC)*. September. www.bacp.co.uk/media/1851/bacp-university-college-counselling-sep14.pdf (accessed 14 September 2018).

Worley-James, S. (2017) Delivering online support: The nuts and bolts behind a student-friendly service. *University and College Counselling*, 5 (2). www.bacp.co.uk/bacp-journals/university-and-college-counselling/may-2017/delivering-online-support// (accessed 1 July 2018).

Yeung, P., Weale, S. and Perraudin, F. (2016) University mental health services face strain as demand rises 50 per cent. *The Guardian*. 23 September. www.theguardian.com/education/2016/sep/23/university-mental-health-services-face-strain-as-demand-rises-50 (accessed 10 September 2017).

9

Risk and Crisis: Managing the Challenges

Nicola Barden

Objectives

There are two fundamental rules in managing risk and crisis. The first is neatly summarised by Parry (1990: 31): 'Half the skill of successfully working through crises is not to make things worse than they already are.' The other is to recognise that the best solution to risk and crisis is to prevent them happening in the first place; investment in prevention is the surest way to minimise the unavoidable stress and anxiety related to any crisis. However, with the best prevention possible, times of crisis and elevated risk are not wholly avoidable, and this chapter focuses on core considerations when dealing with them.

The chapter will consider:

- How risk and crisis is understood in higher education
- Characteristics of the student population in relation to risk and crisis
- Positive institutional approaches to managing mental health risks and crises
- The importance of risk assessment
- Intervention in risk and crisis situations
- Crisis management

What is a risk? What is a crisis?

In any institution there is likely to be more than one perspective on risk and crisis, and in higher education this includes the perspective of the institution, the professional service and the individuals concerned.

Risk in the broader university often refers to, though is not limited to, the risk of academic failure or withdrawal. Mental health states can impact on this: students who are feeling depressed or highly anxious, for example, are likely to struggle more with meeting the demands of HE. A research report in the *Association for University and College Counselling Journal* (Wallace, 2012) confirmed, through student self-reporting, that using university counselling services had helped 79% of them do better in their academic work and 81% to stay at university, showing that mental health support is relevant to addressing this type of risk. Of course not all students with mental health difficulties do experience an impact on their work; indeed, academic achievement can be remarkably stable in the midst of considerable mental disruption.

The institution will need to be concerned with crisis management on levels that are different from the individual practitioner, including the potential media impact, the effect on staff and the wider student body, reputation, safeguarding concerns and, more recently, terrorism and the Prevent legislation (Home Office,

2016). This does not detract from a genuine and paramount concern for the individual student; it does reflect the added layer of responsibility that must appropriately be attended to. It is often at the point when these broader issues may be impacted that the senior management team within an institution will want to be involved in specific situations.

Risk in professional support services is generally understood to refer to a serious risk of harm to self or others, and a crisis state emerges when this risk is no longer felt to be contained, requiring additional action. University support services will routinely be managing varying levels of risk in the students they see, and most of these will never reach the point of being seen outside the professional services at all, let alone as a crisis.

Universities in the United Kingdom originated as residential communities of learning, often with a religious basis, in which moral and social instruction was an integral part of the academic agenda (Lochtie et al., 2018). Despite the vast changes in higher education, this expectation of community prevails, accompanied by a presumption that universities will be able to address the majority of their students' needs in-house, which, by and large, they do.

For the student, the definition of crisis is more likely to be subjective: a point at which they feel their coping mechanisms are not working and the situation is escalating out of their control. Parry (1990) emphasised the uncontrollable, unresolved characteristics of crises, the feelings of loss, danger and uncertainty that accompany them, and the trigger which can be an unexpected event or the accumulation of distress over a long period. For this reason it is crucial not to rely on objective criteria alone to assess a crisis; the intensity of adolescent feelings combined with a potential level of inexperience in self-management can make one person's manageable difficulty into another person's crisis. This is why a good risk assessment relies on a thorough understanding of the situation. If the student is not already engaged with support the risk of withdrawal into themselves is high, and it is often flatmates who notice and try to help – sometimes to the point of their own exhaustion and feelings of being overwhelmed. It can be the crisis point reached by others that brings the crisis of the student concerned to light.

It is helpful to the process of risk and crisis management to have a shared view on what escalates a risk into a crisis, and what constitutes an acceptable risk. To do this, the institutional values and priorities need to be clear and services need to be mindful of them when setting their objectives. If the ethos is 'we will support and develop you as a unique individual throughout your degree', this places a responsibility on the support services and the academic staff that needs resourcing and embedding. If the ethos is 'we will develop your employability and improve your career prospects throughout your degree', this will require a different sort of resourcing and embedding. A wellbeing service that designs itself around the uniqueness of the individual in an institution that measures itself by career outcomes is on track to be at odds with senior managers over support decisions, not because the two things are inimical but because the definition of a successful outcome in a crisis may differ.

Even where there is a shared vision, if there is no communication around the actions taken in individual cases then the mental health professionals in the university can be working towards one objective – for example balancing vulnerability with stress while maintaining the therapeutic relationship; the academics to another – enabling the student to succeed and maintaining academic standards; and the senior management another – avoiding reputational damage at a time of challenging recruitment. This can split the organisational response, leading to an inconsistent message to the student and undermining of staff. In fact, these three perspectives share a common core: that the student should be able to find a way through their difficulties and attain their goals with appropriate support from the university. Recognising this commonality is a good starting point for addressing disagreements over how best to achieve it.

Safety in universities

Managing risk can be a frightening process for all involved, and there is much discussion currently over the expectations of 'safety' in HE: safe environments, safe campuses, safe experiences. The one-time Minister for Universities, Science, Research and Innovation Sam Gyimah's recommendation that universities act in loco parentis (DfE, 2018; HEPI, 2018; and see Chapter 2) to their students epitomised some of this, and there is an established critique of education itself creating unhelpful dependencies through an excessive focus on support, leading students to expect less of themselves in terms of 'getting on with it' and manufacturing wellbeing concerns over ordinary experiences of self-doubt and challenge. Ecclestone and Hayes describe this as the 'diminished self' (2009: xiii), reducing resilience by making the trepidation and excitement of transition into a problem needing support,. This perspective is further explored and challenged in Chapter 4. Vailes (2017), in a more measured way, expressed concern that over-protection could interfere with learning the skills of self-management.

This does raise the role of parents in terms of risk. Parents are more involved in their sons' and daughters' education than previously, but there is uncertainty in terms of how to respond to this when there is a risk of harm. Parents can be the ones contacting the university to raise an alarm, so placing themselves in the process, and the UUK/Papyrus publication *Suicide-Safer Universities* (Clarke et al., 2018) includes parents in the student support network. A suggestion from Education Secretary Damian Hinds, that students should be able to opt into a system on application or enrolment that permits universities to contact their next-of-kin with concerns about their wellbeing (Turner, 2018), has been adopted by some while approached with caution by others. Where appropriate, most university support services would strongly encourage students at risk to contact, or give permission for the university to contact, those they have put down as next-of-kin/emergency names, or other preferred friends/relatives, to support them in their recovery.

Psychiatric input

Another change has been to the place of psychiatry in managing risk. In the earlier development of counselling services (Bell, 1996; Newsome et al., 1973; and see Chapter 8 in this book) health centres were frequently part of the university structure with psychiatric consultancy easily available. Now such consultancy comes through referral by the GP, and as the threshold for referral climbs increasingly higher the GP has a more prominent role as gatekeeper. The usefulness of psychiatric diagnosis can be contentious (Pilgrim, 2009: 12), and has a history of racial bias and misunderstanding (Fernando, 2010); nevertheless, where risk is high it has a valuable place. Some universities buy in psychiatric advice and consultancy for this very purpose. Where there is no psychiatric backup, assessments conducted by university staff are required to be both more cautious and at the same time more robust, as they assess increasingly difficult situations.

Particular issues for a student population in relation to risk and crisis

The most visible difference in the student population is age, and the vulnerabilities associated with this, particularly in terms of impulsivity, have been documented in other chapters. Whatever the age, though, the transition to HE brings with it a certain regression to an earlier state of not-knowing, including for mature students who may have been out of education for some years. A 40-year-old returning to education can feel more daunted by their first assignment than a younger person who completed their A-levels the previous year, is less likely to have a cohort with whom they can identify, and is more likely to feel that they should know the things that they find difficult. The first chapter in this book draws attention to the demographic change in higher education brought about by increased access and widening participation, and this has undoubtedly achieved a greater representation of society at large in the student body, bringing different sorts of unfamiliarity and transitional needs. There are some clear indicators that certain groups of students are more at risk in terms of access to, success in and progression from higher education. Supporting these students is the subject of the Access and Participation plans required of all universities by the Office for Students (OfS, 2019) and which commonly refer to students with disabilities, mental health issues, disabilities, low family incomes and first in the family to enter higher education, as well as other potentially vulnerable groups such as care leavers, asylum seekers, young carers and those previously homeless. The dislocation that is part of all student life exempts no-one; even those who are commuting and returning to familiar environments are experiencing a separation from home and family in terms of shared experience, making an old home feel newly strange. For those who live on campus, there is the untested experience of living in a community of largely young people, without the familiar adult 'brakes' on behaviour. It is easy to be anonymous, to be unnoticed, to feel alone and unaware of the others feeling similarly, particularly in a digitally led, performance-orientated social world. Feeling alone in a multitude will never have been easier.

There are known risk factors in certain groups: for example those with an existing psychiatric diagnosis or with previous attempts to take their own life, or a family history of either of these things, and those who are socially isolated, recently bereaved or with a childhood history of abuse (Hawton et al., 1993; Pritchard, 1995). Translating thought into action can be triggered by access to the means of harm, recent disturbances in the family, a significant rejection, and feelings of shame and fear (Bertolote, 2014). Less is known about protective factors but these include self-esteem, good relationships, access to and engagement with support, a sense of purpose and a feeling of belonging – all of which are helped by positive childhood experiences. Simple social support can be a successful buffer between impulsivity and risk (Kleiman et al., 2012), and it is worth thinking about this in terms of students who by nature of their difficulties may lack this, for example those on the autistic spectrum (Moskowitz and Ritter, 2016). In higher education terms this means that some students will arrive more vulnerable to risk than others, and this can be mitigated by their experience at university, finding friends and settling in, and using the help available. Coupled with the recognition of the place of stress in the development of crises (Greenstone and Leviton, 2002) and the vulnerability to the onset of various mental health disorders (see Chapter 3), the heightened risk to students becomes clear. It also underlines the difficulty in assessing risk as it is about how the student feels as well as known external factors; a risk assessment has to take both subjective and objective aspects into account.

At the same time, there is more help within the university that is free and available than there is likely to be again in their lifetime in terms of easily accessible and tailored support; but students have to feel confident in accessing it, particularly in relation to mental health difficulties. An Equality Challenge Unit (ECU, 2015) report found that disproportionately low numbers of students disclose a mental health condition to their university, and in fact are more likely to tell other students than to tell staff. At the same time it reported that 78% of students accessing a range of mental health support found it helpful, highlighting the challenge of enabling students to confidently engage with the support that will help to prevent future crises from occurring. The student narrative in the ECU report indicated that those who arrived with a positive attitude to their mental health difficulties were more likely to disclose and therefore more likely to access help and find it useful, whereas those with a negative image about their difficulties were less likely to have the confidence to make an approach and, by so doing, to feel more positive.

Institutional approaches to risk

It is natural for institutions to be risk averse, but a principle of risk avoidance in itself does not make for good risk management. In mental health there can seem little to be gained in taking risks. However, the clinical discourse around risk repeatedly affirms that informed risk taking as a result of sound risk assessment is the most effective route to successful risk management. 'We cannot, and should not, seek to avoid risk-taking. The focus needs to be on the quality of the decision-making, not on risk' (Carson and Bain, 2008: 239). Three conditions for positive institutional approaches to risk are:

1. Trust between the institution and its professional services. Institutions can want mental health risk to be clearer than it is in practice, but risk is not binary (Reeves, 2017a), on or off, high or low (Maden, 2011): it is a matter of degree. Assessments are not dealing in absolutes but measure the risk of risk. Facing this is crucial; an institution that expects failsafe solutions from its professional services will place them under unrealistic pressure that can only result in defensive practice which, while it might make the institution feel safe, is unlikely to be in the best interests of the student. Professionals working in a university's counselling and mental health services in particular need to know that they will be supported in their work by the institution, and Baker and Wilkinson (2011) draw a helpful difference between 'defensible' and 'defensive' practice. No-one is expected to endorse a course of action taken without due care and attention; but a poor outcome in itself does not confirm a poor decision. 'The reality is that for most clients with capacity, it will not be the therapist who keeps the client safe, or others safe, but the actions and willingness of the client to act to self-support when away from the session' (Reeves, 2017a: 82).
2. Good communication between different aspects of the institution. This involves respect for the differing levels of confidentiality offered. At times of risk information should be pooled where possible. This does not give blanket permission to override professional and ethical responsibilities to confidentiality (Mitchels, 2017). While organisational policies can influence expectations and levels of individual vulnerability should be taken into account, counselling services in particular have a high level of confidentiality attached to them (BACP, 2018; Jenkins, 2017). Part of the risk assessment therefore includes weighing up the consequences of breaking confidentiality, particularly the risk of damaging the therapeutic relationship on which the management of risk might be relying. The best resolution, of course, is having the consent of the student. That said, sharing of information as clearly as possible on a need-to-know basis is essential to taking a comprehensive view of risk, and serious risk of harm to self or others is a strong factor in a decision to break confidentiality.
3. Tolerance of the anxiety that risk brings. Risk definitions are contextual (Titterton, 2005, 2011) and influenced by institutional values. What risks are

institutions willing to take, and what, in their context, are they entitled to take? Universities are primarily providing education and their support is legitimately shaped around this; reasonable risk for a psychiatrist in an in-patient team will be different from a counsellor in a university service. Accepting that risk is not absolute means an inevitable anxiety in relation to its assessment and management. When risk is elevated, it should be dealt with by senior management teams listening carefully to the information and guidance provided by the mental health expertise available to them from their professional teams, and making a decision based on this.

A skilled professional team, empowering management, a shared vision of a good outcome (Calder, 2011) and clear policies that stand behind this are good bases for a positive organisational approach to risk.

The importance and nature of risk assessment

Risk assessments must identify and balance dilemmas (Carson and Bain, 2008). Supporting a student who shows risky behaviour can make staff, particularly when this is not their main role, feel ill equipped, under-resourced and out of their depth. These issues must be taken seriously; staff are not expected to work outside their capacity. However, there are many ways to address this that do not lead to the student having to give up or even take time out of their course, as is often the first impulse for resolution. The 2010 Equality Act gives students the right to reasonable adjustments in relation to mental health needs, and the institution must fulfil this as a duty. It must manage its own dilemmas over whether and how it can provide what the student reasonably needs in order to continue with their studies; it is a serious business to refuse this. It is when continuing at university is actively contributing to mental health difficulties that a turning point is often reached. If the student at risk 'lacks capacity', that is, the ability to make a decision on their own behalf due to mental illness (NHS, 2018; Rethink, 2018), then a decision may be able to be made for them, such as a temporary suspension. However this is a rare circumstance and will most often happen with the involvement of statutory mental health services. While 'risk' is often cited as a reason to override many rules, that argument only holds good for the very short term and does not override the legal and ethical rights to autonomy and independence that are heavily protected in law (Girgis, 2017). The careful procedures around any compulsory mental health admission in the 2007 and 1983 Mental Health Acts exemplify this (Fennell, 1996).

Assessments can be aided by standard questionnaires and familiarity with known risk and protective factors for self-harm and suicide. However, it is the dialogue between the student and the assessor that is the crux of the assessment (Reeves, 2017b): what is happening for *this* person, *now*. If trust is established it will be possible to assess the risk more confidently. The openness of the student, the knowledge and experience of the assessor, the information available and the attitude of the institution are all part of the picture. An understanding of the individual student's way of looking at things, the connection between the person and their situation, is what overcomes the gap between risk factors in theory and risk in practice (Baker and Kelly, 2011).

It is often helpful for an assessment to come from more than one perspective, particularly where there has been multiple involvement with the student. Talking as a cross-university team reduces the isolation of each section and grows confidence in working together and managing worrying situations. It would be good practice to have clear structures within which this type of discussion can happen. Some institutions will have regular 'at risk' meetings between relevant staff, with clear consent and recording procedures, and this can prevent a risk becoming a crisis. Most universities have a 'fitness to study', or 'supported study' procedure, for when risk has escalated and an action plan needs to be drawn up, and this is outlined in more detail in Chapter 6. Crucially these must be seen as supportive procedures as it is all too easy for the student to see them as disciplinary and to disengage from them. Their purpose must be to support the student in their aims, providing a realistic commitment for the university's part in this and building a platform to assess when the risk of a situation makes these aims untenable.

One other aspect that must be taken into account is the impact of an individual student's mental health difficulties on others. All students have a right to an environment conducive to their purpose in being at university. Most are inexperienced at managing others' mental health problems, although some of course will have had their own experiences with family and friends. The result is often an over-enthusiasm to help, sitting up all night with distressed housemates, not telling anyone else that there is a problem until it all becomes too much. At this point parents can get involved, angry and concerned that their son or daughter is dealing with a flatmate who is self-harming and talking about suicide. The initial reaction is often to regard the unwell student as the one who should leave. In fact such situations can usually be managed once the support services are involved and the strain and expectation is removed from the friends.

CASE STUDY 9.1

Sarah was a first year student who alerted the Disability Team to some mental health difficulties before she arrived at university. She described high anxiety and some obsessive-compulsive behaviours which had been managed in school by means of a shared safety plan that included

(Continued)

(Continued)

early notification of changes so that she could prepare for them. It was easy to predict that Sarah would find the initial transition to university difficult so she attended a pre-arrival orientation day and made the decision to commute from home, avoiding the additional difficulties of living with new people. The Disability Team set up a learning agreement which included advance notice of information regarding her teaching materials and schedule.

In the first week Sarah followed her arrivals schedule meticulously, but found that it was not always accurate. Some of her business management lectures took less or more time than indicated; the members of her tutor and seminar groups were not finalised; the events led by the Student Union changed venue at the last minute. The whole institution was teeming with people using the mainly open style learning spaces which, as a consequence, were crowded and noisy. Even the library allowed food and drink, and shared study spaces seemed to dominate, which had not been the case at school.

Sarah had been allocated a mentor following her Disabled Student Needs Assessment over the summer, but the first appointment was still two weeks away. She tried to access the wellbeing team but was daunted by the queues at the reception counter; she did not have the courage to email them, feeling herself to be a great nuisance. Sarah had not disclosed that self-harm was one of her coping strategies, and she started to cut her legs with a blade. This was easy to disguise through clothing, but at the end of her second week on leaving the bathroom she was met by one of the lecturers on her way in, who saw a screwed-up ball of blood-soaked tissues in Sarah's hand. She immediately asked her whether anything was wrong, but Sarah was unable to answer. The lecturer took her straight to Student Services, who managed to see Sarah in a drop-in on the same day. She was prioritised for an appointment the next day with a mental health adviser, who took a fuller history and did a risk assessment.

In many ways Sarah did all the right things, alerting the university to her needs and getting support in place. She had found ways at school of managing her difficulties, and was optimistic that this could be repeated. What she could not account for in advance was the actual experience of such a massive change to her routine, everything from her work schedule to the food she ate. She had not disclosed the self-harm, partly due to stigma and partly because she hoped it would not recur. To find it returning made her feel a failure, and she quickly thought she had overestimated her abilities. Yet she really wanted to be at university, and held on to the hope that if she could continue things would get better.

Student Services had done everything they thought was necessary, given what they knew. The vagaries of the welcome week and arrivals process were not unusual; it is a time of some chaos where even the best laid plans do not work out and many students find themselves cheerfully able to 'go with the flow'. For some, however, the chaos is a nightmare, and their concerns can easily get lost or dismissed. This can be especially true of students on the autistic spectrum, for whom early orientation and access to quiet space can make a big difference.

In Sarah's case the risks were of withdrawal or possible failure academically, and of worsening self-harm personally. Previous self-harm is one of the risk indicators for future suicidal ideation (Van Rijn, 2017). Sarah's case also raised the potentially protective factor of self-harm: it can be experienced as a coping mechanism when all other expressions of distress fail or are unavailable (Reeves, 2017a) and can reduce suicide risk in the student's perception. Indeed, there is some evidence that no-harm therapeutic contracts can do harm (Bertolote, 2014). While self-harm in itself does not constitute a crisis, it is a constituent component of risk despite these safety perspectives, not least because of the impulsivity factor in young people and the rapidity with which feelings can change.

The mentor had the disadvantage of not having met Sarah before, but the advantage of some background information and expertise in the field. The important thing will be to arrive at a shared sense of future direction so that the student can see a way forward; a sense of hope is key. An impulse to leave higher education and return later could be the right move for Sarah, or it could lead to a collapse in self-confidence from which she does not recover. An impulse to stay and tough it out may exacerbate the problems, worsening the self-harm and leading to a risk to life, or it may be rewarded by a successful transition and improved self-esteem. There is no guarantee either way; this is the skill of the assessment, and the reason why it is a partnership activity with the student.

Intervention

Assessment is the precursor to intervention; its purpose is to provide a basis for the way forward. Another precursor is to understand the institution's expectation of resolution, and ideally the institution needs to agree on the definition of both the problem and the solution (Froggett, 2017). The student's wellbeing and ultimate safety are paramount, but how best to achieve this will be the nub of the discussion.

All the changes in higher education have not fundamentally changed the shape of its delivery, and students with mental health difficulties are still generally expected to manage within a three year programme. This means that resolution is often thought about as returning the student to the state in which they can manage this status quo, without expecting the status quo itself to change. Yet while many mental health difficulties are temporary and do pass with the right support, others are going to be part of the ongoing life of the student, and therefore the institution. Personality disorders, psychotic episodes, bipolar disorder are all conditions that can be managed but do not go away, while also presenting a higher risk of self-harm. They can be seen as outside the boundaries of normal behaviour, or as a challenge to what is thought of as normal (Noble, 2017). Recovery is therefore increasingly seen as the capacity to build a personally meaningful and fulfilling life rather than an absence of symptoms (McCormick, 2009; Ramon et al., 2009), and facilitating this involves some risk taking, exemplified by Sarah's decision to come to university, and now by the intervention the university decides to make.

Sarah agreed to discuss her self-harm openly with her GP and her mentor, and was relieved to be given a list of quiet places that she could book to study. She took advantage of a room for commuting students that she had been unaware of which provided a locker in which she could store things and a place to make hot drinks. The safety plan was re-drafted and renamed a management plan. Sarah agreed that this could be shared with her lecturers. This plan helped Sarah but unfortunately alarmed the lecturers more. Word had spread through the academic staff about the cutting, and they were anxious that she had a level of risk that they did not feel comfortable supporting.

At this point it is easy for the narrative about supporting Sarah to become polarised, with lecturers feeling anxious and unsupported, and Student Services feeling they are doing their best and being misunderstood. While the incident with Sarah should not have been disclosed by the lecturer, it is difficult to keep such information contained and rumours quickly spread. To help with this, it is useful if Student Services can (with Sarah's permission) talk directly with the programme staff to address their concerns and discuss their role. Staff will understandably feel that by handing over to support services they have fulfilled their responsibilities. For support services this is only the start of the journey, and improvement will take time and a continuing involvement from all concerned. Wellbeing is a whole-university responsibility, underlined by the work of Universities UK's 2017 #stepchange report. The student-led mental health charity Student Minds underlined the need to close the gap between academics and student services and to develop 'overlapping interests, principles, culture and language' (Hughes et al., 2018: 88).

The role of the personal tutor has always contained a pastoral element that some tutors felt resistant to, and now 'The increasing prevalence of student mental health problems means that complicated emotions and pastoral issues are becoming an inevitable part of the tutor's role' (Lochtie et al., 2018: 56). At some points academics may take on too much responsibility, finding it difficult to pass things on when the student has struck up a rapport with them and there is no clear guidance on where to draw the line. A 24 hour email culture is not helpful here. Hughes et al. interviewed 52 academics in five institutions and found a common concern over 'ambiguous boundaries' in their academic role (2018: 55), which was not clearly identified in relation to its pastoral aspects. This exacerbated tensions between academic and support departments where each thinks the other should be doing more. In fact for Sarah, the academics needed not to be concerned if she self-harmed but to accept it as a coping mechanism due to stress, and their part was to ensure that as far as possible they informed her of changes in advance, posted information ahead of time and shared any concerning observations with student services.

CASE STUDY 9.2

At 21 Aafiq was slightly older than the other first years; his schooling had been disrupted when he and his family left their homeland in Afghanistan as refugees and came to the United Kingdom. He was 12 when he arrived and, after a long struggle, the family were granted asylum. His mother's mental health was affected by the trauma of the journey and as the eldest son he took on additional responsibilities while his father concentrated on finding work to support them. The family stayed close, but it was difficult. Nevertheless, Aafiq gained his A-levels and a place at university.

He asked to be placed in a quiet flat and found his housemates to be similarly studious, but he was surrounded by another unfamiliar culture, people who had little idea of what he had been through, and separated from the familiarity of his family. He became depressed and, copying his mother, stopped eating and stayed up all night, sitting in the communal kitchen. His housemates were sympathetic and would often sit with him and make food for him to eat, which he would refuse. Their help was welcome but also made him feel like a failure and he became increasingly dependent. His weight loss became very noticeable and other aspects of self-care were affected (not washing or changing his clothes), and the flatmates felt out of their depth. A couple of them talked to their parents, who phoned the housing department saying that something had to be done and Aafiq should be removed.

The problem here was not Aafiq himself but the way in which his understandable difficulties were being handled. In this instance taking a more social perspective was helpful. Aafiq was clearly a young man with resilience and potential, but this had been temporarily derailed. Many universities put additional support in place for refugees and asylum seekers, which means they are linked to a caseworker from the outset, someone who understands their situation and provides support. In this instance Aafiq was on his own, in yet another new environment, set apart by experiences that few others would share. The parents were right to alert the housing services, if not right in their presumed solution; their call may have prevented a risk becoming a crisis if Aafiq had continued to spiral downwards. Thompson pointed out that the right intervention at a point of need provides an opportunity to make a significant change to the individual's coping ability for the future (Thompson, 2011), and the student adviser who assessed Aafiq decided to work on his strengths, including holding a meeting with him and his flatmates so they could all learn something about how to look after each other and themselves.

Crisis management

Just as with Aafiq, Sarah's situation could have escalated into a crisis if the coping strategy had not worked. The line between an escalated risk and a crisis is not exact but can relate to the urgent need for action.

A crisis needs much the same management as any other sort of risk: first comes information gathering, then assessment, then a plan. A good rule of thumb in any crisis is to anticipate that things will not go according to the plan, and the situation will need to be continually re-evaluated (Thompson, 2011). Another is to anticipate that there will be a drive to attribute blame, and a fear of having it attributed. This should be avoided; there is a time for review, but a blame culture around crisis freezes thought and is anathema to the taking of responsibility and learning from mistakes. 'Organisations should aim to develop and promote professional, skilled, non-defensive approaches to risk taking and decision making rather than merely technical accuracy and procedural compliance' (Baker and Wilkinson, 2011: 27). One possibility that must be borne in mind is that there may not have been any mistakes: tragedies happen, and there is no capacity to create absolute safety. One of the hard personal realisations that will be grappled with in the face of a crisis is that 'the world is not as safe as one thought, *and it never was*' (Parry, 1990: 58, italics in original).

CASE STUDY 9.3A

Shui was a British student of Chinese heritage in his second year doing business management. He was being supported by the mental health adviser because he complained of frequent headaches, feelings of being overwhelmed and poor sleep. He was achieving marks in the middle range and this worried him because he felt he had to graduate with a first class degree in order to stand a chance of a decent job. He had seen his GP and discussed the headaches and tiredness; medication was given and counselling was recommended. Shui did not want to see a counsellor. As he was reluctant to talk about his feelings but keen to try things that would be of practical help, the mental health adviser worked with him on sleep hygiene, working patterns, rest and relaxation, but felt that somehow they were missing the point. As his second year assessments loomed Shui became increasingly agitated, abandoned his working pattern plan and library staff reported that he had started to sleep there. The adviser was very concerned.

At this point the adviser would be thinking, if they had not done so already, about whether their concern over Shui needed to be taken anywhere else; supervision would be an obvious place for consultation, and/or a senior colleague or head of service. Most services have a protocol or guide for when to share concerns over risk, or at the least have well-established custom and practice in the area.

At the same time as the mental health adviser was considering this, the Student Services receptionist took a phone call from a Mrs Chen.

CAST STUDY 9.3B

Mrs Chen was concerned about her son and wanted to talk to someone. She was passed to a student adviser who explained that, while she could not disclose information, she could listen to Mrs Chen's concerns and take whatever action may be appropriate. Mrs Chen explained that she had not heard from her son Shui for two days; he normally called her every night. She knows that he has been worried about some exams coming up, and that he can sometimes work too hard and not look after himself. The student adviser thanked her and assured her that they would look into it, although they may not be able to tell her the result. On putting the phone down the adviser quickly checked the Student Services records for the student, scanned the mental health adviser's notes and sent her an email outlining the conversation with Mrs Chen.

In Shui's case, not enough was known about his relationship with his parents to know whether he experienced them as a support or not; but his mother was concerned enough about unusual behaviour to call in. Given what else was known about Shui this was valuable information, adding to the cause for concern. The usefulness of centrally recorded information is clear here; this link could easily have been missed if records were not shared across appropriate support departments.

On the basis of this additional information the Head of Wellbeing asked the University Security Manager to try and locate Chen in his university-managed accommodation. Given the circumstance, a student adviser went with them. They knocked on Shui's door but there was no response so they let themselves in and found Shui lying unconscious but breathing on his bed, with an empty packet of anti-depressants by his side.

This is both a crisis, and hopefully a worse crisis averted. When a crisis occurs, tasks divide into what needs to happen immediately, and then what needs to happen in the medium, short and long term. Immediately, the security team will assess the risk from their perspective and call the emergency services; the adviser will do the same from theirs and address the needs of the other students in the house. Both will inform their seniors, who will consider what other action needs to be taken. The potential list to contact is likely to include:

- A member of the senior management team responsible for student welfare overall
- The Director of Student Services
- The Director of Housing
- The Director of Security
- The Head of Communications
- The hospital
- The personal tutor and head of department
- Chaplaincy.

The uncertainty of outcome is part of the anxiety in this situation, and the crisis leadership must establish a sense of order out of potential chaos. The possibility that Shui may not recover will loom large until more information is forthcoming from the hospital. Nothing is worse for a university than the death of one of its students. It is a tragedy in every sense of the word, and is also a crisis. There is an urgent need for action, but an even more urgent need for thought, and it is vital that the urge to do something does not overtake the need to think about what to do. This is where procedures are so helpful – they provide an automatic guide to the necessary processes, so that thinking time can be spent on the things that cannot be dealt with by a procedure.

How institutions respond to this will vary, but in all events the following things should be considered:

- Continuing communications. Who needs to know what, and how will they be informed. This will include the family, staff and other students. It will also include managing any possible press interest.
- Support. Who will need it, in what form and when, and who will provide it and what do they need in order to do this?
- Liaison. Who will take responsibility for liaison outside of the university, with the hospital, the police, the family?
- A plan for sharing information between those managing the crisis centrally and those involved directly in service delivery.
- A supportive debrief for all the staff involved and a 'lessons learned' meeting to take on board their suggestions for improvement in terms of managing the situation.

If Shui does not recover, a member of the senior management team is likely to lead the response. The level of leadership needs to match the level of authority required to make quick decisions in the situation. If Shui recovers, then continuing actions are likely to be led by Student Services.

As this scenario shows, the immediate response addresses practical needs and information. Do the students feel all right to stay in the house that night? Do they need to talk anything through now, or should they be followed up in the morning? Does the room need sealing off in case it becomes a crime scene, and how should this be explained to them? How much can they be told, and how much can they be asked? What if anything can and should be passed on to the parents at this stage? It is not expected that any single person would know the answers to all of the questions; this is the strength of working as a coordinated and well-led team, that the answers are available between everyone. It would also be at this stage that plans were made to respond to situations of both recovery and non-recovery.

If Shui returns to university, a referral to the counselling service is likely to be helpful. There is good evidence that counselling and psychotherapy are effective in working with suicide risk, and steady, non-judgemental, respectful and validating sessions are deeply appreciated by clients at risk of suicide (Winter et al., 2009). For Shui this will need to include some sensitivity to the possible cultural factors in his background, while avoiding assumptions.

Managing 'out of hours'

When crises occur they are seldom contained within working hours. In an emergency most staff will pitch in where they can to cover urgent need, for example staying until Shui's housemates are settled, or waiting until contact has been established with the hospital before going home. There may be administrative work to do to tie things up for the night, and helplines to be set up in anticipation of a worst case scenario.

This is not the same as the provision of consistent out-of-hours support, which is increasingly in demand in a 24/7 culture in which libraries and learning spaces are open all night. Many universities concentrate on halls of residence, providing wardens or residence assistants who can be called on to varying degrees by students in crisis. It is only a matter of time until the issue of parity is raised for off-campus students, and some student services departments are already opening until late in the evening. For routine services this is less problematic; many counselling services open in the evening by appointment, while being clear that they are not emergency services (Bell, 1996). But any move to offering 24/7 mental health cover is a serious undertaking, and a wish to replace statutory services with a qualified in-house mental health resource should be viewed with extreme caution, and grounded in the university's fundamental purpose as a place of higher education.

Conclusion

Management of risk and crisis is a skilled activity that is best supported by the whole institution working together, with a shared understanding of its ethos and clarity in its processes. Decisions about assessment and intervention rely primarily on human judgement, backed up by good information. Despite the pressures experienced during these situations, time to think is core to good practice.

Risk will always be a part of working with people, and with students there will always be risk associated with mental health difficulties. A century ago Freud, in response to a debate about suicide in young people, exhorted secondary schools to be mindful of their responsibilities to give students 'a desire to live', and to provide 'support and backing at a time of life at which the conditions of their development compel them to relax their ties with their parental home and their family' (1910: 231). Universities continue to do this now, through the provision of both education and support. They are not purposed as therapeutic communities but do have a role to play in helping students through risky and critical moments, supporting their personal as well as their academic development.

Further reading

Feltham, C., Hanley, T. and Winter, L.A. (eds) (2000) *The Sage Handbook of Counselling and Psychotherapy*. London: Sage.
   Provides many excellent chapters relating to risk and crisis, and is applicable beyond the counselling and psychotherapy remit.

Parry, G. (1990) *Coping with Crises*. Leicester: British Psychological Society (BPS) and London: Routledge.

Parry's calm and sensible approach to crisis stands the test of time and helps practitioners to stay grounded in what can be achieved by using a human and professional approach.

The website www.studentsagainstdepression.org is excellent for giving a student's-eye view of what it can feel like to be depressed and not coping, while also presenting a positive approach for going forward.

The Samaritan's postvention tool for universities www.samaritans.org/ universities is a good measure for actions to take in the event of a situation involving suicide, particularly in terms of supporting students and staff should a student have taken their own life.

References

BACP (British Association for Counselling and Psychotherapy) (2018) Ethical framework for the counselling professions. www.bacp.co.uk/events-and-resources/ethics-and-standards/ethical-framework-for-the-counselling-professions/ (accessed 15 January 2019).

Baker, K. and Kelly, G. (2011) Risk assessment and young people. In Kemshall, H. and Wilkinson, B. (eds) *Good Practice in Assessing Risk: Current Knowledge, Issues and Approaches.* London and Philadelphia: Jessica Kingsley Publishers.

Baker, K. and Wilkinson, B. (2011) Professional risk taking and defensible decisions. In Kemshall, H. and Wilkinson, B. (eds) *Good Practice in Assessing Risk: Current Knowledge, Issues and Approaches.* London and Philadelphia: Jessica Kingsley Publishers.

Bell, E. (1996) *Counselling in Further and Higher Education.* Buckingham and Philadelphia: Open University Press.

Bertolote, J.M. (2014) Prevention of suicidal behaviours. In Nock, M.K. (ed.) *The Oxford Handbook of Suicide and Self-Injury.* Oxford: Oxford University Press.

Calder, M.C. (2011) Organisationally dangerous practice: Political drivers, practice implications and pathways to resolution. In In Kemshall, H. and Wilkinson, B. (eds) *Good Practice in Assessing Risk: Current Knowledge, Issues and Approaches.* London and Philadelphia: Jessica Kingsley Publishers.

Carson, D. and Bain, A. (2008) *Professional Risk and Working with People: Decision-making in Health, Social Care and Criminal Justice.* London and Philadelphia: Jessica Kingsley Publishers.

Clarke, N., Mikulenaite, G. and De Pury, J. (2018) *Suicide-Safer Universities.* London: Universities UK and Papyrus. www.universitiesuk.ac.uk/policy-and-analysis/reports/Pages/guidance-for-universities-on-preventing-student-suicides.aspx (accessed 17 January 2019).

DfE (Department for Education) (2018) New package of measures announced on student mental health. www.gov.uk/government/news/new-package-of-measures-announced-on-student-mental-health (accessed 15 January 2019).

Ecclestone, K. and Hayes, D. (2009) *The Dangerous Rise of Therapeutic Education*. Abingdon and New York: Routledge.

ECU (Equality Challenge Unit) (2015) 'Understanding Adjustments: Supporting students and staff who are experiencing mental health difficulties'. www.ecu.ac.uk/wp-content/uploads/2015/02/ECU_Understanding-adjustments.pdf (accessed 12 January 2019).

Fennell, P. (1996) *Treatment Without Consent: Law, Psychiatry and the Treatment of Mentally Disordered People since 1845*. London and New York: Routledge.

Fernando, S. (2010) *Mental Health, Race and Culture* (3rd edn). Basingstoke: Palgrave Macmillan.

Freud, S. (1910) Contributions to a discussion on suicide. In *The Standard Edition of the Complete Works of Sigmund Freud*, Vol. *XI* (Translator J. Strachey). London: Vintage, The Hogarth Press and the Institute of Psycho-Analysis.

Froggett, A. (2017) Leadership. In Feltham, C., Hanley, T. and Winter, L.A. (eds) *The Sage Handbook of Counselling and Psychotherapy*. London: Sage.

Girgis, S. (2017) Mental health law. In Feltham, C., Hanley, T. and Winter, L.A. (eds) *The Sage Handbook of Counselling and Psychotherapy*. London: Sage.

Greenstone, J.L. and Leviton, S.C. (2002) *Elements of Crisis Intervention: Crises and How to Respond to Them* (2nd edn). Pacific Grove, CA: Brooks/Cole.

Hawton, K., Fagg, J., Platt, S. and Hawkins, M. (1993) Factors associated with suicide after parasuicide in young people. *British Medical Journal, 306*: 1641–4.

HEPI (Higher Education Policy Institute) (2018) Are universities in loco parentis? The good old days or the bad old days? www.hepi.ac.uk/2018/04/25/universities-loco-parentis-good-old-days-bad-old-days/ (accessed 15 January 2019).

Home Office (2016) Prevent duty guidance. www.gov.uk/government/publications/prevent-duty-guidance (accessed 15 January 2019).

Hughes, G., Panjwani, M., Tulcidas, P. and Byron, N. (2018) *Student Mental Health: The Role and Experiences of Academics*. Derby: University of Derby, London: King's College London and Leeds: Student Minds.

Jenkins, P. (2017) Therapy and the law. In Feltham, C., Hanley, T. and Winter, L.A. (eds) *The Sage Handbook of Counselling and Psychotherapy*. London: Sage.

Kleiman, E.M., Riskind, J.H., Schaefer, K.E. and Weingarden, H. (2012) The moderating role of social support on the relationship between impulsivity and suicide risk. *Crisis: The Journal of Crisis Intervention and Suicide Prevention, 33*:5, pp273–279.

Lochtie, D., McIntosh, E., Stork, A. and Walker, B.W. (2018) *Effective Personal Tutoring in Higher Education*. St Alban's: Critical Publishing.

Maden, T. (2011) Mental health and risk. In Kemshall, H. and Wilkinson, B. (eds) *Good Practice in Assessing Risk: Current Knowledge, Issues and Approaches*. London and Philadelphia: Jessica Kingsley Publishers.

McCormick, M. (2009) Introduction to Part II: Inequality and policy. In Reynolds, J., Muston, R., Heller, T., Leach, J., McCormick, M., Wallcraft, J. and Walsh, M. (eds) *Mental Health Still Matters*. Basingstoke: Palgrave Macmillan and Buckingham: Open University Press.

Mitchels, B. (2017) Confidentiality, note taking and record keeping. In Feltham, C., Hanley, T. and Winter, L.A. (eds) *The Sage Handbook of Counselling and Psychotherapy*. London: Sage.

Moskowitz, L.J. and Ritter, A.B. (2016) Assessment and intervention for self-injurious behaviour related to anxiety. In Edelson, S.M. and Botsford Johnson, J. (eds) *Understanding and Treating Self-injurious Behaviour in Autism: A Multi-disciplinary Perspective*. London and Philadelphia: Jessica Kingsley Publishers.

Newsome, A., Thorne, B.J. and Wyld, K.L. (1973) *Student Counselling in Practice*. London: University of London Press.

NHS (National Health Service) (2018) Mental Capacity Act. www.nhs.uk/conditions/social-care-and-support-guide/making-decisions-for-someone-else/mental-capacity-act/ (accessed 18 January 2019).

Noble, J. (2017) Personality disorders. In Feltham, C., Hanley, T. and Winter, L.A. (eds) *The Sage Handbook of Counselling and Psychotherapy*. London: Sage.

OfS (Office for Students) (2019) Access and participation plans. www.officefor-students.org.uk/advice-and-guidance/promoting-equal-opportunities/access-and-participation-plans/ (accessed 15 January 2019).

Parry, G. (1990) *Coping with Crises*. Leicester: British Psychological Society (BPS) and London: Routledge.

Pilgrim, D. (2009) *Key Concepts in Mental Health* (2nd edn). London: Sage.

Pritchard, C. (1995) *Suicide – The Ultimate Rejection? A Psycho-social Study*. Buckingham and Philadelphia: Open University Press.

Ramon, S., Healy, B. and Ranouf, N. (2009) Recovery from mental illness as an emergent concept and practice in Australia and the UK. In Reynolds, J., Muston, R., Heller, T., Leach, J., McCormick, M., Wallcraft, J. and Walsh, M. (eds) *Mental Health Still Matters*. Basingstoke: Palgrave Macmillan and Milton Keynes: Open University.

Reeves, A. (2017a) Risk: Assessment, exploration and mitigation. In Feltham, C., Hanley, T. and Winter, L.A. (eds) *The Sage Handbook of Counselling and Psychotherapy*. London: Sage.

Reeves, A. (2017b) Suicide and self-harm. In Feltham, C., Hanley, T. and Winter, L.A. (eds) *The Sage Handbook of Counselling and Psychotherapy*. London: Sage.

Rethink (2018) Mental capacity and mental illness – Assessment. www.rethink.org/living-with-mental-illness/mental-health-laws/mental-capacity/assessment (accessed 15 January 2019).

Thompson, N. (2011) *Crisis Intervention*. Lyme Regis: Russell House Publishing.

Titterton, M. (2005) *Risk and Risk Taking in Health and Social Welfare*. London and Philadelphia: Jessica Kingsley Publishers.

Titterton, M. (2011) Positive risk taking with people at risk of harm. In Kemshall, H. and Wilkinson, B. (eds) *Good Practice in Assessing Risk: Current Knowledge, Issues and Approaches*. London and Philadelphia: Jessica Kingsley Publishers.

Turner, C. (2018) Education Secretary backs system to flag university students' mental health problems to parents. *The Telegraph*. 4 December. www.

telegraph.co.uk/education/2018/12/04/education-secretary-backs-system-flag-university-students-mental/ (accessed 17 January 2019).

UUK (Universities UK) (2017) #stepchange: Mental health in higher education. www.universitiesuk.ac.uk/policy-and-analysis/stepchange/Pages/default.aspx (accessed 18 January 2019).

Vailes, F. (2017) *The Flourishing Student: Every Tutor's Guide to Promoting Mental Health, Well-being and Resilience in Higher Education*. Tadley: Practical Inspiration Publishing.

Van Rijn, B. (2017) Assessment. In Feltham, C., Hanley, T. and Winter, L.A. (eds) *The Sage Handbook of Counselling and Psychotherapy*. London: Sage.

Wallace, P. (2012) The impact of counselling on academic outcomes: The student perspective. *Association for University and College Counselling Journal*, November: 7–11 .

Winter, D., Bradshaw, S., Bunn, F. and Wellsted, D. (2009) *Counselling and Psychotherapy for the Prevention of Suicide: A Systematic Review of the Evidence*. Lutterworth: British Association for Counselling and Psychotherapy.

10

Supporting Staff: Creating the Conditions for Confident Support

Andrew Reeves

<hr>

Objectives

In the context of diverse student need around mental health, this chapter considers how, with training and support, staff in higher education settings can play an important role in providing timely and effective support to students. It also provides direct guidance in some of these areas. More specifically, the chapter will consider:

- How staff in higher education settings might encounter mental health distress in the student population
- The range of training opportunities that should be available to staff to help build capacity and confidence in supporting students, and how the specific role staff hold in the institution shapes the training required
- Reflection on key areas for development and training, as identified by staff themselves, including their limitations and necessary boundaries
- The importance of 'helper' self-care and reflective practice; how supporting others can impact on the helper and strategies that might be employed to attend to the supporter's wellbeing

<hr>

Introduction

As has been discussed in detail in other chapters, university support services traditionally fall into two distinct areas: specialist and non-specialist. The specialist services might include counselling, disability and mental health, for example. By specialist, this refers to services that offer specific mental health support by trained and qualified practitioners, such as counsellors/psychotherapists, mental health nurses, medical and psychiatric staff, and so on. But what of non-specialist mental health support? In some ways this might be defined as those offering mental health support without a specific training or qualification in that area. This might include wider student services staff, support staff, mentors, etc. However, and increasingly the case, non-specialist mental health support has come to include the wider institutional staff team, regardless of job or role. There are therefore multi-layers of mental health support available to students across the institution: from those whose role is specifically designated as offering mental health interventions (and are suitably qualified to do so), to those whose role is more pastoral and supportive and that sits allied or additional to their primary function in the university.

All staff across the institution have an important part to play in supporting students' mental health. It can sometimes (wrongly) be assumed that it is only the specialist services who should be undertaking this work; however, the university's duty of care to individual students around mental health is not confined to specialist staff only; rather, all staff have a duty to offer appropriate and reasonable support to students in the context of their particular role. The importance of recognising and working within the context of the primary role has been further explored in Chapter 2.

The *Student Mental Wellbeing in Higher Education: Good Practice Guide* (MWBHE/UUK, 2015: 33) outlines three levels of information dissemination in HEIs:

- Level 1: including the whole institution's population
- Level 2: staff and students who have more defined pastoral roles or whose roles require particular sensitivity to problematic issues
- Level 3: specialist staff, for example counsellors, mental health advisers.

In broad terms, this relates to the two-level demarcation described around specialist and non-specialist. The training needs discussed here relate more specifically to level 1: across the wider institution. Often institutions will make available in-house training events, which different groups of staff will be able to access. Such events tend to be role-specific, in that they equip staff in particular roles with defined knowledge and skills. This is undoubtedly important but tends not to address the wider knowledge and skill-set required for responding to individual students.

As a consequence, therefore, it is important that all staff have the capacity (knowledge of skills, interventions, and when and how to signpost students to specialist services), and confidence (the confidence in an ability to use such skills and knowledge appropriately in a given situation) so that students can be best responded to. Additionally, and equally importantly, in using skills and knowledge in a confident manner, staff are best positioned to take care of their own mental health and work successfully in the context of appropriate boundaries.

This is particularly pertinent with the publication of the #stepchange: Mental Health in Higher Education policy initiative by Universities UK (UUK, 2017). This policy document emphasises the importance of an institution-wide approach to mental health, across three primary areas:

- Individual: 'Mental health should be part of everyday language in higher education … individuals need to be able to talk about mental health, to know how to keep well and to support others.'
- Institution: 'staff and students should be involved in every stage of the journey to improve mental health'.
- System: 'the higher education sector should lead a national conversation on mental health. The sector should be bold, innovative, collaborative and inclusive' (UUK, 2017).

The supportive collaboration

There can sometimes be a pervading traditional view of what staff–student supportive relationships are like. That is, where academic staff enjoy a one-to-one encounter on a regular basis with their students, building a close relationship over time. While such professional relationships can still occur, they are more generally the exception rather than the rule and it is not uncommon for personal tutors to have limited ongoing one-to-one contact with their students. According to the Higher Education Statistics Agency (HESA), in 2015/16 the average number of students per HEI in England was around 16,000 (HESA, 2018), though this figure includes very small institutions (of under 1000 students), through to much larger institutions with student populations in excess of 30,000 students.

This broad brush overview of number of students is a reminder that current university settings are busy places where staff (and students) may not always have the consistent opportunity to meet regularly and review how things are. The challenge therefore is for students to feel sufficiently comfortable to be able to talk to a trusted member of staff about their problems, and for staff to find the right time and place to offer the support that is needed. That is not to suggest that this does not happen, but it does so in the context of a fast-moving working context.

In acknowledging these challenges however, a greater staff awareness of the potential for mental health difficulties, or a greater attunement to the concept of students' wellbeing on a day-to-day basis, can provide opportunities for students to talk about problems and difficulties earlier on, creating a chance for earlier intervention (which might also include self-help strategies). The importance of the relationship in any helping encounter is well-evidenced (Asay and Lambert, 1999; Cooper, 2008; Wampold, 2001). Considering the evidence for psychotherapy specifically, it might be assumed that the precise techniques used by the therapist are most important. However, from extensive research over many decades, the therapeutic relationship is an important factor in outcome.

The key message here for staff is not to underestimate the importance of the relationship that can be forged with the student. This can build over a number of contacts or, importantly, might include how the student experiences the member of staff even in one encounter. Such factors in the experience of the relationship include the capacity of the member of staff to really listen to the student's problems; taking a non-judgemental position; holding a sense of hope (and communicating that hope) that solutions might be found; and communicating empathy.

The presenting need

It is difficult to illustrate the full range of ways in which students' mental health needs might present within the university context, and these have been discussed in greater detail in other chapters. There may be a number of factors that might influence how both the member of staff and the student experience support. It is important to remember that each student will experience their own mental health uniquely and the ways in which the student communicates their distress will also vary. The student's experience of managing problems in the past (of any type), or if they have not encountered any major problems previously and this therefore is their first experience, can shape how they approach problems in the present, as well as a range of other circumstances in which the student is seen: the professional role held within the institution; the location; and timing of contact with the student.

Finally, the capacity of the member of staff to understand, recognise and respond to mental health needs and their level of confidence in responding to particular situations (different situations are likely to trigger different responses in different staff, depending on professional and personal circumstances) will be key.

Consider the following scenarios.

CASE STUDY 10.1

Jason is an academic tutor with a large teaching load, together with preparation and marking commitments. Jason is concerned about an undergraduate student who is often tearful during tutorial contact. The student is performing well academically, but appears to be struggling with his mental wellbeing and is reluctant to approach student support services, instead preferring to speak with Jason.

CASE STUDY 10.2

Ah Kum works in the Student Union as a sports instructor. She has noticed a second year Chinese student who has been very active in the hockey team. More recently, while the student has continued to attend regularly, her presentation has changed from confident and happy, to withdrawn and quiet. Ah Kum latterly notices some cuts on the student's arms and has considered that they might be self-inflicted.

CASE STUDY 10.3

Sam is a study skills mentor who works with people returning to education. Sam has recently supported a student on an Access course, who is

(Continued)

(Continued)

soon to begin his degree in History; he is 52 years of age, is in a relationship, and has adult children. He tells Sam that he has been depressed for some time and sometimes feels suicidal – although he says he wouldn't act on these thoughts. He is fearful of talking to anyone 'official' about it.

Each of the three scenarios illustrates some of the difficulties staff may encounter in responding to student need.

More specifically, in Case Study 10.1, while Jason is very busy preparing for and delivering lectures with the associated marking of work, he is clearly committed to supporting his students. However, the importance of working within a personal level of professional competence (which could include knowledge and skills but might also include the actual time and availability to offer the student) while setting appropriate boundaries for the relationship, is critical. In this instance, the student has focused the supportive relationship on Jason and, as such, is unwilling to seek out more specialist help. It will be important for Jason to clearly set the limits of this relationship with the student. Explicitly, he will need to agree when he is available, for how long, and what support he can realistically offer to help ensure the student does not retreat from accepting professional help as a result of Jason extending his own support inappropriately. For his own reflections, Jason will need to monitor his own confidence and competence in offering support, depending on the issues that emerge during the discussions with the student.

In Case Study 10.2, Ah Kum has witnessed changes in the student's presentation, including the possibility of self-injury. It is always important, of course, not to make assumptions about what might be an underlying problem while, at the same time, keeping the possibility of mental health deterioration and self-injury in mind. Ah Kum is facing a very real and common experience: if, when and how to approach a student about one's concerns. Ah Kum might feel sufficiently confident to informally ask the student if she is ok, saying that she had noticed she had been quiet recently. Alternatively, or in addition, Ah Kum could consult with student support services who might be able to offer specific guidance about how to have such conversations, and to ensure Ah Kum was aware of what additional support might be available for the student.

In Case Study 10.3, keeping in mind that while a significant number of students will still fall into the 'traditional student' demographic (18–21, recently left home), there is great diversity in the student population and, as such, needs will be varied too. It is key in such situations not to become isolated; consulting with a supervisor or manager, or with student support services, not only provides a space for Sam to consider how he might respond specifically to the student, but also ensures that issues of risk are fully explored, considered, and shared at an institutional level.

Bringing the 'self' into the helping relationship

Should a student present with an imminent or immediate risk to themselves or others, a quick response – following the institution's guidance on seeking help in urgent situations – would be critical. In less urgent situations, however, it is important not to panic, or rush into action without giving the options due thought, or taking the opportunity to consult with others. Personal feelings and responses can shape how a situation is responded to and should be reflected on in all situations, where possible. The experience of the different staff outlined in the case studies will be important in how these students are responded to.

There are a number of factors that might shape a capacity to support students (Charlie Waller Memorial Trust [CWMT] 2019, in Howdin, 2019):

Feeling tired, uncomfortable or ill: It is important to pay attention to the wellbeing of the helper, as well as the student. Recognising an impaired capacity to listen, or be with, a student experiencing mental health distress is important. Rearranging to another time, or finding another member of staff who could meet the student – if possible – might be worthwhile considerations.

There are external distractions: for example noise, concern of being interrupted. Wherever possible, finding a private space to meet with a student is important in respecting their confidentiality, as well as mitigating any external distractions. A simple 'Do Not Disturb' notice on a door can help reduce the chance of interruptions, keeping in mind safe working practices, for example, another person in the department being aware of the student contact.

Feeling pressured to solve the situation: While there might be practical solutions to a problem, it is often the case that the student's problem is multi-layered. The primary task of the helper is to listen, empathise, identify the problem and, if appropriate, signpost to appropriate services. The value of non-judgemental listening should not be underestimated.

Not having enough time: Staff often experience a pressure to respond immediately and to offer unlimited time. Unless the situation presents with an imminent risk, it is important that the student is seen when there is time for them to be seen, even if that means suggesting an alternative time for the discussion.

Being negatively impacted by the content of what is being talked about: It is often not possible to know what the student will disclose and, therefore, the potential exists for a student's experience to have a negative impact on the member of staff. Talking to a colleague or manager, soon after the student meeting, to debrief is very important. Alternatively, talking it through with a staff member in student services can be helpful.

Feeling out of one's depth/overwhelmed: Similarly to feeling that all problems have to be solved, or being negatively impacted by the content, it is understandable to feel overwhelmed at times. It is important, however, that such feelings are honestly acknowledged and that regular consultative support is sought as soon as possible after a student consultation.

Being preoccupied with personal worries: Human relationships are founded on the meeting of people in a relational process. As such, it is highly likely that relationships are, to a greater or lesser extent, shaped by the intrapersonal and interpersonal processes of each individual. Staff members offering support to students are not immune to this process and, as such, may well be focusing on personal problems that can impair their capacity to hear and be with others. Staff need to ensure they seek help and support from family, friends and within their work setting, which might include through their manager or through a staff counselling service, if available.

Finding silences difficult: Often there is a great deal of communication, or important reflection, in the silence between people. However, how people experience silence can be culturally and socially defined. Silence need not be problematic and, when supporting students, periods of silence can be helpful in allowing the student time to consider their options or reflect on feedback offered.

Pre-judgement of the person or the subject, based on past behaviour or other characteristics. It is important to be open to consider judgements made about people based on appearance, characteristics, previous behaviour or information received from others (who, in turn, may have made their own judgements). Taking a non-judgemental position with students is an important contributory factor in creating a safe, supportive relationship, as the student will more likely feel able to talk honestly about their problems.

Faking attention: Appearing to listen, and actually listening, are two different states. Students may believe the member of staff is listening because they appear to be, whereas, in actual fact, the staff member's attention is elsewhere. It is important to be fully aware of and attentive to the student's needs at all times and, if attention has wavered, to double-check information so that important facts are not missed.

How much the staff member identifies with, or fails to connect to, the student's experience: People's experiences can sometimes closely overlap, which can create difficulties in identifying with another's problems, rather than listening to their experience of them. Or, instead, the student's experience might be so different to that of the member of staff that there seems too great an 'experiential gap' to cross. In either situation, it is important that the staff member recognises this might be the case so that more appropriate support can be put in place.

The extent to which the student's problem is similar to that of the staff member. If the helper identifies too much with the situation they are trying to offer support for, it can become very easy for the needs of the student to become confused or conflated with those of the helper. Staff, at all times, need to ensure the individual needs be kept separate and they seek out their own help and support, if required, as outlined above.

With confidence and training, some of these barriers can be reversed so that they instead become facilitators for helping, such as being able to separate the student's difficulties from personal responses, having positive feelings towards the student, or feeling sufficiently confident to be able to listen but without creating additional pressure to 'fix the problem'.

Active listening

When involved in a helping relationship that is not one defined with a specialist purpose, for example, therapy or mental health intervention, the intention is to create a trusting space so that the student's need can be identified and appropriately responded to. To achieve this, the use of active listening skills is fundamentally important so that the student can feel heard, can trust the intention to be helped and, ultimately, the right support quickly identified.

Active listening skills can be defined as 'a way to be totally involved in the concern of another person in order to help them form a clearer awareness of his or her situation and for them to feel understood. We will all bring our pre-judgements and experiences to helping others. What we can do however, is to put them aside – sometimes called "bracketing" our own thoughts/feelings – to help us listen to others effectively' (Howdin, 2017). In revisiting the three case scenarios outlined earlier – Jason, Ah Kum and Sam – they all present very differently in terms of student, context and problem, and yet all can be helped through the use of key listening skills. It might be the act of active listening in itself will be sufficient to offer the student what they need at that point, without the requirement to refer to another person or agency.

The capacity to 'be there' for a student is fundamentally important, and it is important to not assume that someone else is better placed to respond appropriately. The #stepchange policy (UUK, 2017) places emphasis on the importance of an institution-wide approach to mental health, whereby staff feel equipped and confident to talk about mental health in a facilitative and supportive way. This is achieved through the delivery of training for staff, as described earlier, through philosophical change where staff can talk in formal (for example team meetings) and informal opportunities (such as peer support), as well as institutional cultural change, where non-stigmatising mental health discourse permeates the organisation.

Returning to the case scenarios and considering Sam's situation specifically, the student might benefit from counselling at some point, but at this stage he might need someone who is able to listen, without judgement, to his problems to help him feel less isolated. It is not uncommon for a good response early on to mean that additional, more specialist input, is not necessary later.

Developing competence

All staff have a role – to a greater or lesser extent – in responding to students' mental health needs. The case scenarios described previously illustrate the different ways in which mental health distress or concerns can present. Underlying the multiplicity of ways in which students might come to staff attention are a number of key knowledge areas and skills that inform confident responses. Some staff will feel more confident than others in a supporting role, by virtue of previous professional experiences, personal experiences of helping, or of times when they have been supported, while others will be learning about new areas. However, all staff, regardless of their current level of confidence and competence, will benefit from training opportunities.

Given the increasing role staff across institutions have in supporting students' mental health needs, those institutions arguably have a duty to provide staff with appropriate and relevant training to equip them for this, at times, challenging role. Chapter 2 discusses the legal aspects that need to be considered in terms of staff knowledge and training. Whether or not such training should be mandatory is a difficult argument. Mandatory training, on the one hand, helps ensure staff are given information and skills development opportunities while, on the other hand, may lead to some disengagement by staff by virtue of having to do a particular task they might not otherwise have chosen to do (Curado et al., 2015).

Drawing on a recent initiative by CWMT (2019) looking at the development of training resources around mental health for the higher education sector, the areas identified by staff during peer review as being most critical in supporting them to support students are considered here more fully.

Setting limits of confidentiality

While some degree of confidentiality may be afforded, what can realistically be offered is defined by the university itself and it is therefore critical to be aware of those parameters. Most staff are likely to work within a university-wide policy, i.e. confidentiality is afforded at an institutional level, on a 'need-to-know' basis, rather than by individual staff. No individual staff member or service can offer a student absolute confidentiality; rather, confidentiality should be offered in the context of the policies of the institution, which are likely to ensure staff can receive and give information about concerns, as well as successfully signpost students to the most appropriate support. The location of where the support takes place is important too. A busy corridor or common room might not afford the student much confidentiality; but likewise, always keep in mind health and safety – a deserted office at the end of an unoccupied corridor might not be best either. In meeting a student away from a normal working area, it is important to ensure a colleague or manager is aware of the meeting and when it is due to finish. Likewise, ensure the meeting room is set up in such a way that access is not impaired in the case of an emergency; that telephones are available and working; emergency alarms are available (if possible); and that the health and safety of both staff and student are considered fully and addressed absolutely.

Setting limits of time

Paradoxically, those services within the university that work with the most challenging and complex problems generally have least difficulty setting such boundaries. Their contact with students is typically planned and organised around fixed appointments, so the student is clear from the outset what is available. Day-to-day contact with students, both in academic departments and other parts of the institution, including residences, can often be much more informal and supportive discussions might not be planned. The reality is, however, that by not setting time limits future problems surrounding all sorts of boundaries may occur (consider the Jason scenario above). Paradoxically, setting clear boundaries of time can be incredibly important in attending to staff self-care, but also help to contain the student's distress. Wherever possible, it is important for both the student and staff member to be clear as to how long they have available. The benefits of this are several-fold, and include: ensuring sufficient time to help the student in the context of competing work demands; knowing the limits of time available can facilitate a capacity to listen actively, rather than being distracted by other concerns; the student is more likely to feel contained and 'held' safely by the boundaries.

How boundaries are set around time might change from situation to situation, but could include: a planned meeting, such as a tutorial or other formal contact, for example, 'Just to say that we have half an hour available today, so we will need to finish at 3 o'clock'; or an unplanned meeting, such as in a corridor, or in residences, in response to a request for a 'chat', for example, 'yes, I can talk now, but I have 10 minutes – I'm happy to arrange another time if you might need longer'; or, 'Unfortunately, I can't talk now, but let's meet in half-an-hour's time for 20 minutes – is that okay?'

Making such decisions is always a question of balance: what can be offered set against the apparent needs of the student. It is important to remember that some of the most vulnerable students do not present as such: sometimes vulnerability equates to quietness and withdrawal, rather than crying and clear signs of distress. However, checking with the student how much time they might need, putting in place something immediately, or as soon as possible, and then following it up, can create the best environment to offer high-quality support.

Knowing when to refer on

Many staff worry about when to refer a student on to another service. They might be concerned that the student could experience a discussion about another service as a lack of interest on their part, nor do they want to waste the time of others with what might be an unnecessary or inappropriate referral. A referral to another service is rarely an act that takes place in isolation from other support: even if the student would benefit from specialist input, there is a great deal that can be offered to help the student feel heard before a referral discussion takes place.

In making a referral to professional services within the institution it is important to provide as much detailed information as possible, including: identifying information, such as name, age, course, student number or identifier; others involved, such as GP or other university or community services; the nature of the problems; how long the problems have been apparent; the student's account of their own difficulties; whether they are supportive of the referral and willing to accept support; and any risk issues, such as suicidal thinking, self-injury or threats to others. Finally, some academic context, such as problems on their course, non-attendance, etc., can further contextualise the student's needs.

Many institutions have a generic contact point to help signpost referrals to the best services. However, in the absence of such a 'one-stop shop' type of referral point, contact with any key student service department will often provide an opportunity to direct the student to the best service for them. Capacity in supporting others will include having knowledge of university-based services, what they offer (in general terms) and how they can be accessed. Legal requirements mean that once a student has declared a disability to the university it is important they be directed to support departments to consider their needs. The student has a right to decline such offers, but they should be made all the same. Capacity therefore, in this context, is as much about knowing what others can do and how to access them, as well as possessing personal skills and knowledge. However, in providing such information, the importance of the helping relationship with the student and the value of active listening should be kept in mind.

Recording student contact

How and what is recorded in relation to contact with students about their mental health difficulties will be shaped by the role of the member of staff and the types of contact with the student. Day-to-day chats and usual conversations will not typically require a record being made. However, when offering advice and support to a student around mental health, it is good practice to make even a brief note of the exchange. There are a number of benefits of doing this (Ingram, 2017), including: providing an aide-memoire of what happened and what support was offered; creating a time-line of what support has been put in place in the event of further deterioration; helping to inform referrals to external agencies, if needed; and to inform the student themselves in the development of a support plan. Ingram (2017) offers a good overview of what should routinely be recorded:

- Basic information: time, date, location, student's name
- Manner of approach, i.e. how was contact initiated
- What was said to the student about confidentiality
- What the student said about their difficulties
- What the student was advised to do
- What, if any, action was promised to the student
- A note of the action taken and its outcome(s)
- Which other colleagues are now involved as a result
- What if any follow-up is needed and how information will be shared with other services, such as Student Services.

It is impossible to give definitive advice about where to make such records because, as said, so much will be dependent on the particular role and working setting. It is best to clarify this with a manager or person responsible for the area of work, and also to take account of any university policies or guidelines.

Support needs of staff

Regardless of the role held in the university, offering support to students demands careful attention to self-care. It is already widely recognised in many specialist roles, such as counselling, that regular supervision attending to the restorative (self-care) aspects of the role is critical to sustain wellbeing in the helper (BACP, 2016). Staff can feel depleted and emotionally exhausted if supporting others while not paying attention to their own needs. It is critical therefore, in this context, that individual staff and institutions alike pay careful attention to the emotional wellbeing of staff. The Universities UK #stepchange policy document restates the importance of support for both staff and students (UUK, 2017). There are a number of steps, by individuals and at an institutional level, that might be taken to specifically attend to staff care. These could include:

Individual self-care

- Talking to a manager or colleague. Additionally, human resource departments within universities often make available staff support or staff counselling, which a member of staff could access.

- Attending team meetings, where mental health is given time for discussion.
- Making a careful record of support contact with students.
- Consider accessing the institution's staff development department, to review what additional training or resources are available.
- A variety of wellbeing and sports activities, which provide space and time to specifically consider emotional health, such as mindfulness groups, assertion skills, relaxation, yoga, dance, exercise, sports groups.

Staff wellbeing and self-care: A self-reflective activity

It is important to consider self-care in supporting students. As identified earlier, there are a number of important steps a university can take to create a self-care culture. However, there is also an individual responsibility to pay attention to wellbeing. This short activity provides an opportunity for a wellbeing 'audit', to then help formulate an action plan.

- Set a timer on your phone or clock for five minutes. In that time, write down as many things you enjoy doing that make you feel happy. There are no rights or wrongs, and don't censor yourself – anything will do, it is your list.
- At the end of five minutes reflect on the list, and put an asterisk next to five of the things that you enjoy the most.
- Re-write the list in order of 'favourite', with the five asterisked items at the top.
- Review this list, initially once per week, and thereafter monthly, to ensure it continues to reflect your preferred self-care strategies.
- Additionally, review the extent to which you have been able to draw on these activities: (a) what has worked well; (b) what has not worked; (c) what prevents you from paying attention to your own wellbeing?
- This list creates a 'menu' of good things for self-care. Many of these things might be routinely undertaken; the secret is checking in on yourself regularly to see how you are feeling, and if you need to do one of these things specifically – or mindfully – to replenish yourself. In this way you can take deliberate and active steps to look after your mental health.

Care of staff by the institution

- Compassionate leave, may be helpful where staff have a caring responsibility away from the institution. Caring responsibililites can include supporting others around mental health.
- Case review meetings, in which specific students of concern are discussed.
- Debriefing opportunities to learn from previous interventions with students.
- Providing university forums about mental health. These might include forums to consider mental health across the institution, often established by human

resource departments, or mental health events delivered by the student union, for example.

- The promotion of working practices conducive to good mental health, including: staff taking a full lunch break away from their desk or main working area; healthy eating choices in refectory areas; encouraging staff to maintain agreed working hours, rather than routinely working over their hours; and an active promotion of a culture of work–life balance, for example.

- Work spaces that facilitate contact with others, for example, social and communal areas, to provide alternatives to lone working; staff kitchen areas where refreshments can be made, and food prepared at lunchtimes; buildings designed with natural light and easy access to safe outside space.

- Some employers are beginning to embed 'mental health days' into their contract of employment, where staff can take some limited time away from work to attend to their own mental health, without having to provide medical evidence to support the request.

- The establishment of reflective practice groups, discussed in detail below.

Reflective practice groups

Reflective practice groups (RPGs) have been used in a variety of settings for several years, including psychology (Cooper and Wieckowski, 2017), clinical psychology (Lyons, 2017) and nursing (Hernandez et al., 2015), for example. Such groups, when used in HEIs to support staff in their work with students experiencing mental health distress, provide a space for staff to consider, in a structured and supportive format, aspects of their day-to-day work with students. Group meetings are typically facilitated by a member of staff experienced in delivering mental health support, to enable staff to check out good practice, receive support and talk through concerns.

Individual institutions typically identify staff who are more directly involved in student mental health support, for example, academic tutors, disability team members, residence tutors, etc., who might not otherwise receive formal supervision for their student support work on a day-to-day basis. In practice, however, it might be argued that any staff who offer support to students might benefit from a facilitated space to consider what they do and how they do it. There is growing evidence of the value of these groups in a range of settings (Webber and Nathan, 2010), with their translation into student mental health support an increasingly compelling initiative. To illustrate this, see the example of an RPG below.

The success of such groups – as is the case for most groups or teams – is the clear establishing of ground rules from the outset, to clearly set parameters of time, confidentiality, line management responsibility and accountability to the institution, for example. While facilitation is not an essential element of an RPG, given that experienced group members might be able to use the space effectively under their own direction, a person with a facilitator role can help hold the boundaries of the group and ensure all group members have an opportunity to speak, if they wish. Additionally, a facilitator with experience in delivering mental health support can contribute to an educative function of the group. It is important that group members are clear as to the boundary of confidentiality, so that they are better positioned to use the group confidently. Agreements around confidentiality should specifically attend to risk (to students or staff), and how the group (and facilitator) should respond to disclosures of bad or potentially harmful practice. Additionally, and consistent with important factors discussed previously around individual support, other boundaries need to include those of time, location, safety of the meeting space, how or whether discussions would be recorded and the extent to which individual students would be discussed (as opposed to more general mental health practice issues).

CASE STUDY 10.4

Reflective Practice Groups in Action – an example

Alan is a lone learning support mentor in a busy department. His role is to meet with individual students who have disclosed a disability, including mental health problems, or who encounter personal problems during the course of their study. In addition to liaising with student support services, he is expected to offer face-to-face support, as well as organising key departmental meetings throughout the year. There are a number of such staff across the institution in different departments, but they rarely meet as there is no forum to do so. The institution established an RPG, meeting for one and a half hours twice a term (six times per year). All learning support mentors were invited; the group was facilitated by a mental health lead in the institution. The aim of the group was to offer support and a space to discuss practice issues. The group quickly established itself with 15 people attending regularly. Over the course of the meetings the group set their own agenda, discussing issues including: self-disclosure; supporting international students; and, latterly, suicide risk. Alan reported to the group that prior to meeting, he had begun to experience some personal anxiety about his work and a loss of confidence. However, in being able to 'benchmark' his own practice and receive support from others, he not only felt more personally confident, but had been able to transfer into his own department examples of good practice shared by others.

This example illustrates the variety of ways in which RPGs can provide a safe space, not only to support staff and discuss particular concerns, but additionally to share good practice across the institution.

Conclusion

The primary purpose of this chapter has been to outline the different ways students might experience mental health distress and how all members of the university community have a role in offering support. It is not uncommon for people without a specialist training in mental health to assume that all types of student problems inevitably sit beyond their competence. This chapter has, hopefully, demonstrated that while there is clearly a place for specialist input, a capacity to listen, to not judge, to not always try and fix, and to communicate a willingness to take an interest can go a long way in helping the student through their difficulties.

Additionally, the policy direction in HEIs is for an institution-wide approach to good mental health practice, both for students and staff. In achieving this goal it is key that universities provide both adequate training (such as key information around mental health, how mental health problems might present, as well as key intervention strategies), and a culture of positive mental health and support across the organisation (such as dedicated discussion time in team meetings, case review meetings and reflective practice groups).

Finally, and drawing on feedback directly from staff, the chapter has focused on the key areas for training and development in supporting students with mental health problems, with examples for good practice.

Further reading

Keeping Mental Health in Mind: e-Learning for Higher Education Staff. http://learning.cwmt.org.uk

The Charlie Waller Memorial Trust e-learning resources are free and designed for non-specialist university staff building knowledge and confidence in supporting students with mental health problems.

Minded. www.minded.org.uk

Hundreds of free e-learning sessions to support the development of skills and knowledge in supporting young people, from birth through to mid-twenties.

Student Minds is a leading UK mental health charity focusing on the mental health needs of students, and provide some really helpful information. www.studentminds.org.uk

Universities UK (2015) *Student Mental Wellbeing in Higher Education: Good Practice Guide.* London: Universities UK. Available at: www.universitiesuk.ac.uk/policy-and-analysis/reports/Pages/student-mental-wellbeing-in-higher-education.aspx (accessed 4 March 2019).

Universities UK and the Mental Wellbeing in Higher Education Working Group have developed an important good practice document around student mental health, and it can be downloaded for free.

References

Asay, T.P. and Lambert, M. (1999) The empirical case for common factors in therapy: Quantitative findings. In Hubble, M., Duncan, B. L. and Miller, S. (eds) *The Heart and Soul of Change: What Works in Therapy*. Washington, DC: American Psychological Association. pp. 35–55.

BACP (British Association for Counselling and Psychotherapy) (2016) *Ethical Framework for the Counselling Professions*. Lutterworth: BACP .

Cooper, L.D. and Wieckowski, A.T. (2017) A structured approach to reflective practice training in a clinical practicum. *Training and Education in Professional Psychology, 11*(4): 252–9.

Cooper, M. (2008) *Essential Research Findings: The Facts are Friendly*. London: Sage.

Curado, C., Henriques, P.L. and Ribeiro, S. (2015) Voluntary or mandatory enrollment in training and the motivation to transfer learning. *International Journal of Training and Development, 19*(2): 98–109.

CWMT (2019) Keeping Mental Health in Mind: eLearning for Higher Education. - http://learning.cwmt.org.uk (accessed 6 March 2019).

Hernandez, B.C., Trimm, D.R. and Kim, L. (2015) Use of collaborative reflective teams for practice discussing sexual issues with patients. www.nursinglibrary.org/vhl/handle/10755/602054 (accessed 26 January 2018).

HESA (Higher Education Statistics Agency) (2018) Data and analysis. www.hesa.ac.uk/data-and-analysis (accessed 4 March 2019).

Howdin, J. (2017) Keeping mental health in mind: Key Skills – e-Learning for Higher Education: Key Skills. Charlie Waller Memorial Trust. http://learning.cwmt.org.uk (accessed August 2017).

Howdin, J. (2019) *Key Skills: Keeping Mental Health in Mind – eLearning for Higher Education*. http://learning.cwmt.org.uk (accessed 6 March 2019).

Ingram, S. (2017) Keeping mental health in mind: Key skills – e-learning for higher education: Key principles. *Charlie Waller Memorial Trust*. http://learning.cwmt.org.uk (accessed August 2017).

Lyons, A. (2017) The Experiences of Reflective Practice Groups as Part of Doctoral Clinical Psychology Training: An IPA Study. D. Clin.Psy, unpublished thesis, University of Hertfordshire.

MWBHE/UUK (Mental Wellbeing in Higher Education and Universities UK) (2015) *Student Mental Wellbeing in Higher Education: Good Practice Guide*. London: MWBHE/UUK.

UUK (Universities UK) (2017) #stepchange: Mental health in higher education. www.universitiesuk.ac.uk/stepchange (accessed 11 December 2017).

Wampold, B.E. (2001) *The Great Psychotherapy Debate: Models, Methods and Findings*. Mahwah, NJ: Lawrence Erlbaum.

Webber, M. and Nathan, J. (2010) *Reflective Practice in Mental Health: Advanced Psychosocial Practice Children, Adolescents and Adults*. London: Jessica Kingsley.

Conclusion

Nicola Barden and
Ruth Caleb

Some of the issues considered original to the predicaments of higher education in the twenty-first century are not as new as might first be thought. If the reader goes back far enough, the discovery awaits that universities in the United Kingdom have, at various points in their existence, been fee-paying, employment-focused, politically influenced and growing in both the number and range of people attending them since Oxford and Cambridge received their royal charters in the thirteenth century (Palfreyman and Temple, 2017). While this long view allows for quite a sanguine perspective on the situation today, it does not make the current changes any less real or finding a response to them any less urgent.

One narrative that has found a new foothold is student mental health; its profile has risen steadily over the past 20 years and more. Always talked about in student counselling and mental health circles (Bell, 1996; Rana et al., 1999), it seldom reached the level of senior managers and was certainly not an agenda set by them. By degrees, however, this has changed, and the persistence of professional services in drawing attention to it may have paved the way, along with the changing student and higher education profile, as outlined in earlier chapters. Mental health is now a priority issue with the National Union of Students, Universities UK and the government, as well as with universities and students themselves. There is also a broad public conversation around mental health, which has created a little less stigma and greater acceptance of the challenges.

It is clear that students with mental ill health at any point in their course have an equal right to attend and progress at university, and to have an equal chance of success. There is no doubt that there has been progress within universities and from the government towards this aim, but it is by no means complete. This book has provided many opportunities for reflection on what institutions can and should do to support mental health in their students, illustrated by some of the good work already being done.

Many academic staff are enormously sympathetic to students experiencing mental health difficulties. They will gladly take on reasonable adjustments, change their teaching methods, and make time to talk to students, to learn about their challenges and grow more confident in their own ability to offer appropriate help. Similarly, professional staff will work to resolve difficulties with accommodation and finance, manage out-of-hours emergencies, talk to worried third parties, provide counselling and mental health support at times of potential risk, and stay alongside the student in their journey. There are other times, however, when academic staff find the continual demand of individual adjustments too much, feel out of their depth and irritated by a pastoral demand they may have had little or no training for, and that feels remote from their chosen teaching role. Professional staff, always struggling with resources, may feel weighed down by unrealistic expectations of what they can achieve and the dread of being blamed if things go wrong.

There is potential for the two groups to become opposed, with the academic staff assuming it is the support services' role to deal with all emotional or psychological issues and the support staff feeling aggrieved that the academic staff assume that these challenges are nothing to do with them. These tensions can be turned against the narrative of equality and against the student who is the subject of that narrative. What this pinpoints is the reality that while the student cohort has broadened, the structure of higher education has not; it still works to a largely full-time undergraduate and postgraduate framework, as does the student loans company, and anything outside of this, once it is embarked on, can only be negotiated as an exception. Staff and students alike are operating within structures built for a different era. Turn this around and make the exception the rule, and it might be possible to design a framework for higher education that more accurately fits its students, and offers effective support. This follows the inclusive practice that is encouraged by the 2010 Equality Act and its anticipatory duty that disabilities should be reacted to not with surprise, but with familiarity and recognition. An ambitious view for equality in student mental health not only rests in the student being able to engage with the institution's requirements, but that the institution is also engaged with the requirements of its students and allows their own practices to be changed by so doing.

What can be concluded?

The majority of students are part of an age group that is at a vulnerable point in terms of developing mental health difficulties. Regardless of age, it is a cohort embarking on a time of transition which is stressful and that will have an impact on life beyond the subject studied. A significant percentage of those studying in the UK are international, likely to experience additional cultural stress, and it could be said that there is a shock felt along the many other cultural boundaries that are crossed in a university community.

Of course students are not the only group in society under stress, and this is not about seeking special status for them. It is about redressing a longstanding perception that they are somehow protected from problems and less prone to mental health difficulties than other people. The authors of this book have provided a clear case to the contrary, and shown that while there are specific support services available, and in this sense students are privileged, this privilege exists only in relation to the additional risks and demands that have to be managed, and the penalties that occur if they are not. Perhaps because of this perception of privilege, the debates about safety on campus (trigger warnings, no platforming, safe spaces) can be met with some cynicism and quickly become polarised. Universities must manage the tension in providing an experience that is both educationally challenging and not unreasonably stressful. They must be truthful to students about what to expect, and this can vie with a recruitment agenda that has to meet targets related to university budgets. Budgets are a reality and without enough students universities will not survive; but equally, without enough knowledge of what the university of their choosing may actually require and offer, the student may not be able to manage the demands that face them.

While discussions about mental health difficulties in higher education are often problem-focused, the opportunity to provide well-timed and accessible interventions promises a high chance of success with the cohort, in part because of the very capacity for change that brings the risk. Learning and using new coping skills and protective habits, and developing insight into themselves and understanding their emotions and behaviours, will stand students in good stead for years to come. The message is therefore both cautionary and optimistic. There is a problem, and something can be done. The right response at the right time will build capability, and there are many opportunities for that response to be given.

Who should be taking such action? A clear message from this book is that mental health is everybody's business: it is a whole-university responsibility, and beyond the university, it is the responsibility of the statutory services too. Professional support services have led on this for many years, innovating and adapting provision. Expanding this into positive multidisciplinary working across all aspects of higher education provision is the next step. This needs leadership from senior management teams, and leadership will require the matching of direction with resources. There are often concerns that the mental health agenda is a bottomless pit in terms of resources. This is not so, unless the institution seeks to be everything to everyone. Where it clearly identifies its priorities for mental health and facilitates its staff to work towards them, objectives are achievable. Students are allies in this; there is little appetite from them to leave university in a state of dependency.

This book has attempted to show how mental health can and should be supported by both small actions and large ones: by a kind word at a vulnerable time, or by multi-agency involvement at times of intense need. Mental health risk can be frightening, but it is always worth remembering that the student at the heart of it is likely to be just as frightened as the lecturer, or accommodation manager, or member of security who has come across them, and a willingness to listen, be sympathetic and seek help will always be useful.

It is the authors' hope that this book will encourage everyone involved in higher education to see mental health as something that they can contribute to in a positive way from within their role, and find their own practice enhanced in so doing. For staff whose main role is working with student mental health, it is hoped that this book will provide recognition and commendation of their achievements, and bring them greater support from the community within which they work. For senior managers, the hope is that the book gives some a direction of travel that is useful and encouraging, while also stretching. Lastly, for any students who read it, the hope is that they find recognition in these pages, and are glad that they were written.

References

Bell, E. (1996) *Counselling in Further and Higher Education*. Buckingham: Open University Press.

Palfreyman, D. and Temple, P. (2017) *Universities and Colleges: A Very Short Introduction*. Oxford: Oxford University Press.

Rana, R., Smith, E. and Walkling, J. (1999) *Degrees of Disturbance: the New Agenda* (A report from the Heads of University Counselling Services). Rugby: British Association for Counselling.

Index